AN INSTINCT |

Antonella Gambotto was born in Sydney, Australia, on the nineteenth of September, 1965. In 1988, she won the *Cosmopolitan* New Journalist of the Year Award in London and was accepted as a member of British MENSA. A guest commentator on SBS, the ABC, and Channel 9, she has worked for the *Australian*, *Elle*, *GQ*, *HQ*, the *Independent on Sunday*, *Mode*, the *New Musical Express*, *Penthouse*, *Playboy*, and the *Sydney Morning Herald*, as well as having contributed essays and short stories to a number of anthologies. Her first anthology, *Lunch Of Blood*, was published in 1994. Her first novel, *The Pure Weight of the Heart*, is due to be published internationally in 1998.

Also by Antonella Gambotto

Nonfiction
Lunch of Blood

Fiction
The Pure Weight of the Heart

AN
INSTINCT
FOR THE
KILL

**ANTONELLA
GAMBOTTO**

HarperCollins*Publishers*

HarperCollins
An imprint of HarperCollins*Publishers*, Australia

First published in Australia in 1997
by HarperCollins*Publishers* Pty Limited
ACN 009 913 517
A member of the HarperCollins *Publishers* (Australia) Pty Limited Group

HarperCollins*Publishers*
25 Ryde Road, Pymble, Sydney NSW 2073, Australia
31 View Road, Glenfield, Auckland 10, New Zealand
77–85 Fulham Palace Road, London W6 8JB, United Kingdom
Hazelton Lanes, 55 Avenue Road, Suite 2900, Toronto, Ontario, M5R 3L2
and 1995 Markham Road, Scarborough, Ontario, M1B 5M8, Canada
10 East 53rd Street, New York NY 10032, United States of America

National Library of Australia Cataloguing-in-Publication data:
Gambotto, Antonella, 1965–.
An instinct for the kill.
ISBN 07322 5891X.
1. Celebrities — Interviews. 2. Celebrities — Australia — Interviews.
3. Biography — 20th century. I. Title.
920.00904

Printed in Australia by Griffin Press, Adelaide

9 8 7 6 5 4 3 2 1
01 00 99 98 97

To Michael Harmer,
a white velocity.

To Stephen Liggins,
unbreakable thread of snow.

To Timothy Gillespie,
seminal opal disseminated.

To Mark Burrows,
an increment of stars.

All newspaper writers are, for the sake of their trade, alarmists: this is their way of making themselves interesting.

Arthur Schopenhauer

ACKNOWLEDGMENTS

I am passionately grateful to the following individuals for being part of my life, and for all that they have taught me:

Gillon Aitken; Quentin Bacon, depraved magician; Candy Baker, woman on the same wavelength; Libby Bessell-Browne; darling, darling Caesar and the Honourable Devil Reptile, for the Scrabble, so much encouragement, and unimaginable kindnesses; George Capel, my genius negotiator; Warwick and Joanne Capper, who possess the courage to be true to themselves; Anthony Cheetham; Wayne Chick; Paulo Coelho; Edward de Bono, dear and irascible constant; Lionel Docker; Christine Farmer; William Fraser, for first suggesting a critique; Edward Grieve, for his intelligence and skill; James 'I don't believe in literature' Hall; my leggy Camilla Harvey; Gerard and Anne Henderson; Ian Hicks; Barrie Hitchon, for first suggesting an alliance; Barn Hoskyns; Miss Jism; Michael Korda, for his informed heroism on that burning deck; Maria Kozic; Angelo Loukakis; Zaid Lozi; John le Guay; Shona Martyn; Warwick McCarthy who inspired the A Team; Mick Mercer; George 'Chicken Legs' Michelini, whose lack of diplomacy as a flatmate ensured that I remained in my study; Lisa Mills, for her tolerance; Big Bad Barry Oakley, for his unexpectedly wonderful enthusiasm; Alan 'The Spook' Pilkington, God bless; the inspiring Puck; Ros Reines, for her generosity; Alicia Richardson; the chivalric, altruistic, and handsome Dennis Robertson; Dom Romeo; Sean Ryan; Sex Rocket; Luke Slattery; Mat Snow; Fenella Souter; Deborah Thomas, Valkyrie, editor, cherished friend; the late Michael VerMeulen, forever in my heart; Vietnam, however distant; Murray Waldren, for inspiring the title; the divine Simon Watt and his many, many voices; Jacqui Wolf; and the unusually humane Peter Wurth.

CONTENTS

FOREWORD

THE AUTHOR OF this book has asked me to write that she is brilliant. So I must. It would be unchivalrous and even dangerous to do otherwise. Readers will, in any case, discover this for themselves.

But is it the dazzling brilliance of fireworks, the shimmering brilliance of a peacock's fanned tail, the clear brilliance of a diamond, or the brilliance of a juggler who controls eight knives as they curve through the air? Make up your own mind. It could be the precocious brilliance of a child who does not want to grow up — ever.

On Fifth Avenue in New York City you often see dog-walkers with about six dogs on six leashes heading for Central Park. You marvel at the control because you can imagine the chaos if each dog chose a different direction. The author of the pieces in this book gives the same sense of impending chaos as language and thought struggle to dominate each other. But in the end the control is there, as it is with the dog-walker. Both dogs and words are under excellent control.

The pieces in this book are fierce, fascinating, and funny. The author often gives the impression that the subject of her attention should conform to those pre-set images which make her interviews more interesting. Why be nice when it is funnier to be fierce? At the same time, enough truth seeps through to suggest that the author's view may have its own special legitimacy. In a strange way the author manages to convey that her view may not be the only one, but that it is nevertheless valid — and always interesting. This is a considerable feat with some of the raw material. The author is an impresario who produces and directs interest. She could probably make a desert seem like a jungle of violent tensions.

I have always felt that the main purpose of reality is to fuel the beautiful myths that give colour and value to life. The Italians and the Irish, in different ways, believe that a good story deserves to be true even if it is not. Why tarnish style with banal reality? So readers of this work have a double offer of enjoyment: enjoy the style and learn something about a wide slice of humanity.

The author has a manic sense that her sharp-edged judgments are not only fair, but accurate. From such certitude and near-fascist lack of doubt comes the acuity of perception that makes the subjects come alive as caricatures of themselves. Caricatures are never meant to be photographs and yet can be more truthful than photographs. People come to look like their caricatures but rarely resemble their photographs.

The purpose of art is to make reality more real and the author has the art to do that. Yet behind the web of words there is an energy that makes the writing more than just an exercise in word-weaving. This is not the energy of rage which becomes boring if sustained for too long. It is more like the energy of a hound that has just caught the compelling scent of the trail.

So who is the author? Antonella is a slight figure with big opinions and small ears. Somewhere in her there is a sweetness which she fears because it may lessen the passion of energy which drives her writing. There is almost a Slavic sense of anguish in her that makes for sharper feelings or perhaps it is the Italian passion (her ancestry) that has to find something about which to be passionate. Even the humour is passionate. As is the acute attention to detail that make the reviews and interviews come alive.

I first met Antonella when she met me for an interview. The process was disarming and charming and the outcome perceptive except for an unexplained obsession with my ears (which are, much as she believes otherwise, a perfectly normal size). Since then, we have sporadically met (which is the way of frequent travellers, busy lifestyles, and Antonella's exigent temperament). There is, however, an exciting vitality that makes her difficult to forget and marvellous to know. Sometimes you want to shake her to dislodge some of the quickset opinions which are held because they are more fun to hold. Antonella's mind is like a fast-shutter camera: one blink and it is permanence. This may not matter if several shots are to be taken over time.

The pieces in this collection range from the hilarious and affectionate double interview of Warwick and Joanne Capper to the witty dismissal of Gore Vidal as someone whose need to be stylish cannibalised all other values. In each case the piece stands on its own as excellent reading and does not depend on its relationship to a person or a book. Each piece has its own intelligence and vitality. Occasionally the energy outruns the meaning so that the reader needs to treat the overlay of images as poetry rather than prose. Nowhere is there a hint of doubt in Antonella's conviction. Nowhere is the writing boring. The pieces stand in the great tradition of writing that is to be read for its own sake, as with the classic essayists.

That much of the fun is at the expense of some victim arises from Antonella's belief that the only sin is to be boring. The enjoyment of the attack may be contrary to my own preference, but powerful in its own right: vinegar is also a flavour.

Observation is concerned with 'what is' and design is concerned with 'what can be'. The Greek gang of three (Socrates, Plato and Aristotle) set the habit of Western thinking by supposing that if we could find the 'truth' then everything else would follow and we would always know what to do. Ironically, the great successes of Western thinking in science and technology are only in part due to this search for the truth. They are mainly due to the derivative energy of the 'possibility' system as with hypotheses in science and vision in technology. While I am concerned with what can be, Antonella often indicates that she is concerned with what is (the truth). In fact, there is a considerable overlap because the truth is seen through a designer's eye. This is what makes Antonella's truth interesting and not boring. Truth needs designers to dress it just as a stage demands stage designers. At the same time, Antonella must deny this because anything less than a search for the truth would come across as contrived coyness (for which Antonella condemns Gore Vidal).

Perceptions and ideas have their own life and their own momentum. Once born, they breed and develop related ideas. The trick is to keep all these offspring in contact — somehow — with the subject matter. Antonella handles this with ferocious skill. You never feel that the idea-creatures have broken loose on their own to rampage through the prose. Yet there is always a sense that they just might — as with the Fifth Avenue dog-walker.

Intensity is a characteristic of Antonella's writing. Words and ideas crowd together like vultures on a carcass. Words crowd around each idea. There is a reason for each of them. The effect is Gothic, for every detail is there to catch attention — not just the classic outlines of Palladian proportions. There is a bold abundance and almost a horror of the spare and simple. It works well like any style that is true to itself. Style without confidence is like a flag without a flagpole. Confidence holds aloft the style and waves it about proudly so all can see. Approval does not matter so long as the attention is caught and sustained. Antonella prefers see-saws to balances. Black and white is better than shades of grey.

Whatever else, readers will enjoy this book for its sheer expressive energy written out with wit, passion, perception, and a powerful ease with words. Antonella is not afraid of words, ideas, her own opinions or the opinions of others. Perception is personal so truth is also personal. This is much more like Protagoras than like Plato. For Protagoras, perception was the only truth — but it was changeable. For Plato, the fascist, truth was what you had reached when you thought it was the absolute. So when you read this book, you choose to look at the world through Antonella's sharp eyes. See and feel what the world looks like to her.

FOREWORD

Antonella believes that feelings are the real reality. Feelings guide perception and perception guides feelings with a circularity that breeds belief and conviction. It is the unusual combination of feeling, intellect, and word-skill that makes this book wonderful to read. Take it only as seriously as the author intended.

Edward de Bono
Venice, 1997

THE ART OF THE INTERVIEW

I RECENTLY VISITED a temporarily crippled associate of mine in hospital who had, during the course of his convalescence, chanced upon an interview with me in a national publication, an interview in which I discussed — which as much candour as the word-count would allow — my wild and crazy upbringing. My slope-levelled friend, a man well-versed in the internationally acceptable sadomasochistic strategies of the stockmarket and a decorated veteran of the even bloodier carnage of love's battlefield, sat up as I entered the room. 'You are an absolute *socio*path,' he declared. This was an intriguing, if unexpected, greeting. And so I asked why he, a skilled manipulator of human vulnerabilities and shark emeritus, thought that I (at best a tender and retiring sort of individual) was an absolute sociopath. 'It's *ob*vious,' he said. 'Who but a sociopath would have spoken to a member of the press in such a frank fashion about *fam*ily problems? How *could* you have aired your dirty laundry for all and sundry to read? This is the literary equivalent of a *beave*r spread.' The morphine coursing through his veins did not dilute his outrage. 'Have you no self-*control*? Have you no sense of pro*priety*? Have you no *pride*? How on earth do you think your father felt when you described him to the nation as a "hard and tyrannical *fascist*"?'

In actuality, my father was tickled pink at the description. My sick associate had made the error of assuming that I was in some way rebelling against the prim zipper-lipped strictures of my parents whereas I am, as anyone familiar with my richly emotional and colourful family knows, a mere chip off the old black shirt. My father would have been mortified had I described him as a sentimental old sweetheart, but was much flattered by the ideological ramifications of my words and their reinforcement of his perception of his masculinity. This was something my sick associate, an outwardly proper Anglo-Australian Anglican, could not understand, and his reaction was depressingly predictable.

Control. Propriety. Pride. Behavioural modes that not only gave D. H. Lawrence the night sweats but which are, in however distorted a form, responsible for most of the ills of our ailing society. They are Puritan hangovers which make the best of us queasy and fill the worst of us with a passionate intensity.

Being one of the worst — the *very* worst, I should add; an absolutely slouching monster of anthropocentricity and solipsism — I am always in a state of passionate intensity over something, be it my own dirty laundry or that of our civilisation. What some would call baroque emotionalism I see as a profound interest in the psyche. In *Seduction of the Minotaur*, Anaïs Nin asked: 'How did this heavy wall build up, these prison walls, these silences? Unaware of this great loss, the loss of the transparent child, one becomes an actor, whose profession it is to manipulate his face so that others may have the illusion that they are reading his soul.'

The themes of every man's life evolve from his 'transparent' childhood, and it is only through an understanding of this childhood that a man and his actions can be appreciated and then placed into a wider context.

To illustrate: the Prince of Wales recently cooperated with Jonathan Dimbleby, a journalist he thought suited to write his biography. In this biography, Charles was frank about the emotional deprivations of his childhood and the inadequacies of his parents. His father, a man who, it has since been discovered, regularly played curious party games during his marriage, went on the record as saying: 'I've never discussed private matters and I don't think the Queen has, either.' A friend of Prince Philip's described Charles' behaviour as 'repugnant' and told the press: 'I would not expect anyone to criticise their parents in public.' Another high Anglican ally of Prince Philip's added: 'Prince Charles has broken one of the universal rules of family life — that you don't air your grievances in public.'

In a world in which form is valued above content, such hypocrisy is unsurprising. The maintenance of superficies is considered to be the *sine qua non* of Western social acceptability. Truth is the first casualty in any war, and the maintenance of propriety is the most violent of wars: it is a war fought against natural human instincts. Whether or not a man's private life is bizarre or miserable is seen to be irrelevant on the condition that he maintains a conservative façade. Our puritanical socialisation trains us to demand and reward such emotional repression. We strive for bloodlessness, for bodilessness, and regard silent suffering as heroic. These expectations are implicit in what we understand to be 'decorum', and they are pressed upon us by every authoritative body.

The intellectually gifted British MP who was discovered dead on his kitchen table wearing black stockings, a garter belt, high-heeled shoes, and with a plastic bag taped over his head was a martyr to the puritan cause. Better that he die than subject the world to his enduring mortal pangs; better that than his challenging the imposed schizophrenia of the puritan ethos.

When Prince Philip's churchy chum expressed his horror at the 'breaking' of one of the 'universal rules of family life' he was, however inadvertently, endorsing deaths such as the one mentioned. We have been conditioned to be ashamed of the truths of our lives, and in this shame lies a denial inimical to mental and emotional equilibrium. What purpose can this distaste for emotion serve beyond instilling in us an essential sense of inferiority to some impossible ideal?

The 'respectable' Western media is the organ of the puritan ethos in that its 'objectivity' presupposes a disregard or contempt for emotion. This onslaught of 'objectivity' has caused us to become desensitised both to ourselves and to the world around us. Verbal and visual depictions of despair or horror are stripped of their meaning by the method of the reportage. Such detachment facilitates intellectual absorption but destroys emotional impact, thus withholding the whole truth of the information. Implicit in this homogenised reportage is a recoiling from instinctive responses and the suggestion that the only validity of any situation rests in its 'objectivity'.

The Oxford English Dictionary defines 'objective' as: 'Belonging not to the consciousness or the perceiving or thinking subject, but to what is presented to this, external to the mind, real.' To the puritan, that which is 'real' is the tangible, the quantifiable — a definition which excludes emotion. In its reflection of this limited 'reality', the media essentially perpetrates our hostility toward one another and to our instinctive selves; we learn to respect our form, to despise our content. The message is subtle but effective: the expression of emotion is 'vulgar'; the airing of grievances is 'repugnant'; the acknowledgment of fallibility is mocked; feeling unrelated to form is inappropriate — in short, the full expression of our humanity is penalised. In our mania for objectivity, we have become masters of objectification.

This clinical objectification is the axis of Western respectability. High level publications worship at its shrine, relegating emotionally charged journalism — now known as 'personality journalism', previously known as 'writing' — to the ghetto of the arts and women's pages. This ensures that 'news' and 'human interest' are perceived to be mutually exclusive. But what possible value can 'news' have if it holds no 'human interest'? And what is 'human interest' if not 'news'? Every editor knows that his publication is anthropomorphised by its readers. A magazine aimed at adolescent girls plays the role of a big sister; a newspaper aimed at the blue-chip set plays the role of a mentor. The information imparted by these publications helps shape our perspectives and our behaviour. In however small or grand a manner, it alters all our lives — from the way in which we present ourselves to the goals towards which we strive. The advertising industry pivots on this knowledge (which in itself may be enough of an incentive for us to reconsider our definitions of reality and relevance, our definitions of information).

Saul Bellow has often spoken of our need for a greater culture, a culture that 'allows the greatest latitudes to certain natural human needs and simplicities'. This plea of Bellow's is regarded as significant, but still that of an egghead. Our culture remains one in which emotion is tyrannised.

The role of the journalist in this war between objectivity and subjectivity is important. Journalists should never claim to be objective, as this 'objectivity' is only ever a pretence; it is a self-aggrandising sham. A journalist's choice of subject matter, the angle he takes on the material, the tone he adopts — all are subjective matters. The mood of the journalist, the time he has been allotted to gather the information, the proximity of the deadline — all are subjective matters. The location of the story in the publication, the headline under which it is run, the length of the article, the day on which it is run — all are subjective matters. And yet we persist in pretending that this information is detached from the informant, as if it had been dictated from some Divine source, lucid and unsullied by feeling — the 'they' who 'say', the 'general' who imparts his 'opinion', the 'it' which makes points 'understood'.

Writing of any description can only ever be a form of propaganda to support that writer's ideological metasystem. Does this fact in any way detract from the significance of the writer's contribution or the validity of the content? It shouldn't, but it does. The possibility that the information we are fed is somehow dependent on emotion is frightening to many. As children we are reluctant to perceive our parents as anything but gods (or, as Philip Roth so cleanly put it, 'giants'), and many of us carry this reluctance into adulthood, when we pretend that the 'authorities' — the media being one — are not collections of fallible individuals, but macroscopic and objective organisms to be blindly respected and obeyed. And through this fearfulness of reality, we not only limit our understanding but cripple it.

On the 1st of April this year, the *Spectator* ran a cartoon. A hooded executioner is distracted from his work at the rack by his irritated superior, who scolds: 'There have been complaints about your interviewing style.' Its resonance was a source of humour to my friends. Over the years, I have been regularly accused of 'prying' into my interview subjects' lives, of 'making' their lives a 'misery', of focusing on the man at the expense of his work, of amateur psychoanalysis, of *subjectivity*. I lost no sleep over these prognoses but did find them boring. God forbid that any journalist should abandon the Olympian prose-style of the newsman and personalise his voice! God forbid that any journalist should, through this very personalisation, dare to pretend to be anything other than omniscient, omnipotent, and omnipresent! The bravery and intelligence of these paragons of objectivity was made clear to me one sunny afternoon. Having just stepped off the bus to walk to the gym, I saw trundling across the road towards me the lemon-haired current-affairs bollard-thighed troll who had savaged my first book in a newspaper. This woman's professional reputation was built on footage of her squinting at the sun on location for war-stories, et cetera. Tough and uncompromising, fearless and intelligent, objective and ambitious, this was a woman who felt herself to be terribly superior to weathergirls and game-show hostesses and subjective journalists. I stopped to stare at her, surprised at her lack of height and maternal width. She looked up and saw me. Dressed in trackpants and an OHIO BUCKEYES T-shirt, I did not think myself particularly threatening, but we agreed to differ. She froze on the pedestrian crossing, turned on her heel and sprinted back into the comparative safety of the Neutral Bay Foodhall. I often wonder how I could ever be perceived as scarier than stoned Third World soldiers brandishing machine guns. Perhaps she thought I was going to whip her into submission with my gym towel? Or perhaps it was the possibility of fulfilment of this secret fantasy that so unsettled her.

But enough of my amateur psychoanalysis and more of my history. Whilst still at school, I had a short story published in the literary magazine *Billy Blue* and a satirical poem published in the *Sydney Morning Herald*. Terrified that my editors would somehow discover that I was a schoolgirl and thus unworthy of publication, I wrote both pieces under the pseudonym Clavis Lumen — in Latin, 'key [of] light'. This was a serious identity crisis. For years I wrote under various pseudonyms, thinking myself 'objective' behind my shield of letters. I won a national journalistic award in England under the name of my first fiancé, Richard Gray. When the organisers called to invite Mr Gray to the awards ceremony, I was faced with my own fear of subjectivity: how could I be my own baroquely emotional self and still be objective enough to be a journalist?

This was a turning point. I broke down and confessed. I was, as embarrassingly subjective as it seemed, only myself. A former schoolgirl, in fact. I later realised that I had been seeking respectability by hiding behind 'objective' personae, personae who were not tortured by my overt sensitivities, personae who were privy to Platonic truths and not slaves to 'certain natural human needs and simplicities'. In itself, my name seemed to me a synonym for subjectivity — all those passionately intense vowels, nothing like the sturdy organised consonants of a Woodward or Dunne or Johnson. Nevertheless, the name was mine and I finally accepted it, and it was with this acceptance that my writing began to change.

My first interview was commissioned by an editor of the *Australian*, a kindly man who guided me with the words: 'Here's the guy's telephone number.' No training, no advice, no nothing. My first lesson in the art of the interview. In retrospect, it was a great lesson in that it forced me to develop what I have been told is a style of my own, but it was also to cause me certain difficulties. My understanding of an interview was that you asked what you felt like asking, wrote what you felt like writing, and the result was always published. This understanding was flawed.

I moved to London at the age of eighteen, where I reviewed and interviewed rock stars for the music press. These were wild and crazy times. Popular musicians are the ideal training ground for any interviewer as they are, as a genre, non-verbal, substance abusing, and emotionally retarded. This allows much scope for the writing itself to grow. It is a real skill to hold the attention of an exhausted moron at three in the morning after he has just injected himself with heroin, performed for 250,000 people, or downed ten port-and-beers (as one Irish subject so memorably did). If the interviewer doesn't learn to hold their interest, there is no interview. In this respect, concert reviews were immeasurably easier — a few hundred words of opinion and a byline, *c'est entendu*? Not quite. That most exemplary of forgiving Christians, Cliff Richard, so objected to my review of his performance that he sued the paper in which it was published for almost 50,000 pounds. This was a lot of money at the time. My third lesson was in the art of libel, and I learned it well.

Mr Richard's lawsuit, justified as it undoubtedly was, made me realise that what I had thought to be 'unreal' (that is to say, the feeling invoked by words) could have some very real repercussions. The words had become real enough for this one reader to call his lawyers in to defend his otherwise unreal feelings in order to be compensated with some very real capital. The words became real enough to inspire other readers to threaten me with GBH or write me the most extraordinary love letters. These varied responses caused me to examine the 'human' angle, they led me to consider its significance. I began to take my work a little more seriously and to investigate what I had been taught was the province of tabloids and the 'glossies': emotion.

In exploring the emotions of my subjects, I was surprised to find the blueprints of their lives. Freud, of course, had come to this realisation some time earlier. Increasingly I became interested in the experiences that were later translated into their work — the emotional and physical brutalisation which inspired Maria Kozic's art; the stereotypical machismo which caused Paul Mercurio to rebel through the means of ballet; the poverty and ugliness which fed Gerard Depardieu's need for fantasy; the terror of truth in John Pilger's childhood, a terror of admitting an imperfect social pedigree, a terror which he translated into the saving of 250,000 lives.

Each interview became an absolute challenge. Imagine a time-pressured situation with a complete stranger, a stranger known to you through the words and images of others, a stranger who has been trained to be evasive and mundane, a stranger experienced at presenting himself as an easily-digestible cartoon designed to promote his work, a stranger who does not and will not (if he can help it) trust you. This paranoid lack of trust often works to the subject's detriment. Kylie Minogue, for example, demanded that I sign a little contract prior to the interview stipulating that the interview was not to be published anywhere other than *Elle* magazine without her permission. Bored but loyal to the magazine, I signed the contract. Her minders then rang *Elle* and claimed that the little contract stipulated that the piece be shown to Ms Minogue prior to publication. As this was not the case, the editor refused and they resorted to that prissy little threat so beloved by foot-stamping soap-stars: the withholding of suitably glamorous shots. Those unforgettable portraits of Ms Minogue wearing big rabbit ears and fishnet stockings would not be given to the magazine unless the piece received Ms Minogue's approval. Predictably, the piece did not receive Ms Minogue's approval. My experience of her as a charmlessly narcissistic and robotic dwarf did not correlate with her experience of herself as an incandescent, gifted and alluring siren. The result? *Elle* ran an anodyne interview and Ms Minogue allowed them to publish the photographs of her wearing big rabbit ears. A waste of time for everybody.

The best interviews are both illuminating and exhausting, mental chess, terrific fun. The worst — dispiriting and infuriating as they may be for the parties involved — are often a joy to the reader. I have to be bullied by editors to write discordant interviews as I prefer not to be reminded of the experience. In the case of Elle McFeast — a woman who, in the name of publicity, recently entered a dog competition — I wanted out. I rang my editor to inform her that as the interview had been such a fiasco, I wanted *out*. No dice. I was ordered to write it as I experienced it. And so I did. My depiction of McFeast as a repellent and manipulative bully was considered to be a touch too close to my experience and so I was told to 'tone it down'. The final result displeased me and McFeast for different reasons — she felt I had crucified her; I felt I had been too soft. The readers loved it. I was just as helpless with the

Kafkaesque Nick Cave. It was to be a cover story, the deadline was rigid, my experience of the mostly incoherent and partly incomprehensible Cave had to be written. Again, I detested every minute and again, the readers loved it. Cave was so incensed by the article that he implied in an interview with another journalist that some kind of sexual high-jinks had taken place between us. This was, I might add, wishful thinking on his behalf. Unfortunately for Cave, I possessed the tape. The journal was persuaded to run an apology. A minor storm. The unreal world of emotions was to produce far more interesting rumours.

It was when my first book, *Lunch of Blood*, was being auctioned to publishers that I was made to understand that my approach was not endorsed by all within the profession. I was informed by my agent that various publishers had been told that I was dying of AIDS. This was an easily disproved rumour, and not without consequence. The individuals who had been told that I was dying of AIDS refused to name their source, quickly understanding that there would be some ugly legal action. I then discovered that I was bedding every man with whom I had ever worked. According to the grapevine, I was not only sleeping with my publisher, but with my literary editor, my publicity director, an academic with whom I had once shared a cab after a literary function, my lawyer, every male journalist who had ever reviewed me favourably, and most of the men I had interviewed. Close male friends were magically transformed into my writhing sexual victims; doors closed for meetings guarded a bacchanalia for which I only wish I had the strength. I received a number of fantastic letters slyly suggesting that the postscripts to certain interviews in the book were incomplete, that I had (in my nyphomaniacal mania for secrecy) omitted certain sordid details. One of my ruffled subjects fired off a letter suggesting that I should be 'careful' that the story of me and 'the cake' didn't 'get around'. I read this letter twice, wondering what lascivious act I could have possibly performed in the minds of my detractors with a *cake*. The mule and the black rubber mat I could understand, but a *cake*? Not only was I dying of AIDS and in a constant state of erotic ecstasy, but I was now mating with pastries.

How is it that the exposure of essentially benign and commonplace truths can arouse some to such fury? Why are so many people humiliated or enraged by ordinary honesty? Why is it so damning to be revealed as fallible or imperfect? The psychiatrist Alice Miller has this to say on the topic: 'The more one-sided a society's observance of strict moral principles such as orderliness, cleanliness, and hostility towards instinctual drives, and the more deep-seated its fear of the other side of human nature — vitality, spontaneity, sensuality, critical judgment, and inner independence — the more strenuous will be its efforts to isolate this hidden territory, to surround it with silence.'

By surrounding our public figures with silence, we not only diminish their dignity but belittle ourselves. We belittle ourselves by treating ourselves as children who are incapable of embracing the concept of a multifaceted human being. It is an insult to our intelligence to have our leaders — whether they be political, artistic, financial or intellectual — presented as cartoons, and ultimately profoundly damaging. Those in the public domain are our role models and have a responsibility to be honest. If they cannot be honest, then that responsibility is passed on to the press. The beauty of anyone's life lies in its truth and not its conformity. Instead of recognising this, we cling to the linearity of the eschatological doctrine, a doctrine that allows only for polarity and conflict.

By accepting these 'objective' cartoons, by degrading human detail and feeling, by relegating this detail and feeling to the lowest stratum of consideration in the media, we denigrate ourselves. Acknowledgment of humanity is essential and never exclusive to excellence or relevance. Man is defined by his passion. This acknowledgment must begin with those whose voices are more audible than others. Our culture must return to one that is anthropocentric; those certain natural human needs can only be trivialised at the risk of all we love. My sick associate still disagrees with me on this matter. Unwilling to confront his personal demons, he re-channels the energy of stress into aggressive skiing. His neurosurgeon warned him that the next accident would probably be fatal. A zipper-lipped puritan to the end, my associate has now hired a team of physical therapists to get him back on those slopes as soon as possible. Effects are always so much easier to deal with than causes, after all.

Speech delivered to the Sydney Institute, 1995

UNDER THE DOUBLETHINK:
TORI AMOS

ON STAGE, SHE silences. The impact of her voice — that ethereal, that demoniacal, that rare instrument — is overwhelming; it is, in its own way, a means of real evisceration. She is dwarfed by all theatres, only a fraction over five feet tall, and yet by the end of every performance she has both commanded and changed the quality of the audience's concentration. Her mastery of the piano is mesmerising. Her playing demands the transcendence of pure listening. Her performance style, wrongly classified by some as mannered, is liberatingly sensual. The ferocity with which she can attack the keys will often cause her to spring from her stool until she is standing, hunched over her rippling hands, her carmine hair trapping the spotlight like a halo, her face tipped to the sky, her eyes closed: it is as if she is being electrocuted. At each show she is wrung clean of encores. She once said that it took her years to realise that she had 'some kind of calling'.

In the winter of 1991, Tori Amos' first solo album, *Little Earthquakes*, was released. She had been shipped to London by representatives of her American record company who felt that her work was too introspective and individualistic to penetrate the 'hardest market in the world'. Publicity for the album was minimal; the reaction was phenomenal. By the time her second album (the more abstract *Under the Pink*), was released, her beautifully asymmetrical face was on the cover of every major music publication and her singles were selling by the million. Her rapture, it seemed, was infectious.

Beyond that are the issues that her songs address — female shame, female fury, human delicacy, and, in particular, violence and sexuality. The evolution of these themes has been a complicated process.

A child prodigy, she was enrolled by her Methodist minister father at the Peabody Institute of Baltimore's John Hopkins University. At the age of five, Amos was the youngest student the Institute had ever accepted and startling if only because she had never learned to read music; she played Mozart and

Beethoven and Lennon by ear. Her precocity was to be her downfall. When she played her own composition for her yearly assessment at the age of eleven, the elite academy rejected her. It would take her many years to recover her musical confidence.

For months afterwards, she only felt comfortable singing at her maternal grandfather's graveside. Her father was disturbed by her depression and in an effort to restore her self-esteem, suggested that she find a part-time job as a pianist. Clerical collar in place and to the amusement of certain patrons, he chaperoned his daughter every time she played cocktail piano in the gay bars of Washington DC. Amos was a minor playing major in cheap glittering evening gowns and lip gloss, belting out lounge standards and learning how to handle hecklers with grace. Her father commented, 'Even [as a child] she talked of being a rock star.' In 1980, the *Washington Post* quoted the incandescently wilful Amos on her ambitions: 'I want to be a legend.' At the time, her father was writing letters on church stationery to established stars requesting that they assist his gifted daughter. The fact that Michael Jackson and Frank Sinatra did not reply to the Reverend's dinner invitations did not lessen his belief in the youngest of his three children.

Amos moved to Los Angeles when she was twenty-one. She had already changed her name from the staid Ellen to Tori, leaving behind in the process an identity with which she no longer felt comfortable. Her hunger for the success she felt she had been denied was powerful, and her new image was the antithesis of her reality: emeritus Rock Chick — long, teased hair, plastic snakepants, scalloped bra-tops, thigh-high boots. She recorded *Y Kant Tori Read?*, an album which, when released, was murdered by the critics. She was also raped at gunpoint by an acquaintance who had asked her for a lift home after a performance. The experience brought her close to suicide; she vowed never to discuss it. Her way of dealing with the aftershocks of the brutality was to write the a capella 'Me and a Gun', the song which led the Atlantic Group and Warner Music to fund RAINN, a nationwide toll-free sexual assault helpline. The response to the song was a catharsis in itself for Amos, who is now tentatively moving beyond the mourning.

The floor of her eleventh floor suite in Sydney's Sebel Townhouse is littered with gutted suitcases, bizarrely designed and coloured shoes (her one true 'fetish'), her famously mismatched clothes (blue A-line dresses worn with white patent-leather five-inch platforms, grey woollen tights worn with fragile golden spindle-heeled slippers, batik T-shirts, tartan skirts, flared seam-emphasised jeans, et cetera). The glass doors are opened to a dingy afternoon, a view of the city skyline. Loose-limbed in straight-legged jeans, *'bitchin'* Timberland boots, and a cropped sea-coloured chenille or velour top, Amos is all fragile warmth. Her apple-cheeked face halves in a melting smile, she cries hello hello hello, she wears her every emotion.

'Experience,' she announces as she crashes back into the sofa, 'was the only thing I lacked before the age of five, but I didn't have *shame*, either. That whole Christian thing hadn't sunken in yet. I mean, I was playing the scores of musicals when I was four. Music was *everything* to me, eight hours a day. Playing the piano was like *diving* into a world apart.' She frowns as she struggles to articulate her perceptions. 'Music was really about how I understood *time*. It was almost a chronological device. I didn't listen to what people were *saying*; I listened to the music of the time. Music told me everything I needed to know.'

Her absorption in her abilities was beyond pride; music has always been her primary mode of communication. 'I had to *learn* how to pee in a toilet, but I *never* had to learn how to play the piano,' she says as she begins to fiercely twist a rubber band between her fingers. 'I mean, I could play before I could *talk*. When it all went wrong at the Peabody, I felt I had failed as a concert pianist. I had things to prove. I had rebelled, yes, but I also turned on myself and let my abilities go. Now I understand that I had let them go because I didn't really feel that they were going to serve me.' She pauses, flicks the rubber band onto the table beside her, her cheeks pale with lamplight. 'I felt that I was not the thing that everybody thought I was. I believed them when they told me that I had regressed; I believed them when they told me that I didn't have what it took.'

The release of the film *Amadeus* was a watershed for Amos, who went to see it twelve times in a two-month period. 'I went every day and *wept*,' she says with a rueful half-smile. 'The struggle of not being *heard*! Before *Little Earthquakes*, I had been working on my own compositions for seven years. After this period of failure and rejection, I began *chasing* success. At that point it became more important for me to make it than to be a musician. I had lost faith in my work. Instead of telling myself that approval was irrelevant and that all that mattered was the truth of my expression, I became *desperate*.'

The critics, now so hagiographic, were cruel. The *New Musical Express* called her a 'Grade A, Class One, Turbo-driven Fruitcake'. Another critic wrote: 'She is destined … to enter the realms of eternal obscurity.' In England, she is still regarded by some as a 'lovable loony' and her surrealistic lyrical images are seen to be 'incomprehensible'. In part, these dismissals reflect an unwillingness to acknowledge the significance of her more disturbing material, but they also reflect a widespread confusion. Amos frequently expresses herself through metaphor, citing tastes or smells to convey a feeling, offering an image in place of an insight. Such labyrinthine processes are similar to those of the English novelist Jeanette Winterson, with whom she shares a fundamentalist indoctrination. Simply viewed, theirs is a different way of thinking. Raised on allegory and hymnody, Amos, who has long abandoned the doctrine, learned to perceive the world in religious terms. The constant use of metaphorical devices is also a means of establishing a safe emotional distance from others.

'There is a real logic to intuition,' she says as she leans forward, her expression intense. 'If I get called a Californian New Age kook one more time, I'm going to cut somebody's penis off. I mean, it's offensive. The thing about writing is that it's a *craft*; it's not like I just throw some words up against a wall and see if they stick. Just because a topic is significant to me doesn't mean that anyone else wants to know about it, which is where the craft comes in.' Her mouth, shaped in a smile even in repose, works every word. 'Lyrically, I like to work with archetypes, with myths — the myth of the sisterhood, the myth of masturbation. I think it's essential to open yourself to your shadows. My whole problem with the New Age movement is that they're only looking for the light. I believe that in looking for the dark, you'll find that light.'

This 'dark' surfaces through her songs in a sudden sweep of rage, her voice gaining in volume, in depth, in breadth. Amos used her rage to escape 'a place where I was really dying'.

Suddenly distressed, she folds one arm across her belly. 'The little person I used to be disappeared for a time,' she says in a small and broken voice, referring to the period after the assault. 'I went *loco*. Pretty much gone. Vacant. Just totally *vacant*. I mean falling *apart*, yes. Fragmentation. Disintegration.'

Prior to the assault, she had been enthusiastically exploring her sexuality — she was, she says, a girl who drove down the road, saw an attractive man, thought, '*Mmmmmmmmn!*' and could act on that thought. She has spoken of having wanted to be 'the baloney in between the wholewheat bread' of two bisexual male models, of having relished all the hedonism of the pre-AIDS era. Now thirty-one, she feels that the only place where she can integrate her sexuality, spirituality, and emotionality is the stage. 'Never, ever anywhere else,' she says.

Her withdrawal into a quietly panicked monologue is sudden. 'Instead of *respecting* the fact that you're juicy and intelligent, a passionate woman, certain people are *threatened* by it; they try to make you feel *bad* about it. And then when you submit to their judgments, when you *do* feel bad about it, then you *scar* yourself.' Her rainwater eyes are desperately steady. 'So many survivors of sexual assault sell their bodies — very *expensively* sometimes. I know girls who go and sell themselves and say: *I'm getting them all back!* And I'm, like,' here her palm shoots out and she inclines her head, as if attempting to understand, 'hang on a minute … hang on a minute … you're getting them back? You're a $1000 a night girl! Hang on a minute … this is not your liberation! I mean, I love hookers; they're my buddies. There is something in them that was made to feel so shameful about their passion, and other women exacerbate this shame by being critical.'

Simultaneously overcome by different feelings, she becomes agitated. 'As a woman,' she urgently says, 'you are really forced to choose sides. Intelligent women always laugh at a particular kind of woman, the Pamela Anderson kind of woman. Now Pamela's coming to my show tonight, she's a big fan. My music speaks to her because like every other woman, there's a part of her that gets really hurt.' With a quick and childlike movement, she tucks a lock of that carmine hair behind her ear. 'I've been through the whole loop of denying my real passion for years and not being honest about anything. It was a reaction.'

She openly acknowledges the difficulties she has had in being intimate with men since the assault, and has been quoted as saying that there are times when she finds it necessary to pretend to be a prostitute during sex to divorce herself from the fear. These are difficulties shared by all survivors of sexual abuse, and recovery can be tortuous. Amos was helped on her journey by her lover of eight years, the producer Eric Rosse, from whom she parted late last year. 'God, the *mirrors* of the men I've pulled into my life! The things they've shown me about myself!' She shakes her head, folds her hands palm-up in her lap, nestles against the backrest. 'I mean, Eric is probably the dearest person in the whole *world* to me because he helped me through so much — through the whole "Me and a Gun" thing. He really took the brunt of all that. But it's too hard for you to be supportive of each other when you're professionally competing. We both decided that we needed some time apart. We'd been such a creative entity together and really didn't have *time* any more to just be boy and girl.'

Her shoulders relax and her smile becomes tricky, playful, sensual. 'I *love* tecchies [technically inclined men]. Eric is a tecchie. I like men who can *fix* things. If I'm in the middle of fucking nowhere and the car breaks down, I don't want a man who says: *I gotta call my agent.* That's why I don't get involved with musicians. We're too similar; we know our instruments too well we all know how to get around a studio; we *compete.* But tech guys are into rugby and dirt bikes and this whole other world. They're not *precious* like I am about certain things. They don't call room service when something goes wrong. They don't hire people to do their laundry. They're into getting their hands dirty. You know, people in my position have *runners* because sometimes we work from 8 am to 2 am. And because you have people who will do things for you, you get precious.'

Her laughter is high and light. 'People can get *too* used to things, though. For example, going through middle America is such a trip. That level of mediocrity is absolutely *accepted*. The corporations are getting away with murder. The people aren't challenged. They don't challenge *anything*. They stop rejecting; they no longer *question* what they're given. Telling someone that they must change, that they must question the established order isn't enough. *It has to go back ten layers.* What do your internal voices say? What messages have you absorbed? How do you develop the tools to be creative? Because without creative expression, you are dysfunctional.'

Tucking one slender leg beneath herself, she smiles again, a subtle smile. She props her chin up with her hand, her eyes satisfied. 'You know the character I could relate to most in *Amadeus*?' she asks. 'The maid. They portrayed her as a real dingaling, but she probably knew a *lot* more than they ever realised.'

Elle, 1995

AIMING TO PLEASE:
JEFFREY ARCHER

'HOW *OLD* IS he?' Lord Archer asks of my recalcitrant beloved, a fork heaped with spaghetti suspended in the air between the plate and his wide smiling mouth, his grey eyes shrewd, lucid and upturned over those rimless spectacles. He frowns with a philanthropic measure of concentration as he listens. 'I *could* just say to him: you are a *fool!*' His laughter is a blast of hail against a corrugated iron roof; he almost drops the fork into his lap. 'You need a decent *young* man,' he then decides. There is a pause. He crosses his grey flannel legs, parks the fork into the pasta, darkly hums, steeples his fingers, makes a thinking noise. 'If he's a *literary* man,' he murmurs, waggling his recently-trimmed eyebrows, 'he's a big *thinker* ... and big thinkers are dangerous because you never know what they're going to bloody do *next*.'

He refuses to be interviewed until he has heard my story. He insists that he is bored; that he has been yattering about himself for weeks; that it is Friday afternoon and he deserves a break; that he is more interested in my problems than a 'tedious' analysis of *The Fourth Estate*, his superbly structured number one bestseller. 'Jeffrey has always had an *insatiable* curiosity about most everyone he meets,' remarks a friend. Any attempt to ask a question is met with a Ferdinand snort. He squeals if deprived of a single detail. In full flow, he is hilarious, captivating, brilliant, mad. 'I think,' he says in a conspiratorial tone, 'women should be treated *better* than that. He's obviously got no style. At *all*. Upper class arrogance.' His handsome broadbean face contorts as he hisses: 'Arrogance! *Arrogance!*'

For a moment, he stares out at the Sydney Intercontinental's Australia Suite view of the Harbour Bridge and all the sumptuous green inlets of the lower North Shore. 'Where was he educated, do you know?' he suddenly asks. When I tell him, he spreads his palms and evenly grins: all has been explained. '*That* school is famous for producing such men,' he cries. 'Gosh, what a boring *toad!*' And this is his cue. Leaping from the chair, he begins to prance around the table, slapping his thighs, rubbing his hands, literally *shouting* into the tape recorder. As he waves his arm, a cufflink in the shape of a castle turret glisters in the sunlight. 'He's a boring TOAD! You need a nice young man AND NOT THIS BORING TOAD!' He leans into the microphone and loudly snarls. He narrows his eyes, tips his chin, flashes the black onyx signet ring his mother gave him on his twenty-first birthday, burns with medieval outrage. 'YOU ARE A BORING TOAD!' he shrieks, as if addressing the boring toad in question. 'WHAT A P'THETIC CHAP YOU ARE! WHAT A P'THETIC MAN!' And as if struck by lightning, he suddenly slumps back into his chair. 'Ah,' he whispers wistfully, 'it's very sad …'

His gaze is one of avuncular concern. 'All those high-end literary men are like that, by the way,' he says. 'They sort of live in that refined world all of their own and imagine they're sort of godlike.' He considers this. Raises his voice a decibel or two. 'GODLIKE!' A thoughtful pause. 'And people like myself, for example, who write popular novels, well — we can't be seen with them in public. I know them well; I've met them all.' Short shrug. 'You see, I am earthy — man of the people.' This phrase is by him much enjoyed. 'MAN OF THE PEOPLE!' Adjusting his rumpled Hilditch & Key ladybird tie, he is again sombre. 'But your friend is ethereal. This is Oberon we're discussing — must get this right. I'm Puck.' His sense of comic timing is a masterpiece. 'Mind you,' he confides, 'what we have to decide is whether you're Titania or Hermia.'

The man is bewildering, a true paradox. He is England's bestselling author and he cannot spell. He is an arch-Conservative who loathes tradition. He is a traditionalist who insists on change. He is a conventional individualist. He is a prude who flirts religiously. He is a lord contemptuous of the establishment. He is a Machiavellian naïf. He trashes his achievements and defies others to match them. He is a sentimentalist entranced by ruthlessness; touchingly shy and a bombastic extrovert; an Englishman who stands for all that is American. Jeffrey Archer has become part of the modern mythological pantheon, a latter-day Mercury — patron of travellers and rogues, both messenger and thief. Posts with a marble head of Mercury were in ancient times erected where two or more roads met to point out the way.

'The English,' he remarks, recrossing his legs, 'are an introverted race, a race which does not like enthusiasts. We think it's just *not on*. We think we should all be very *quiet*. We *mask* our aggressive impulses. I think the English are *killers*. The English and the Israelis are still the two leading killers in the world today.' His chuckle quickly transforms into the purest indignation. 'And the *snobbery*! I mean, the treatment of John Major has been *total* snobbery!'

One of his most admired diplomatic feats has been his ability to remain close to both Thatcher and Major who are, if not clawed enemies, certainly not friends. 'Here is a man who comes from Battersea,' Archer continues, 'a *beautifully* mannered man — *intensely* loyal, thoroughly decent, a man who comes from Battersea to Downing Street only to have *people like your fellow* run him down all the time. *They* couldn't do one *tenth* of what he's done! They're just *p'thetic* compared to him!' He scowls dramatically. 'The English don't *welcome* success; this is the result of centuries of understating everything. They don't let themselves *go*! They're all pent-*up* inside!'

Comments such as '[England] is no longer a country of aristocrats standing by while [it] becomes a second-rate power' have not endeared him to the establishment. 'Their attacks are *never* direct,' he says. 'I mean, you get people like a certain MP who wrote: "My friends think that I should write a Jeffrey Archer novel." ' A hissing pause. And then he cracks — outraged, exhausted by the memory of such disparagement, and he leans forward as his right hand slices through the air like a blade. '*Be my guest!*' he manages through gritted teeth. 'If you think it's *that* easy, get out and do it, kid! If you think I sell 150 million books by doing something you can do, you second-rate little *creep*, pick up a pen and *go* for it!' Slamming back into the chair, he clenches his jaw and stares at me miserably. 'They think that what I do is *easy*. Oh, of *course*! "I, too, can be a bestselling author!" ' There is the sense of impending thunder. '*BALLS!*' he suddenly explodes.

Another pause. 'Oh,' he wretchedly sighs, *'forget it.'* His feelings of dismay are understandable: Archer is lionised in every country but his own, where he has always been ridiculed for his (many and varied) mistakes without having his (many and varied) achievements acknowledged. The regard he feels he deserves is denied him, and despite the recently bestowed rank of peer, he has never been allowed to forget that he is — in his softly mocking words — 'a pleb'.

'I suppose I've reached a stage now where I know how long I've got left,' he glumly says. 'I've prob'ly reached a reflective point in my life.' Again, he sighs. The ladybird tie lies flaccid in his lap. 'It's my thirtieth wedding anniversary this week; I'm fifty-six — an old man, my love. I've achieved everything I can in the sense that — I mean, *how many more books can I sell?* I mean, yes, I can sell a few more ...' The tinge of defeatism in his words annoys him. 'OF *COURSE* I CAN!' he trumpets. And then, unhappily: 'But I want to do something *important*! I don't want to go to my grave recognised only as a "bestseller"! I think that's *worthless!*'

Wincing, he turns away. Pouts a bit at the wall. 'Would the ultimate be to be elected Prime Minister?' he crossly asks himself. 'NO!' he bellows. A minute passes. And then: 'Of *course* the ultimate would be to be elected Prime Minister! *And I never will be!*' Self-loathing fills his voice. 'I am,' he announces, staring coldly into my eyes, 'a *failure*. I have felt like a failure all my life. I didn't make school prefect; I didn't get into Oxford the right way; I didn't get into the British relay team and stay there … I keep *not* quite making it. And now I'm the number one bestselling author in the world and *it isn't what I want!*'

Absurd as this statement may seem, it holds truth. It can be said that Archer's evident ambitions are no more than an inheritance: it was his mother, Lola, a resourceful provincial journalist, who dreamt of literary fame; it was his late father, William, a charming and incorrigible criminal, who fantasised about political power. Archer's love of the Tory ideology is and has been, in a sense, his only means of actively loving his father, a way of demonstrating to himself that there was something in his father to admire and respect. Much of his youth seems to have been troubled by his need for approval from his erratic guardians, and he seems to have dedicated his life and unique energies to fulfilling both parents' frustrated dreams without really considering his own.

The dissatisfaction with himself that he has always felt can only be the result of attempting to be all things to all people. Michael Crick's exhaustive 1995 biography, *Stranger Than Fiction*, examines Archer's peripatetic childhood, which engendered in him a near-insatiable need to feel worthy of attention, to feel deserving of love: simply *being* has never been enough. Archer has always felt he has to work for affection. Crick reports that the seven-year-old Archer was placed in a weekday 'kind of foster home'; Archer claims to have no recollection of being in any such institution. His father, sixty-five years his senior, was home only intermittently during his early years and there are no reports of him visiting his son at Wellington, the direct-grant boarding school at which Archer was enrolled at the age of eleven. Crick writes: 'Some people at Wellington were under the impression that Jeffrey didn't have a father.'

'I never knew much about my father,' Archer says as he begins to fidget with his shirt-cuffs. 'I never had a very ... *verbal* relationship with him. You must remember that I was very immature, possibly very ... sensitive.' The weight of shame or hurt or betrayal he feels has silenced him. In thirty years of being interviewed, he has referred to his father only fleetingly. William Archer died of complications after an operation in 1956. Pausing as he looks down at his knees, Archer says in a very small voice, 'I remember my *work* not going very well at school after he died. I never blamed him for that, and I —' suddenly gesturing, he hits the tall glass of fruit juice to his right; with a smash, the glass topples over and the juice begins loudly trickling onto the tiled floor. Archer freezes, but he does not flinch. Without even turning his head, he continues, his expression effortfully controlled. 'I was very *sad* at the time. I think I just became a little bit ... *intro*verted ... didn't *work* for a time.' It is as if the words are being torn from him. 'I was downstairs in the gymnasium when I was ... told the news.'

His voice is near-inaudible. 'I went and hid in the changing-room ... and then the ... ah ... *padre* — very gentle chap — came and took care of me ... and I think I went to pieces for about — oh, two or three months.' He clears his throat. 'I didn't *work*,' he again stresses. 'Didn't do any sport. Didn't try anything. Just gave in. I lost my father. Certainly,' he quickly adds, 'I felt more responsible towards my mother. I went out to work in the holidays. We became closer, of course. She's still alive — a *very* remarkable woman.' One of Archer's favourite novels is *The Prodigy*, by Hermann Hesse. 'Why,' Hesse asks in the book, 'had they ... intentionally estranged him from his friends at the grammar school, forbidden him to go fishing and wander around, preferring to instil into him the empty and commonplace ideal of a wretched ambition. Why, even after the examination had they not allowed him to enjoy the well-deserved holidays?'

The juice has formed a wide red pool beneath the table.

A victim of bullying, he is remembered by one schoolmate as having been 'a loner ... badly disliked ... there was a fat boy who used to sit on him occasionally'. Such memories are still painful for him. 'I was tiny and was called puny,' he murmurs, 'I was — I think *bullied* is the word. I was aware that I wasn't — ah — called puny by *mistake* … I was very … ah … *small* … and underweight and under … *every*thing.' With an expression of despair, he suddenly looks up at me. 'I recall *desperately* wanting to be included!' he cries. 'Oh, yes! I always wanted to be part of the team — I'm a team man! I like being *in the team*! I *hate* not being part of the team! *Hate* being outside!' Exasperated, he widens his eyes. 'You just get *lonely* and you can't get anything *done*! It's very hard doing things on your own! You can write a *book* on your own, but you can't do much *else*. I was in the relay team. I always liked being in Margaret Thatcher's team. I liked being in the Conservative Party's team.'

Thatcher was, in many ways, his idol, and he conscientiously solipsized her dedication. He begins reciting their dialogue, as if rehearsing for a play. ' "See you at breakfast, Jeffrey?" "Beg your pardon, Prime Minister? It's two o'clock in the morning now!" *"See you at breakfast, Jeffrey."* ' He smiles nostalgically. 'Never join in the game if you don't. And it's only a game. During the election campaign, we were down to two hours' sleep a night. Only for three weeks. One couldn't do it forever.' As his excitement increases, his sentences shorten. 'You're under *tremendous* pressure. Three weeks to go. Two weeks to go. One week to go. Some big problem arises —

you're all tired; you might make some very bad decisions. I've seen both Margaret and the Prime Minister snap. We all understand. We all *know*. We all know the game we're in. And the next morning, it's forgotten.'

He easily acknowledges that the world of politics is one of ruthlessness, and peopled by those who are unaware of 'the world outside themselves'. Here he leans forward, ecstatic, wired, as if defending his worth. 'But I actually *like* pressure! I actually *enjoy* it! I absolutely *love* it! I can't *wait*! The three week election campaign? I *LOVE* IT!' His voice has risen to a thrilling squeak. 'THIS IS *BATTLE*! *ABSOLUTELY*!'

His best documented battle was the one which led him to resign from his position as deputy chairman of the Conservative Party. In 1986, the headline *TORY BOSS ARCHER PAYS VICE GIRL* galvanised England. Archer sued for libel. His resignation followed newspaper reports that 'he associated with the prostitute, Monica Coghlan, 35, and paid her 2000 pounds to avoid a public scandal ... Archer told the court he gave the money to Ms Coghlan because he felt sorry for her'. The case became the stuff of international dinner-party conversation, and Mary Archer's defence of her husband is remembered as one of the great displays of impassioned loyalty. She has since commented that righteous anger is a very sustaining emotion. Awarded a record 500,000 pounds, Archer donated the money to charities and to a disabled schoolfriend; he has never ignored or rejected old friends in difficulty, and was admired for standing by Thatcher at the end of her political career.

'I had the *very* great privilege of being with Margaret the week before she left [politics] and the week after,' he says, knitting his brows. 'It was, for me, emotionally draining. She was a *broken* woman.' A thoughtful inclination of his head. 'Never saw her wear grey before. Never seen her sit in the corner of a sofa. Never seen her not speak until she was spoken to. Never seen just no *command*, no *control*. I have to say, though, that I never saw Margaret as a *woman*. She'd use it occasionally; Norman Tebbit used to say that when she starts losing battles, she becomes a woman. She only did that to me three times in fifteen years. But she was on top so much of the time that she didn't *need* to.'

Whilst he empathised with Thatcher's deep grief, he was and is more philosophical about political ambition. 'There's nothing to *lose* at the end, really,' he remarks. 'At the end, you're either the Government or you aren't.' A slight West Country accent infiltrates his otherwise House of Commons voice. 'But yer *life* isn't over! You do actually get *up* the next morning! You're still wearing the same *suit*! The driver's still there to take you to *work*!' The incongruity of this last statement is lost in his emphatic sincerity. 'People who are declared bankrupt go

through *ten* times what we go through in a general election —
ten times! *OH!'* Closing his eyes, he shakes his head and
mutters, *'Ten* times! There's nothing like it.'

Crick's conclusion was that Archer is a 'man of many
outstanding qualities [who is] repeatedly brought down by the
serious flaws in his character'. But Archer is an acutely
intelligent man, no stranger to calculation or to human nature,
and famous for achieving that which he wishes to achieve.
Given that this is the case, why did he arrange to have Monica
Coghlan paid? Why would he have taken that, and other,
extreme risks had his political career been of *genuine*
importance? It seems more plausible to conclude that Archer —
the Jeffrey Archer whose ambitions range beyond those of his
parents — has never genuinely wanted to be Prime Minister,
which is why he subconsciously engineered escape routes from
a situation in which he felt uncomfortable. He is, by nature, a
conqueror and not a tyrant. The position of Prime Minister
would restrict him in every sense — emotionally, intellectually,
creatively, financially. Archer was a sprinter; he has never been a
long-distance runner. It is only a strange propriety which
prevents him from acknowledging his anarchic tendencies and
his passion for erecting hurdles over which he must leap.
Ultimately, his greatest ambition is to be loved for what he is: an
altruistic entrepreneur.

'I *live* for challenges, which is why I have two lives,' he admits with an immediate grin. 'One, being in a room on my own — slogging, fighting, the introvert life of writing. And then politics, which is about being with lots of people, and I *love* people.' Reaching out to pluck a strawberry from the overflowing bowl on the table, he pauses to bite into it. 'I *like* the double life I lead,' he says.

Elle, 1997

ACCELERATING TOWARDS BETHLEHEM: THE BENETTON FORMULA ONE TEAM

THE MUSIC OF a Formula One car is Wagnerian — that swell of decibels and all the tyranny therein, a soundtrack for anxiety: repetitive, fantastic, jarring. An alarm sounds in the pit-lane as the cars approach; the mechanics and NASA-standard engineers disperse at an equipollent speed. During each two-hour race, these cars brake before their pits, are just as rapidly fuelled and adjusted by a team of men, and as the lollipop BRAKE signs are flipped to show every driver his team's logo, the cars begin to paw and snort, to bump the tarmac with ever-increasing urgency, desperate to snap back on the track after eleven or so seconds, and their cry in that moment is almost human: *let me go, let me go, let me go.*

Melbourne has never known such technocratic heat. Sunday morning, and the stands — painted a patriotic green and gold — are bristling with boys and men. 0930: F1 warm-up. Jean Alesi, of the reigning Benetton, pulls his B196 into the pit-lane only to slip on the too-glassy surface. The eloquent skid-mark is black; it could have been shorthand for death. News spreads that one of the Benetton mechanics has been hit. Outside the pit, sixty to seventy members of the international press corps are waiting with their cameras, microphones and pads — *what happened? Is he dead?* Within seconds, an ambulance. Men quickly wheel a stretcher into the pit. Within, the mechanic lies supine and with his right arm balanced on his brow. In the shadow cast by his arm, the man's expression is one of shock; for a moment, it looked as if he were about to cry.

Blue bags of ice are pressed to his ankles and both legs are eased into inflatable and zippered bags. No more than bruising and a cruel surprise. Surrounded by stacks of densely-scented thousand-dollar tyres and the people he calls his family for nine months of every year, the man is lifted onto a stretcher and consoled. Rough strips are adhered quickly to the tarmac. Such 'teething difficulties' were expected; the new Benetton engine was designed to shave two seconds from the previous year's lap-time and has yet to 'settle in'; added to this, the omnipresent unpredictable. 'Before any Grand Prix,' one of his team comments, 'the atmosphere in here is *death*. You never know what will happen.'

The engineers are running on two hours' sleep. Tad, the Pole frontlining design and research, smiles through a yawn. 'In Brazil last year,' he says, 'we worked all night on the Thursday, the Friday, the Saturday. We had a big panic on the Sunday morning when there was an engine blow-up; by the time the race had started, we were in hyperdrive. It was literally a case of the mental keeping the physical going. That night, most of us could barely make it through the hotel door. After the last pit-stop, mechanics were sleeping on the garage floor. There is no room in this sport for people who can't hold themselves and their colleagues together.'

In Formula One, the passion for winning amounts to fetishism. Official prize money is never published and 'only' a matter of hundreds of thousands. 'Success,' explains John Postlethwaite, Benetton's marketing director, 'can mean *millions*.' The reverence in his voice is mystical. 'For a football club, the 40,000 people coming in through the stiles are a source of income; the 20,000 people coming through the stiles here are not. Sponsors are pivotal, and their payback is huge. You're talking about your logo being exposed for 1500 seconds a race in 200 countries. If you tried to buy that airtime in terms of spot-cost, it would be impossible.' Michael Schumacher, who won the World Championship with Benetton for two consecutive years, was lured to Ferrari by a reported US$45 million. Former World Champion, Niki Lauda, now owns an airline. Bernie Ecclestone, head of the F1 Constructors' Association, is said to be worth in excess of US$200 million. Benetton's F1 MD, Flavio Briatore, lives in a world of monogrammed white bathrobes, custom-made watches, private jets, and yachts that are drolly referred to as 'boats'. Less understandable is the devotion of the assistants, mechanics and general staff.

Briatore is 'looked after' by Dave Morgan, an affable Englishman who returns to his rural 'other life' (in which he has a wife he married at sixteen and adult children) for a month or two every year. Seated at a vinyl-covered table in the makeshift dining area, he reasons: 'It makes perfect sense to me that rates of depression are doubling in industrialised countries every decade. What other response can there be to a lifetime of office or factory work? When I go to my local and see the men in there, I think — *there but for the grace of God go I*.' His smile is one of relief. 'I see men locked to their mortgages, their cars, their jobs. These guys are stamped on, they're *caged*. The local paper, watching soaps on the telly, cleaning the windows, taking the dog for a walk … it's great for three days, but then I get panicky. I miss life in the fast lane.'

The popularity of F1 is a testament to this global sensation of being 'stamped on' — 500 million people avidly follow the sport, if only to observe the consequences of daring to challenge conventional limitations. Such a level of fascination indicates a real human need for excitement, for an arena in which men can express strong emotion. Rock-fishing may well claim more lives than the circuit, but its soul is too ancient; F1 is the spirit of all modern men — its goals are material, its success quantifiable, it demands ambition and ruthlessness, cunning and money. Above all, it is violence without an ideology to justify it.

'Here there is no ideology,' explains Briatore in his elegant Italian. A playboy in the classic European mode, he is resented within the F1 fraternity for his achievements. Through restructuring and the implementation of a long-term programme, he made it possible for his team to eclipse Ferrari, Williams, and McLaren. 'There is no consideration in this world for higher levels of thought. This said, the people here are the best in their fields.' He pauses to light a Malboro and then exhales. 'There are children in Bosnia who take bigger risks walking to school. They get a bullet in the head for free; here, at least, they're paid.'

Formerly a player with the Milan Stock Exchange — 'where the ability to decide quickly is more important than the validity of that decision' — he moved to Benetton's marketing department, and then again to F1. Whilst he appears to be remarkably self-possessed, the fact that he cannot eat lunch before a Grand Prix for fear of throwing up suggests an unnatural investment of self-worth in performance. Like many of the others involved in the sport, he was raised by a 'hard' father and has often spoken of 'claustrophobia' engendered by his childhood experience. He shares with his colleagues a nervous need for constant action. 'F1 is extreme,' he says, gesturing gently with his cigarette. 'Where there is a big game, there are big players who play for big stakes and as a consequence, the pressure is enormous. After a time, the pressure becomes as familiar as a lover. We live in a world in which every man runs, but never takes the time to reflect on his direction. It's a logical evolution of industrialisation — too much, much too fast.'

The millions invested by sponsors ranging from beer companies to tobacco conglomerates create stressful expectations. Despite Tad's assurance that 'Motorhead on a twenty-city tour have *nothing* on us when we let go,' the ferocity with which they work is a contrast to 'the old days'. What was a sport spearheaded by characters such as the Englishman James

Hunt, the handsome and sexually voracious 1976 World Champion whose death at the age of forty-five was fuelled by drinking binges and cocaine abuse, is now a *Campus Martius* for the disciplined. All drivers are expected to display the rigorousness of athletes in their approach to fitness, skill, and sponsorship commitments.

Postlethwaite cites this 'public relations work' as the most numbing — an exhausting round of press conferences, interviews, photographs, corporate backslapping, and eye-wateringly dull black-tie functions at which the drivers are expected to 'pretend to have a good time'.

1115: each driver perches on the backrest of a soft-top Austin Healey Mark 2 for the parade. The response is one of awe, and very loud. *'GERHARRRRRRRRRD!'* a swooning man screams as Berger, veteran of 180 races, eleven pole positions, eighteen fastest laps and nine wins, mechanically waves. Spattered with logos and strangely petite, the drivers fulfil their responsibility to heroism. Tall substandard models stand gripping flags at perfectly spaced intervals on the sidelines. With their white smiles and dazed stares, they must hope that their usefulness to society will extend beyond that of human pole-mounts. The men in the stands cheer and clap, ignorant of the amused contempt with which the girls are regarded by the F1 high rollers and photographers (one of whom was overheard asking them to 'have a little wrestle' for the camera).

The corporate boxes above the pits (sold for up to AUS$250,000 each) sag under the weight of dyspeptic meritocrats — bored men who guzzle oysters and ignore the blondes who will never be as interesting to them as an annual report. These bare-knuckle businessmen and their mahogany wives paid $600 a head to attend Friday night's Grand Prix ball (marred by bald pates over which dyed strands of long hair had been hopefully combed, and fifty-year-old women in tiaras and fox-fur and ruffled gold wraps). This event was later described by an F1 official as being 'boring as fuck'. A corporate lawyer patiently explains: 'These guys are here to network. Corporations are always looking for reasons to blow money on their clients, and so try to entertain them at an international level. To maintain loyalty, they have to make the client feel as if they play with the Big Boys, and F1 is the Big Boys' domain. It's all about *power*.'

Berger is an old hand at the power-game, a pal of Gianni Agnelli's and the only driver allowed to see his close friend Ayrton Senna's fatal head wounds in hospital. At the age of thirty-seven and seemingly indifferent to the spoils of his sport, the Austrian describes F1 as no more than 'a chob'. He is slim and fair, boyish in his Versace jeans and white socks, Benetton cap and studded belt. Despite his marriage to a model and two children, he is still plagued by a reputation as a playboy. Asked about his excess and sexual exploits, he ingenuously replies: 'When naughty zings heppen, I close my eyes. I see nozzing.'

The interview takes place in his makeshift office and as we speak, he delicately slips off his azure suede racing boots and then settles down on the blue foam-form sofa, legs apart and eyes shaded by the brim of his cap. Berger will hold your gaze until you are forced to avert yours; to him, power is that which must on every level be asserted. 'If I were to begin to zink I were different to ozzer people,' he says with a shrug, 'I would get mad in ze head, you know?' After indicating the area in question, he frowns. 'I was somebody liking extremely risky situations until 1989, when I crashed. I remember zinking: *I am gonna die*. In my mind, I knew ze speed, I knew my weight, I knew my angle, I knew I was going about 280, I knew zere was a wall and I went straight into it. So I put my hands here,' he defensively crosses his chest, 'off ze steering wheel, and waited for ze bik beng.'

He pauses before returning his hands to their natural position (on or around his groin). 'I changed completely after ze accident because I realised how close it is to dying, and if you die it's over, which is not good because I like my life. In zis sport, ze luck you have is like cheques in a chequebook. My chequebook is getting zin, I know it.' His laughter mitigates what otherwise could be construed as an obnoxious and patronising attitude. 'I don't want to die at all, you know?' He shakes his head. 'No. I don't want to die. I am not going to die. Definitely not.' He also plans never to retire.

'These guys are thousands of miles away from home,' Postlethwaite says, 'and sometimes the female temptations are difficult to resist. People just switch off. A lot of the guys feel as if they're in another world. They have two different lives.' Briatore agrees. 'The relationships we have are never normal. How could they be?' he asks, resigned. 'The only people you trust are those with whom you work or the people you knew *before* you were successful. The more successful you are, the more people you know, but somehow, you're even lonelier.' His current relationship has been one of his most stable, but will end after the season when his girlfriend will be photographed in a relatively compromising vertical position with a certain muscular sex symbol. 'I am now with a person I'm comfortable with and I hope it lasts, but *love*?' The pathos with which he infuses the word is real. 'I would give *anything* to be "in love". Friends of mine talk of "losing their heads" over a woman. It makes me so jealous. I have yet to find myself in the situation where my feelings for a woman overwhelmed me.'

Briatore's attitude is more representative of the fraternity than that of Alesi, who is mocked by many for his shameless romanticism. Divorced in 1994, the thirty-two year old is now engaged to a celebrated twenty-one-year-old Japanese actress. 'I didn't think that I could be loved only for my money,' he admits in Italian blurred by a French accent, 'but I was. My response to the divorce was to say: *bon!* I won't bother searching for love any more.' His sudden smile is infectious. 'And then I met Kumiko, who earns a great deal of money in her own right. Let us say that my talent is fidelity. I am *so* in love — I am *insane* for this girl! I believe in being kind to the girls they call "groupies" — sure, I'll pose for a picture and sign autographs — but I only have eyes for Kumiko.' An engineer who has observed Alesi's gentle caresses and love-play curtly comments: 'It's enough to make a man *vomit*.'

Patrizia Spinelli, Briatore's PA, analyses Alesi's nature. 'Jean,' she says with affection, 'is a typical Latin. He could not *live*, he could not *exist* without his family and his girl. Kumiko's a very famous actress but she's Japanese, you know? Different culture. She could play the star, but she doesn't. Yesterday, she was sewing his *overalls*. If she were an American or Italian actress, you wouldn't catch her *dead* doing that.' Her large jewel-coloured eyes widen. 'The wives and girlfriends of the drivers are not of strong character. Because *really*, you have to devote your *life* to them — you have to cope with their moods when they are *beasts*; you have to spend hours and days in motor-homes and garages; you have to be in bed at nine on weekends; you have to follow them around the circuit. These women cannot have a career.'

Late the previous afternoon, the photographer asked me to interrupt Berger's meeting with his engineers. 'Ask him if he'd consent to a bare-chested shot,' he said. I knocked and entered the room (men, tools, papers, screens). As I spoke, Berger stared at my breasts as if they were making the request. 'What do you zink, guys?' he asked, glancing at his colleagues. General laughter, if mostly embarrassed. Returning his gaze to my breasts, Berger raised his voice: 'My shirt off, eh? Only if you take *your* shirt off. I want to see what's underneaz.' His eyes dropped to my pelvis. 'Is zat skirt twenty centimetres lonk or twenty-five? Make it *schorter*. I want the skirt to be *schorter*. And zen you take *your* shirt off.' On leaving the room, I realised that he had not once referred to my face.

Alesi, a gentle man from a background far less privileged than Berger's, saves his hostility for the circuit. 'We all change when we get into our cars,' he says. 'The aggression I need to drive means that a personality shift is inevitable, but it is an aggression I don't have in everyday life. The violence I feel when I'm racing is only an adjunct to passion — the two are inextricably connected, but also compartmentalised. On the track, I feel *suffused* by pleasure — it's like being on a rollercoaster, you know? *Wild* pleasure. Even so, it must be tempered by calmness. You cannot drive like this —' laughing, he crosses his eyes and jerks an imaginary steering wheel. 'You'd be dead in the first lap.'

The archetypal F1 driver is a man who feels liberated by excessive risktaking. Even the 'cool and independent' Berger acknowledges experiencing a 'certain' release of tension ('not zat I am tense, you know?'). Implicit is also a need to prove themselves, to compound their sense of masculinity through the approval and envy of other men. 'The ultimate talent in a driver is sensory,' Tad explains. 'They become one with the car. Alesi drives from the heart — he bypasses the physical side so that he doesn't even notice the forces of the car: they go straight to his heart. Senna [who died after an horrific crash at Imola in 1994] was much the same.' The accepted wisdom is that the drivers drive 'on gut-feel' and only analyse when confronted by a problem; the engineers, on the other hand, design through analysis and solve problems 'on gut-feel'. 'When you see the view from the on-board camera in the wet, all that's visible is the brake-light of the car in front,' Tad says. 'Every corner must be memorised. That's when you realise how gifted these guys are and how *brave*.'

Preparations for the race are underway. The cars glide into their positions. Helmeted, the drivers are recognisable only by emphatic features — Berger is all cheese-paring nose, Alesi all glowing and thickly-lashed eyes. The sun throws the mechanics' shadows over the tarmac. Umbrellas bearing the teams' logos are held to shade the drivers from the heat. The smell is of oil, petrol, rubber and fear.

Perched on wooden benches in the F1 paddock toilets, the tips of their strappy sandals touching the concrete floor, designer-drunk women natter to their friends — an index finger in one ear and a mobile telephone pressed to the other. Briatore is briefing Berger on the track. In the sky above, red plumes of smoke disintegrate in the wake of spiralling Red Arrow jets. No one stands as the national anthem is played. Alarms are activated: ten, five, three minutes to go before the practise lap. As the last alarm sounds, the mechanics and MDs and engineers sprint back to the pits.

The vibration of the engines rocks the floor of every corporate box. One of the cars overturns and crashes; the roar of terror from the crowd is tinged with delight. Unharmed, the driver walks from the wreckage and winks at his wife. Briatore, safe in the pit, frankly remarks: 'F1 is a spectacle, a circus. We represent a dream. At times, it's a dream for us. I don't think we exist in the real world. Reality is people who have problems paying the rent, people who have problems raising their children. Real life is not 250 people working all year long and millions added to millions of dollars to produce two cars.'

1400: the race begins. Through the earplugs every sound is removed: it is to be in cloud. In an effort to overtake Ferrari's Eddie Irvine, Alesi is 'bumped off' the track with no chance of regaining time. He will not finish the race. After a mesmerising one-hour battle, Damon Hill overtakes his Williams' teammate, Jacques Villeneuve, and wins. Irvine takes third place, Berger fourth. On the podium, Hill knocks Irvine's cap from his head and Irvine responds by spraying him with champagne from a magnum balanced on his groin. Bizet's 'Toreador' booms from the loudspeakers. Unnoticed and with a bowed head, Schumacher retreats to his pit. Alesi is in his office, talking his disappointment through with his ever-present older brother, Jose. Berger storms into his office and slams the door behind himself. The team is quietened by the result, but soon returns to its humour. It is only the first race of the reason after all, and then there is Luigi's pasta to anticipate.

Earlier in the day, Briatore leaned forward in a white plastic dining chair to sip some coffee. 'The car,' he said after a pause, 'is an integral part of a man's life. It symbolises independence to him, it is the means through which he expresses himself, it is his *friend*. And F1 is a logical extension of this symbiotic relationship, an extension taken to its limit.' Another sip, and then the muscles of his face stretched into an uncharacteristic smile. 'Think about it. Your average man spends more time in his car than he does in his wife, no?'

As he laughed for the first time in three long days, he looked like a man unburdened.

Elle, 1996

NUMB AND NUMBER

THE MYTH OF Bacchus is a sad parable of the sins of the father being visited upon the son. Bastard issue of the union of the deity Jove and mortal Semele, the god of wine and its resultant revelry was punished with insanity by Juno, Jove's vengeful wife. Unhappy tale, and rich with truth in that the bastard issue of deception and deception can only be escapism and escapism as a maxim is madness. All alcoholics know this, but madness is not as threatening to them as truth, something they fear — and sometimes rightly — would raze their deceiving progenitors.

Similar tragedies colour the rational materialism of this century red, they colour it black.

Thirty-six-year-old economist Timothy E. Donohue and thirty-three-year-old journalist Caroline Knapp, an improvident 'skid-row' Jeremiah and bourgeois 'high-functioning' alcoholic respectively, have written — with opaque logic and some distemper — accounts of their 'disease'. *In The Open* is a diary of vagabondage spanning a four-year period; in it Donohue casts himself as an amalgam of Hesse's Knulp, Sam Shepard, and John Maynard Keynes. He wanders the deserts, the shores, and the cities. He contemplates suicide and belligerently soils his pants in cars. Interpolated between manic-depressive cockcrows and orgiastic descriptions of his viscid illnesses are bizarre bar graphs and percentiles and musings on government policies. The absolutism of AA is eschewed by him in favour of the great and perverse American tradition of self-destruction.

At the core of Donohue's soul is a wretchedness he justifies with butch posturing. He knows imperviousness to be the axis of machismo, and duly immunises himself against sensitivity by drinking. Apathy is worn by him like the *Legion d'Honneur*. God, he believes, inflicts such misery on him that he cannot help but cite it as the 'prime cause' of his alcoholism. 'When suffering becomes so unbearable,' he writes on page 32, 'then its source impresses us as a vindictive creator who is simply inflicting some token misery on us to remind us of His love.' And on page 35? 'He wants to make sure that we share in that pain and doubt by coercing us into despair and rendering our hope for life impotent in the face of His countervailing antagonism.'

A vindictive creator? Countervailing antagonism? Our Father who art in Heaven? Or just *his* father? '[The cause of my father's death was] an aggressive tumour that invaded his neck and salivary gland,' he reports on page 38. 'The growth ... wrapped itself around his carotid artery ... to me, the death seems more like a cruel murder than a demise from natural causes. He was ... a lawyer still in vigorous contention with both life and his legal foes.' The tumour is 'aggressive'; it 'wrapped' itself around his carotid artery. Donohue's anthropomorphising is transparent. What stifled longing lines his likening of the death to a 'cruel murder'? And how much further does he have to stagger before he finds himself snarling about 'countervailing antagonism'?

His father must not be exposed in his terrors; even in his lesser panoply, Jove still annihilated all mortals. The only truth allowed is that in the guise of madness, for in madness lies the cure to an allergy to responsibility. Page 31: 'A strong, callused hand grabbed the muscle between my shoulder and neck and squeezed till it hurt. In my weakness I managed a terrified bellow, pivoted, and flailed my arms wildly in the darkness. But nobody was there!' Whose hand is he remembering? What experiences taught this man the meanings of 'weakness', 'terrified' and 'flailed'?

Drinking — A Love Story is another cloudy homage to terror. No 'common drunk', Knapp was a cool and collected

LBD-clad newshound: 'You hide behind the professional persona all day, then you leave the office and hide behind the drink.' Where Donohue feels able to 'safely' express only rage (an emotion that does not compromise his understanding of masculinity), Knapp is conversant with every emotion *but* anger. Despite a dram or two of Jewish blood, she is the Protestant poster girl — uptight, strung out, twice removed from her feelings, and discusses her alcoholism using a traditionally 'feminine' argot. In the prologue, she writes: 'It happened this way: I fell in love and then, because the love was ruining everything I cared about, I had to fall out.' Like Donohue, she sees her alcoholism through the lens of gender identity; unlike Donohue, she is made of sugar and spice and everything nice. No paeans to pus or cacky plus-fours for Miss Knapp. *Her* drinking is defined by 'passion, sensual pleasure, deep pulls, lust, fears, yearning hungers'.

Yearning hungers? An 'esteemed psychoanalyst', her adulterous father would come home every night to the martini-pitcher prepared by his wife and sit in crepitating silence until the anaesthetic took effect: 'The difference [in him was the] sense that he'd shifted from slightly disengaged to slightly more available ... the martini seemed to take some core stiffness out of him, to ease a deep sadness, and sitting there watching them, I'd feel like I'd been holding my breath for a long time and finally could let it out.' The early associations of alcohol and relief were set. But relief from what?

Knapp is a waif in darkness, nervously singing to comfort herself. She prettifies Aeschylean agonies, crafts daisy-chains from overtones of incest, and slaps her hand with facts and figures when the going gets too tough. Donohue prefers the ignominy of being a 'bad boy'. The perpetuation of his perception of himself as a victim — of society, of the economy, of theology, of fate — is as necessary to him as oxygen. He does not dare transcend his assigned role. To identify his 'vindictive creator' would be to assert himself; to assert himself would be to not be a victim; to not be a victim would deprive him of the only security — that is to say, sense of identity — which he knows.

Like Jove, the omnipotent father-figure in both books is mendacious and inaccessible. And just as Semele was reduced to ash by bitterness, the mother-figure is emotionally or physically absent. Donohue may well extract pleasure from degradation and Knapp may know her pleasure in the *escape* from degradation, but degradation is the common denominator. To both, alcohol substitutes the father and they respond to it accordingly — Donohue lies prostrate, ever tortured; Knapp allows herself to be partially ravished, ever Daddy's Little Girl. The transference is remarkable, and at no point do either of them realise that their fathers' qualities are being projected by them onto an intoxicant (with which they have obsessive relationships as complicated as those they suffered with their fathers).

The authors are not, as they seem to believe, struggling against alcoholism; theirs is the struggle of the motherless Bacchus against the overpowering excesses of his father. Alcoholism is a symptom. It has never been a cause.

The Sydney Morning Herald, 1997

THE BLOND LEADING
THE BLOND: WARWICK AND
JOANNE CAPPER

THE COOLANGATTA MORNING is moist and sultry, heavy with tropical birdsong. I am being driven to a house on the brink of an amusement park called Dreamworld, a place where life as we know it recedes into the blue, blue distance and where conventionality dissolves into a glittering enchanted consciousness. Love is really in the air. My driver rolls his cab down narrow streets flanked by dense foliage until we reach the foot of a steep and winding concrete driveway, a driveway rumoured to have cost something in the vicinity of $65 000, a driveway leading to the home of the southern hemisphere's

most improbably famous couple, Warwick 'The Wiz' Capper
and his firm-thighed wife, Joanne.

Up, up, up the magic mountain we drive — past bracken
and ghostly gums, past wildflowers and rotting undergrowth,
up and up and up further until we finally reach the summit.
Before me stands the biggish uglyish brown million-dollar
house in question. Warwick, an apprentice-boilmaker-and-
concreter-cum-AFL-legend-cum-fashion-designer-cum-
stuntman-cum-male-centrefold-cum-radio-announcer as well as
would-be actor, passes the greater part of his life here
organising the finer points of his stardom whilst Joanne, a
horse-strapper-cum-page-three-model-cum-receptionist-cum-
cosmetic-dental-person-cum-centrefold-cum-new-mother, takes
exceptional care of him and their mutually enriching industry.
'Capper's Rock Words' may be SEA FM's newest sensation, but
'The Wiz' has never been one to rest on his laurels. Warwick
also plays football for Southport in the position of centre half-
back, has shares in Five Star Films, and will be featuring in a
national twelve-month advertising campaign for Nike. If
Mammon allows, he and his wife will travel to America later in
the year to have 'a bit of a sniff around' Hollywood. Life has
been an unprecedented rollercoaster ride for this man who was
first photographed for the *Sydney Morning Herald* with an
orange bollard on his head.

The house is guarded by a biggish uglyish brown dog encumbered by an enormous studded collar, a dog who lollops up to me with a wagging tail as the cab pulls away. I walk to the porch and shout a greeting, whereupon the door is wrenched open by the lady of the house, all of 5'4" in her diminutive bare feet, her twenty-five-diamond engagement and wedding rings sparkling in the sunshine, her eight-month pregnant belly distorting the clean line of her cerulean tent-dress. *'Hoi!'* she announces in a friendly buzzsaw voice. 'Carm in!'

I am surprised by her loveliness. She is so very *nice*. Her smile is brilliant, her beautiful eyes are the green of stormy water, and she assures me that she has no fillings. In her November 1992 *Penthouse* spread she looked like a trampy rat-haired blonde with a mercilessly freckled cleavage and pubic hair as white as the froth on a pint of Castlemaine, but in the flesh she is (beneath the frosted lipstick, blue eyeshadow, and pancake makeup) quite classically delicate. Her mumbling husband lumbers about in the shadows as she leads me to the kitchen. 'Yew must be doying fer a cawld drink,' she kindly says. 'Oi'll make yew a loime cordial.'

The man whose lips once had him dubbed 'Suction Cups' steps into the light. Tall and strong and as brown as his rooftiles, Warwick Capper is clad in a pair of satin Superman boxer shorts, a black singlet, and black flip-flops. His hair is long and ragged and unevenly streaked, he has a tattoo of a red devil with a football on its pitchfork on his back, and sports a chunky gold hoop in each tanned earlobe. Refreshingly unselfconscious, he continually rearranges what he has referred to in the past as his 'credentials'. He cannot for the life of him remember my name, but he is mesmerised by my cleavage. 'Take yer jacket off,' he suggests a number of times, 'it's hot in here.' I gingerly remove my jacket. Warwick's eyes are glued to my breasts. 'Nice big ones,' he breathes, 'could be in *Penthouse* with those, couldn't she, Joanne?' His wife waddles over with my lime cordial and explodes into a warm and extraordinary cackle which can only be reproduced in print as *'Schhhhhhhhhhhhhyyyyyeeeeeeeeaaaah HAR HAR HAR!'*

The first of their two living rooms is wide and high-ceilinged and virtually devoid of ornamentation. Along one wall, a 15' bar decorated with empty beer cans and a tasteful black-and-white portrait of Joanne and her startling nipples. In one corner there is a television and a video recorder, and in another, a Hugh Hefner pinball machine. There are two worn and faded sofas; between them, a coffee table laden with magazines in which the Cappers are featured. Laminated posters of these magazine covers have been blu-tacked throughout the house — in the toilet, on the kitchen wall, in the games room.

They sit beside each other on one of the sofas, Warwick leaning forward with his elbows on his knees, Joanne resting back with her arms behind her head. Never known as advocates of establishmentarianism, they have been applauded, ridiculed, and misunderstood by the media, and, in particular, criticised for their avarice. They have agreed to do this interview without 'cabbage' [payment], but generally charge ten to twenty thousand dollars for the privilege. Even so, why should they be castigated for exploiting a medium which has exploited them? They see the situation simply enough: *quid pro quo*, and hold the mustard. Like two creations of a contemporary Twain, they are both innocent and wily, delightful and lewd, crude and charming. Warwick may well be an intellectual savannah, but the surfeit of tenderness in Joanne's every look transcends the cold opportunism of which she has been accused. The more sophisticated amongst us probably have something to learn from their unpretentious joy. Theirs is the Great Australian Love Story, and no mistaking it.

'I watch 'im,' she says, 'like, I'll be sittin' in the kitchen and he'll just do somethin' like bite into an apple or smile … and I'll be sittin' there thinkin': yair, *shit* I love yew!!' The swell of emotion in her voice rouses Warwick from a reverie and he turns to her. 'Do ya?' he asks. She screams with delight. He grabs her right breast and fondles it like a grapefruit. 'Quite a beautiful girl, isn't she?' he asks me. She chortles, ever more pleased. 'I think yer a good-lookin' girl!' he says. Her look is pure lanolin. 'Do ya, darlin'?' she asks. 'Yew are!!' he insists. 'Yew certainly are!!' And, turning to me again, he says: 'Grate, isn't she? I don't think I'll be able to get any better, nah.' He shakes his head. *'Nah.'*

'He shows his emotions a lot more openly since we got back together,' she says, ruffling his hair as he stares into space. 'I mean, he really is the idyllic husband now. I wouldn't want to change him in any way, yew know? We hold nuthin' back from each other, since our separation we've learnt that. *Nuthin'* is held back, no matter what. Yew've gotta be really open — communication is *everythin'* ... especially in our lives with him being who he is, yew know?'

Their passion flowered long before their notoriety. They met at a parentally-supervised party in their hometown of Melbourne in 1978, when they were both fourteen. Warwick expressed his interest in Joanne by attempting to monopolise her attention all night. 'I've had horses all me life,' she explains, 'and I was more into horses than boys, but he chased me.' The two relinquished their virginities to each other, an event which Warwick remembers with the words: 'She was pretty tight.'

Their long-awaited 1988 wedding made national news. They married before 120 guests at Melbourne's Uniting Church in chic Collins Street. Joanne's $7000 Christopher Essex chiffon-and-tulle gown was designed to fit her so tightly that she was forced to mince up the church steps sideways, while Warwick awaited her at the altar in white leather-and-lace tails and tight white leather elf-boots. A fortnight later, both outfits were up for sale — his a snap at $900, hers at $3000 o.n.o.

Nevertheless, there was trouble in paradise. Warwick's great career in football was going down the tubes and he compensated for this humiliation by becoming increasingly self-obsessed. Joanne made repeated efforts to remedy the situation, but to no avail. It seemed that the most important person in Warwick's life was Warwick, and in 1991 the golden couple separated. It was a traumatic time for both of them, a time during which she exposed her body for money, during which he catapulted her new lover through a window, during which they warred in print: a vale of terrible tears.

'I took her fer granted too much,' he admits in his strangely high and monotonal machine-gun voice. 'Egomaniac. I got a bit too far up meself, I think.' 'And with all the little seventeen and eighteen year olds who were trying to get into his pants at nightclubs ...' she adds. 'I tried to talk to him but he just wouldn't listen. Nah. But not many women have the balls to pack up and say: *I'm out!* There's not a lot of women like me with a bit of a pigheaded head on their shoulders who won't accept that kind of behaviour, yew know? Most women say: Okay, yer goin' out with the boys every Friday night to come home at 3 am blind drunk, that's gonna be the ritual, is it? I couldn't live like that. We had all this' — she indicates the airy domicile — 'and I just up and *left* it. I had *nuthin'*.'

Joanne was unable to find work. Out of desperation, she posed for *Penthouse* magazine. 'She just wanted the cash,' he says with satisfaction. 'I *did*!' she whinnies, 'I did it for the money! Pure and simply *for the cash*!' Warwick smirks, and with as much sarcasm as Warwick can muster, says: 'Mate, she was *grate* when she left me. Couldn't get a job. Serious. She was on the dole, cryin': *Give me a job, you bastards!* On 'er arse.'

J: He took everythin' —

W: I was pissed off!

J: He took everythin'. He took the car —

W: I was *mad*, mate!

J: He took all our belongings —

W: I wanted to go and give it to 'er. I was really *daaaaaark*.

J: *Everythin'!*

W: But now I'm over it! *Happy!*

His spectacular grin is sudden enough to be disorientating, but that's the way it generally is with 'The Wiz'; very little permeates. The one thing that did get through was his wife's absence. During those fourteen months, she suffered innumerable nuisance calls, was followed, and found the petrol tank of her car filled with sugar. She and her new lover, the signwriter Darren Watson, were living together in an apartment on the Gold Coast the night Warwick kicked the front door down at 3.30 am. When Watson rose to investigate the noise, he 'felt a blow to the left … side of my head … and then a shove' which propelled him through a window. He then said that the person he saw was Warwick Capper, who pointed at him and said: 'I'm going to have you killed.' The *Canberra Times* reported that Capper claimed he was struck first and that a fight ensued when he defended himself. A year later, Capper was cleared of breaking and entering and assault charges at the Southport District Court.

'I just felt a bit … hurt and a bit jealous, I s'pose,' he says uncomfortably. 'I just got a bit pissed at the time and heard a few … a few … a few rumours, so I sort of — I just felt a bit of — a bit of — a bit of hatred. She was in there rootin' this other guy and I didn't like it. Upset. I did martial arts for a year and a half. Pretty heavy stuff. Tai Kwon Do. I kicked the door in. There was a bit of a scuffle in the dark. I gave him a roundhouse kick — a flying kick — and I got him under the chin and he went right through the window and I thought: *Jeez!* I got a bit scared. I thought: *I don't need this!* And that was it. It was over in a few minutes. It made me feel better. But I felt even better when I was acquitted,' he says, his eyes fighting black. 'The message was: *Don't fuck with Wizard Capper.*'

He is still for a moment, and then says: 'I was a bit … lonely. I felt like there was a big … hole in me life at the time. She warrn't there to talk to. I … cried at night. Couple of times. Alone. In bed. By meself.' At the time, he was living in a 'small, shabby flat under a friend's house' and working as a part-time swimming pool tiler and film extra. Getting Warwick to articulate precisely what it was that he missed about his wife is a Sisyphean task. 'Nice … bottom,' is his first offering. 'It's good to have someone to talk to financially,' is his second. His third is that she is a 'good cook'.

Joanne watches him intently as he flounders; she is hugely interested in his responses and refers to me conspiratorially, identifying with the difficulty that I am having with him. I tentatively suggest that perhaps it was Joanne's honest love which he missed, rather than her buttocks or her ability to balance a chequebook. At this, she claps her hands and with an astonished admiration, says to her husband: 'She's a real psychopath!' 'The best!' Warwick exclaims with a winning grin. His wife claps again. 'She's just mappin' it all out!' she says. 'A real psychopath,' Warwick agrees, 'Jeez, she asks some good questions, darrn't she? She's *grate!*'

The word they want is 'psychologist', but such pedantry, I feel, is a little irrelevant at this particular juncture. The festal enthusiasm with which they approach life more than compensates for their energetic ignorance. Warwick seems to enjoy his ignorance, as if he feels that any wisdom could compromise his *joie de vivre*. When emotional topics are raised, he begins to crack puerile jokes, he loudly slaps his knees, he jiggles his feet and interrupts with catastrophically facile remarks. At one awkward point he vanishes into the kitchen and returns with a jar of chocolate-covered nuts which he waves under my nose whilst humming, 'mmnnnn … yummy … yummy … m m m m m m m m m m m m nnnnnn' in an effort to distract me.

'It's very hard to get emotional talk out of Warwick,' his wife sighs. '*Very* hard. The only time he'll show emotion is by himself. During our split, he wouldn't have shown it to his friends.' 'No,' he agrees, 'I don't think I did.' 'Anyone who was with him at that time would have seen him playin' the grain-o'-salt plenty-o'-young-bunnies-out-there tough guy,' she says with feminine resignation.

Raised by a 'hard' mother and a 'supportive' father, the young Warwick loved football, ice-skating, skateboards, and his pushbike. His near-pathological need for attention would tend to indicate that he was never paid sufficient attention as a child.

'I wasn't overadored by my parents,' he shrugs. 'Just average. The occasional backhander. I used to throw rocks at cars, stuff like that ... lemons ... plums ...' 'He was shy, I remember,' Joanne interjects, 'yeah. Because when I met him he was shy, and then when he went to Sydney to play football, that's when he really changed a lot ... came outta his shell.' 'I was the Number One Boy in Sydney,' he says with no trace of irony. 'I was the King.'

His look suggests something pitiful. 'I was the Man of the Moment. It was great. I thrived on crowds. I captured everyone's heart in Australia, yew ask anyone. I don't love meself, but that's how it was. When the Fall From Grace happened, it was a bit crushing. I couldn't sleep that good. I still love the game. It hurt, but I s'pose I'd pretty much achieved everything I could in football, yew know?' Suddenly reaching over, he grabs a copy of the *Australian Women's Forum* which featured him and unfolds the centrespread. 'Nice 'n brown, eh? Turn you on? Better with the penis hidden, don't ya think? Bit o' mystery.'

After their reunion, they decided to tackle a double spread in *Penthouse*, in which they were 'artistically' photographed miming various sexual acts. The very mention of it inspires rhapsodies. 'We like sexuality!' he bubbles. 'We love nudity! Big breasts! Like yours!' 'I wouldn't care if Warwick was sittin' here watchin' a porno with lezzos!' Joanne laughingly cries. He tears his eyes away from my cleavage to look at his wife. *'We like all that sorta stuff,'* he emphatically declares. Joanne becomes intense. 'If he's sittin' here watchin' a porno with lezzos here — you know how some women get [she screws her features up in a parody of horror and disgust] like really pissed off? *How DARE he look at a different fanny on the TV!'* 'How dare he masturbate in front of a porno!' Warwick jovially chips in. *'He should do it in front of ME!'*

The smile is fixed to my face as they carry on as blithely as children, oblivious to the effect they have on others. 'I'm a lot tougher-skinned than him,' Joanne eventually explains. 'I don't care what I say to people, know what I mean? I don't care about anybody any more except Warwick, my family, and the small handful of people that I love. That's it for me.' Her toughness belies a tenderness that is less evident in her husband, who is as direct and self-centred and playful as an untrained dog.

In 1983, Joanne's mother, a propagator of African violets, died of cancer. 'I don't think you ever get over that,' Joanne says, her eyes suddenly moist. 'Her death really hardened me a lot. She was just such a wonderful person and I sorta thought: *Well, you know, how could this happen to such a good person?? How DARE this happen!* Somebody takin' my mother away! It — it was, yew know, *hard*. Warwick knew her. She used to *love* him. Used to ride around on his pushbike.' Visibly agitated at his wife's recollections, Warwick mutters: 'I don't like talkin' about death.' Joanne looks at him with loving patience and continues. 'Since then,' she says, 'I don't believe in God any more. My attitude — since our separation, too — has changed a lot. Yew realise that yew've gotta be happy today and not worry. I'm not afraid of death any more.'

Having said this, she must leave for an appointment. She changes into a smart navy-and-cream outfit. Her bottled milk-white hair brushes against her husband's face as she kisses him goodbye. Warwick and I are left alone, and his manner becomes considerably less belligerent. It seems that when he is around his wife he needs to impress her with his manliness, but now he is perfectly amenable and sweet, eager to make me comfortable. He stands, ready to give me a tour of his home. I follow.

The house is spotless. You could eat chocolate-covered nuts off the bathroom floor. To the left of the first living room is the kitchen; to the left of that, a corridor sprouting two guest bedrooms, a guest bathroom ('cedar spa with gold swan-neck taps'), and baby Indiana's room — a buttercup yellow affair with a teddy motif, its windows overlook Joanne's stables. There are fluffy white toys, a white lace cot, and a foot-high toy castle encrusted with purple glitter and featuring a glittering purple wizard, a crystal ball, and a glittering purple dragon. 'Cost seventy dollars,' Warwick informs me, 'not bad, eh?'

In the laundry, one of Joanne's pre-pregnancy confections droops from a coathanger: a worn strapless white leather party dress with a petticoat-cloud of magenta and sky-blue tulle. For all her natural appeal, Joanne's fashion sense has always oscillated between The Magic Roundabout and the Crazy Horse Strip Club. Happily conversing with himself, Warwick leads me back through the first living room and into the second, which looks exactly like the first, but emptier. We trot down some steps and he announces with a grand sweep of his hand: 'This is the wine cellar and the gym.' I peer into the tiny room. A couple of battered Nautilus pieces and two walls of empty shelves. I point out that the 'wine cellar' is devoid of wine. Warwick suddenly looks enormously embarrassed and shuffles his feet. 'Yeah,' he says, leaving the room, 'don't like wine. Prefer beer.'

The Master Bedroom is, appropriately enough, situated at the crest of a flight of stairs leading up from the second living room. On the partition wall, a giant cream and baby blue banner is diagonally pinned: 'I dreamed a dream,' it reads, 'Do you remember our first kiss? How our hearts pounded with excitement [sic]. Nothing has the intensity of the first time. I love you.' With justified trepidation, I walk past the banner and almost brain myself on a swinging gilded cupid suspended from the ceiling. Their bed is a simple white lace affair topped by a white leather bedhead. On a cane chair, there is a fluffy white bunny toy wearing a pink rose-sewn cloche hat; below it is another fluffy white bunny toy with blue ears. Above the bed is a wooden plaque: 'Last night I dreamed that you and I were locked in a room. The night did not end. My chest exploded with excitement … we made love forever …'

My chest is also near exploding with excitement as Warwick encourages me to view his pride and joy: an ensuite egregiously monstrous liver-coloured clam-shaped spa-bath overlooking the rollercoasters of Dreamworld and the hinterland. We are both reflected unto the Apocalypse within the many, many mirrors. I am speechless. Warwick suddenly begins to undress and the banner was right, it was right: *nothing* has the intensity of the first time. When he retains his boxers, I breathe a sigh of relief. He starts tugging on a loose batik shirt. It is time for me to leave for the airport. He accompanies me to the door. An overwhelmingly awful smell of sewage drifts in from the window. I wrinkle my nose and Warwick jumps. 'That wasn't me!' he cries. 'I didn't fart!'

Destined to return to the real world, I climb into the waiting cab and watch his silhouette behind the flyscreen, merrily waving.

Mode, 1994

LAYING DOWN THE LAWS:

DEEPAK CHOPRA

HE HAS BEEN accused of hawking 'leveraged spirituality'. Extremist religious groups despise him for believing that 'man makes distinctions, God makes none'. Christian fundamentalists angrily picketed St Mary's Hospital in Grand Junction, Colorado, when he was invited to speak by the resident Catholic nuns. 'The signs they carried,' Deepak Chopra wryly says, 'read: SATAN GO HOME!' His few factual errors have been cited by many as irrefutable evidence of quackery. Certain defenders of the Western scientific tradition, disturbed by recent academic surveys showing that those with powerful spiritual beliefs enjoy far superior health, yearn for the opportunity to expose him as a charlatan. Dr William Jarvis, president of the National Council

Against Health Fraud, recently expressed his anxiety that 'people with serious diseases may turn their backs on legitimate medical care and follow his path'.

The calibre of his acolytes has also enraged his detractors. Prince Charles recently invited him to an academic forum to discuss ways of integrating 'non-traditional forms of healing into the Western scientific framework'. When he gave a keynote speech at the State of the World Forum at an international science convention in San Francisco, Mikhail Gorbachev was beside him. Jackie Onassis regularly breakfasted with him at the Four Seasons. Demi Moore calls one of his bestselling books, *The Seven Spiritual Laws of Success*, her 'bible'. The disgraced junk-bond genius, Michael Milken, 'testified that after he was diagnosed with prostate cancer, Chopra's medical attentions shrank his lymph nodes by ninety per cent'. Sarah Ferguson, Michael Jackson, David Lynch, Oprah Winfrey, Donna Karan, David Stewart, and George Harrison have passionately expressed their admiration for his work. Even Hillary Rodham Clinton has acknowledged that his theories are 'very interesting'.

Married for twenty-five years and the father of two grown children, Chopra has written seventeen bestselling books which have been translated into twenty-five languages, their sales exceeding six million. For the past seven years, he has been conducting seminars all over the world on mind–body medicine. Toastmasters International named him as one of America's top Five Speakers of 1995. Chopra acknowledges that he is the hub of an extraordinary industry, one of those on the cutting edge of a new consciousness. 'The media is recognising it,' he acknowledges, 'Hollywood is recognising it, the general public is recognising it. A paradigm shift was inevitable. I hope that it's irreversible, that we're moving towards a more healing world, that we want to be more loving and compassionate, and more caring. I just happen to be part of the tide; if it weren't me, it would be somebody else.'

A physician, an endocrinologist, and a mystic in the ancient tradition, Chopra is, at heart, an alchemist. Chafed by the limitations of the conventional either/or framework, he has studied medicine, physics, and metaphysics to form an holistic synthesis in which the mind is not treated as alien to the body. This 'web' principle — that of the interdependence of mind and body — was recognised in the days of magico–religious medicine but buried at the turn of this century. The grave remained undisturbed until soaring health budgets and disturbing increases in the rates of suicide, depression, and other manifestations of twentieth century malaise caused the public to question rational materialism. The US health budget alone amounts to AUS$1995 billion, and serious problems with the Australian health budget have resulted in attacks on symptoms and not causes; it is, after all, easier to blame 'hypochondria' or 'the victim mentality' rather than address the deeper implications of the situation.

What Chopra calls 'the superstition of materialism' is killing people. Loneliness and alienation, he points out, are carcinogens every bit as effective as nicotine. He believes the immune system to be a 'circulating nervous system', and the supporting evidence is startling. Examples? Those who feel loved by their partners are statistically more likely to recover from cardiac complications. A 1987 Yale study showed that breast cancer spread most effectively amongst women who had 'repressed personalities'. 'Similar findings,' Chopra writes in *Ageless Body, Timeless Mind*, 'have emerged for rheumatoid arthritis, asthma, intractable pain, and other disorders.' The pioneers of psychology — Freud and Jung, in particular — long ago discerned the connection: the human body literally embodies or enacts the mind's conflicts and tragedies. This knowledge was ignored in an effort to retain public faith in pharmaceutical products and technology, a public faith that was necessary to private profit.

Chopra has often spoken of having felt like no more than a 'licensed drug pusher' during his medical career, and this frustration and a sense of moral futility caused him to explore alternative healing methods. His attention locked on the ancient Ayurvedic doctors of India, whose cardinal belief was that as the body is created out of consciousness, consciousness is where healing must begin. The tag of 'mind–body medicine' may be broad, but reflects the on-going process of a field searching for methods and values. Its axis? That emotion cannot be separated from the body which produces it and as such, is inextricably related to illness. Inquiries into the extent and nature of this relationship have been instigated by academics and enlightened medical professionals throughout the world, many of whom feel that technology and resultant emotional detachment of those who use it have replaced humaneness in medical practice.

His critics have always spuriously used the fact that he earns millions of dollars a year as evidence of his 'McSpirituality', and yet the only way in which his income relates to his perceptions is that it indicates a widespread public dissatisfaction with the structures of the current system. Few of these critics seem to care that Chopra has not charged for a consultation for ten years or that he retains only the royalties he makes from his books; profits from his seminars, products, treatments, and forays into television are donated to his Seven Spiritual Laws Charity (created for those requiring money for transplants or medical help), and to his new California Chopra Centre For

Well Being, into which he has invested over six million dollars. Offering instruction in yoga, meditation, practical philosophy, and a comprehensive system of eastern and western therapies, the centre also provides world class cardiac and cancer programs to assist those with more acute needs.

Although he describes himself as 'playful' and 'carefree', he is by nature an intellectual — serious, concerned, a creature of abstract thought. Chopra wants to fix things; he is a relentless self-improver. Those unfamiliar with him imagine a hypnotic-eyed cult leader wreathed in turbans, an urban seer, a prince of the Fourth Dimension. These are common misconceptions. Although there is an unspoken or untranslatable quality about him, he is essentially pragmatic and shy. 'A wizard's heart has triple-thick walls,' he writes in his first novel, *The Return of Merlin*, 'and only those who have the courage to breach the fortifications can discover the hidden treasure within.'

The blue and blinding Sydney day is filtered by curtains in his standard Sheraton on the Park suite. A desk, some chairs, occasional lamps, a coffee table littered by notebooks which he has filled with writing. Now fifty, he rarely stops; half the year is spent on the road, talking, talking, talking. He is a driven man who enjoys a lot of attention. 'My wife would agree with that,' he chuckles. 'Nobody else would say that! I used to resent it when she said that to me, but now I don't; I agree. I do need approval, and I'm working on that.' Having just completed a new translation of the eleventh-century Sufi poet Rumi's work, an essay entitled 'Does God Have Orgasms?', and overseen the publication of his new book, *The Path to Love*, he is finalising the details for an ongoing television series based on *The Return of Merlin*.

The effect created by his black collarless shirt, black socks, black loafers, and houndstooth trousers is austere. It is said that his shiny abundance of black hair is dyed, but his eyes are naturally clear — in them, astuteness and a certain heaviness of intention. Two hours of weight training at the gym each day have not eradicated his gentle paunch. His tone ranges from the learned indolence of the British Raj ('I presume', 'yah', *'fancy'*) to American amiability ('I guess', 'you know?' 'sure!'). Only when recalling his childhood or speaking of healing does the see-saw enthusiasm of his native Urdu become evident; his voice is otherwise resigned. 'It's tough to be in medicine because you *constantly* see suffering,' he explains with a deep sigh. 'During every shift I did, two or three or four or five people *died*. One person comes in after an automobile accident, another comes in after a gunshot, another comes in after a heart attack, another comes in with a stroke … and they are all *terrified*!' The emphasis with which he invests the word is chilling. 'They're absolutely, totally *terrified*. You watch them going through terror, helplessness, resignation — the full gamut of emotions in a few minutes! It is not easy to deal with that.'

Chopra left India twenty-five years ago with $100 which he impulsively spent at the Moulin Rouge during his stopover in Paris. He had been given the money and a free plane ticket by the New Jersey hospital which was to employ him as an intern (during the Vietnam War, a severe shortage of medical staff in America led to this 'incentive' system). 'Very unhappy people, physicians,' he says, directly holding my gaze. 'The relatives of patients with whom they deal are demanding, litigious, intimidating. That's the environment of medicine. Most of my fellow colleagues were very stressed; a lot of them were addicts. I used to experience the most extraordinary frustration and *tightness*.' He pats his solar plexus. 'My great fear was getting into *trouble*. Malpractice suits are a big deal in the United States.'

Determined to succeed, he relocated to Boston, where he worked sixteen-hour shifts at a veterans' hospital. 'Having moved to America,' he continues, 'I was suddenly in a position where I wasn't taken seriously. There was a certain vulnerability, yah. I was treated in a condescending way by the senior physicians, not necessarily invited to social occasions with the American staff, and *definitely* not given the same opportunities for higher education. There was a distinct bias against foreigners, particularly Asians. But again, I was so competitive that I used all this as a spur. *I'll show them!* You know?'

Paid a salary of $500 a month, he had no free time, and when his cramped apartment became too small for the family, he decided that the only option was to double his workload by working until dawn in a suburban emergency room. One of his most traumatic experiences was performing an emergency Caesarean on a murder victim. 'A pregnant woman had just been shot in the head,' he murmurs. 'She still had a heartbeat. Her eyes were very fixed. I don't know — I just — she was … *dead*. I automatically reacted — cut her open. The baby was *alive*.' During those years, he suppressed all natural emotional and physical responses to such stress and instead chain-smoked, gulped litres of coffee, and used Scotch to maintain some outward measure of equilibrium. 'Life,' he acknowledges, 'was *crushing*.'

Superficially, he could explain the desperation of his patients. The profound shift in his thinking was triggered when he saw that a terminal diagnosis led to many of them exhibiting a palpable *relief*. Chopra appreciated that implicit in sickness is escapism; he also knew there had to be more to the situation. Disease, he ultimately realised, offers opportunities denied by ordinary life in that it permits the sufferer to explore his feelings about and place in the world. This caused him to wonder how destructive the demands of everyday Western life could be if terminal illness seemed like the only escape. It is disturbing, he has remarked, to think that our culture provides us with so little opportunity to confront the basic meaning of life that sickness and death have filled the void by becoming conversion experiences.

'Our culture is *psychotic*,' he says, his hands lightly outspread. 'We take ethnocentrism, bigotry, hatred, violence, prejudice, religious intolerance, genocide, poverty, inequality, murder, rape, and child abuse for *granted*. We sensationalise it on television!' Recently at a party in London he met a former senior KGB man who asked him what he thought had destroyed Western culture. '*Star Wars*?' Chopra humorously suggested. 'Reagan?' 'No,' the former KGB man replied, 'it was "Dallas", the soap opera.' He begins to laugh, and slowly shakes his head. 'You go to Rwanda or Bangladesh or Zaire, switch on the television, and you see "Santa Barbara" or some stupid American soap opera. People are such *victims* of this hypnosis of conditioning! So few actually realise that it is happening.'

During his seminars, he speaks eloquently of the imprisonment of conditioning and the boundaries that are, as a consequence, created. He walks his audience through the physiology of perception — arbitrary, and limited not only by time but by the five senses. 'We perceive less than one *billionth* of what is actually occurring,' he says as he paces the stage, cupping his microphone with his left hand, 'and what you perceive is that which reinforces original beliefs. The human body, for example, is perceived to be an anatomical structure fixed in space and time, but seen through the eyes of a physicist, the human body is null and void.' Action, memory and desire he refers to as 'the software of the soul' — 'without karma, there is no memory; without memory, there is no desire; without desire, there is no action'. And without action, there is no life.

'When I address top-ranking executives,' he remarks, 'I see a predatory world. They are male predators, aggressive achievers, and they're getting *ill*. They're getting prostate cancer, heart attacks — they are beginning to see that they are victims of their own predatory instincts. I tell them that bringing back the feminine softness and nurturing, intuition, a contextual approach to relationships and love, will make their lives easier.'

It is precisely this kind of simplicity that is forgotten in the desperate complexity of materialism, a philosophy antithetical to ordinary human vulnerability. The more violently a natural response to a situation is suppressed, the more complicated and extensive is its impact. In the case of illness, most people are subconsciously aware of its 'cause' — that it is a metaphor, an emotional war fought on the body's terrain. 'It would be easy for me to claim that your sickness is meaningless,' he writes in *Unconditional Life*, 'that it is just the result of some random disruption in your body, [which] is more or less what medical training drums into us. Even after you salve the ulcer, unblock the intestine, or cut out the breast tumour, the patient returns with trouble in his eyes.'

Traditional western healing exclusively concerns matter, a premise which struck him as self-defeating. 'Training to become a doctor reinforces this bias again and again, from that moment in medical school when you first touch a dissecting scalpel to a cadaver's grey skin,' Chopra writes in *Unconditional Life*. To cope with the onslaught of traumata and the barbaric hours, most doctors learn to mechanically react to situations which, in turns, leads to them treating patients as if they were no more than components of a machine. It is this sense of alienation and lack of caring (and not, as Dr Jarvis postulated, Chopra's theories) which is driving patients away from conventional medicine. The increase in demand for attention-rich therapies, both physical and psychological, is indicative that a 'sense of specialness, of being charmed, of being the exception, of being eternally protected' is a necessity and not the luxury that many old-school medical professionals had presupposed.

'You have to understand,' he explains with a vehement hand gesture, 'that I was absolutely *fascinated* by the phenomenon of death. Seeing people alive and then dead — that was a very dramatic experience for me, and totally bewildering. I guess that was the beginning of my spiritual yearning. I went through many phases. The first was a very radical scientific, mechanistic world-view throughout medical school, which is where I read Albert Camus and Jean-Paul Sartre, took LSD, smoked marijuana — these, you understand, were hip things to do.' Chopra also worked as a lecturer at Tufts University and Boston University Schools of Medicine and at the age of thirty-eight, a 'master of the post-colonial medical system', he was made Chief of Staff at the New England Memorial Hospital. 'I mean,' he cries, 'I was a doctor when I was twenty-one! I finished my training when I was twenty-five, and I was Chief of Staff when I was thirty! I always felt anxious about not being good *enough*. And then my consciousness shifted. It was a gradual process.' The shift visibly began when he read Krishnamurti's work and in 1985, he met the Maharishi Mahesh Yogi, from whom he learnt Transcendental Meditation.

'My curiosity really goes back to the day my grandfather died,' he says, hooking his thumbs in his belt. 'My father was in England at the time. My grandfather was looking at alternative means for his heart disease, and my father thought all that was nonsense. We received a telegram informing us that my father had been made a member of the Royal College of Physicians and my grandfather took us out to celebrate. We saw *Ali Baba and the Forty Thieves*, went to a restaurant, had a great party. In the middle of the night, my brother and I woke up to the sound of wailing. My grandfather had died. I mean, that was a major experience in my life. The following day they cremated him, and brought him back in a bowl this big — ' he cups both hands together and extends them to me with a quizzical expression. 'All that was left of him was ashes. And I said: *where did he go?* You know? My grandfather with whom I went to the movies last night — where did he *go?*'

Such a line of philosophical inquiry was alien to his father, an eminent cardiologist and committed Anglophile who wanted his eldest son to become a doctor. A lonely and profoundly intelligent boy, Chopra was more interested in Keats, Shelley, Shakespeare, Kipling, and Byron than in medicine, but when he discovered that the novelists Arthur Conan Doyle and William Somerset Maugham had been physicians, he relented and was, at the age of seventeen, enrolled at the prestigious All India Institute of Medical Sciences in his hometown of New Delhi. 'My father was very "British",' he admits. 'He spent a lot of time in England and was very influenced by that. He was Lord Mountbatten's ADC [Aide-de-camp] for a time.' Whilst Chopra is visibly proud of his 'British' father, it is evident that this pride is uncomfortably mixed with the shame that was at the root of his father's Anglophilia. The tiger hunts, cricket matches, and afternoon teas derided the ancient pulse of his country. However indirectly, he had been taught to disdain 'primitive' Indian culture in favour of 'sophisticated' English culture and with it, absorbed a non-holistic view of medicine and a denial of his own nature and heritage.

'When my father was a medical student,' he says, beginning to run his index finger along the armchair's upholstery, 'the British were still in India. He was selected from a few thousand to be an officer in the British Army, which I presume was a big deal in those days. Most Indians were soldiers, they were never officers. He was actually quite militant in the beginning about patriotism. He had this schizophrenic love/hate relationship with the British. In Burma during World War Two, a British officer said that Indian food was horrible and my father actually *beat up* the officer.' A delighted laugh. 'He was almost court-martialled as a result.'

This 'schizophrenic love/hate relationship' was Chopra's first awareness of the dualistic nature of perception. 'I saw the British through my father's eyes, and thought my father's world was fascinating,' he says. 'The army, the parties, the drinking, the socialising. Servants, celebrations, the adults drinking. I thought British culture was very attractive. Fancy compared to Indian beer-cans and tinned food.' Conscious of having used the word 'drinking' twice, he briefly glances away. 'My father *did* drink too much,' he hastily says, 'but then he stopped when I was in high school. He was never aggressive when he drank, he was a storyteller. He'd have three or four glasses of scotch and then he'd tell us these stories. We couldn't wait for them to start.'

The one flaw in Chopra's argument is precisely this reluctance to address dark emotional issues. Contrary to the perspective of humane psychiatrists such as Alice Miller, he has referred to anger and anxiety as 'negative' in his work, rather than as potentially positive and liberating expressions of feeling. During his Sydney seminar, a high-profile socialite took the microphone and began speaking of a desire to 'erase' her tortured childhood. Chopra's expression changed as she continued; a discomfort seemingly antithetical to his native poise became evident. 'The only pain I would be trying to avoid,' he says in a low and careful voice, 'would be connected to the Irish Christian brothers who ran my school. The corporal punishment. If I spelt anything incorrectly or even bowled outside the leg-stump, Father McNamara would take me into his room, pull my pants down, and whip me. *Hard.* I was bruised, very badly.' He inhales and awkwardly swallows. 'I was *so* terrified that I never told my parents, because I didn't want them to know how badly these men treated us. There was a *lot* of fear. I was *terrified* of Father McNamara — *terrified!* I used to say to myself: *if only my father knew!'*

The few references to this difficult period are treated with levity in his books — passing comments, their emphasis comic rather than painful. 'Really!' he suddenly exclaims. '*Enough* of the cane! It was a constant feature. I was also hit in the face. Slapped. By one of the priests. For not wearing my school tie, for being late, for speaking out of turn. So there was a lot of fear of being evaluated.' Here his voice becomes sing-song: 'I never told my father because it was an amazingly good *school*, they had such a respected *staff*, it was difficult to get *admission*, and, I suppose, I like to keep things in.' His silence is long. 'I used to cry alone as a boy. A lot,' he says, almost as an afterthought. 'I have only remembered that just now. I used to make sure nobody was watching and go and sit at the end of the long verandah at school and just … cry.'

Chopra's embracing philosophy has evolved not only from a deep intellectual curiosity, but also from the desire to transcend intensely felt pain and isolation. He represents tolerance, inquiry, synthesis. Like his father, he wants to heal. Like his Ayurvedic ancestors, he wants to treat man as a whole and not two halves. Like Aristotle, he wants people to understand perception as a *conference* of reality rather than its absorption, an understanding infused with real potential for change. Late for a radio interview, he stands — portly, clean-skinned, calm — and shakes my hand. As he leaves me at the door, I remember a tract from *The Seven Spiritual Laws of Success*: 'We're not human beings that have occasional spiritual experiences, it's the other way around: we're spiritual beings that have occasional human experiences.'

Elle, 1997

THE MAN WHO FELL TO SURF:

IVA DAVIES

IVA DAVIES IS not despicable or brutal or poisonous or repulsive, but he is tense. Extremely tense. His laughter rings out like a gunshot — short and sharp and far too highly pitched, it expresses no mirth, no warmth, no charm, only defensiveness. His syntax is nothing short of tortured. He frequently substitutes verbs for nouns ('It's just a complete diffuse'), and as a philosopher, he makes a good composer ('I can't see how people were meant to wear clothes, by design'). His greatest expression of contempt is to describe someone as 'not very bright' or 'not educated' (curious comments from a man who summons truly affecting gravity to tell me: 'contemporary dance has not always existed, you know').

During a one-and-a-half hour interview, he uses the words 'art' and 'artist' seventeen times. It is the years Iva spent at Sydney's Conservatorium of Music and not his great success as a popular musician that are, to him, what those sweating minutes spent kneeling in Hugh Grant's white BMW are to Divine Brown: the anvil upon which identity is hammered.

It has been well over twenty years since Iva (or 'Ivor', as he was then known) had palpitations over his ability as an oboist. Gifted enough to play with the Elizabethan Trust Orchestra, the Conservatorium Chamber Orchestra, the Sydney Symphony Orchestra, and the ABC National Training Orchestra, he sabotaged his classical career through panicked crises of confidence. At the age of 16, he fell into a profound depression, refused to take his exams, and escaped the city. When he returned, his concerned parents asked him what he planned to do. 'Don't know,' was his reply.

A certain aimlessness is and always has been a distinguishing characteristic. 'My career has been a series of accidents,' he admits. Flowers, the band he eventually formed, specialised in versions of songs by Lou Reed, Bryan Ferry, Marc Bolan and other men who were not born in Wauchope, NSW. Photographs from the period show Iva in full Aladdin Sane mode: plucked eyebrows, statement hairdo, the dazed expression of an abuser of cough syrups. In 1980, the band released its first album. Girls squealed, boys idolised him. The name Flowers (aptly inspired by Cocteau by way of Kemp) was then superseded by the more sophisticated Icehouse.

Despite or because of his weak vocals and derivative tunes, the now-original band sold over one-and-a-half million records and their album, *Man of Colours*, went super-platinum. 'I'm like this big kind of blender,' Iva told the *Bulletin* in 1993, 'you can put in the ingredients to make up this filthy cocktail and it will always come out as a strawberry milkshake.' To amuse himself, he wrote the scores for the film *Razorback* (which starred a large rogue boar) and *Boxes*, a piece produced by the Sydney Dance Company (from the ranks of which he chose his bride, the 'stable' Tonia Kelly). *Berlin* is the second Graeme Murphy/Iva Davies collaboration, and its press release not only features a photograph of Iva looking like a supernumerary from *Wings of Desire*, but the words 'destruction', 'resurrection', 'illusion' and 'decline'.

Within every artist, however great, there is an ordinary person, and as a person, Iva is desperately insecure. So insecure that he compares his failures to those of Puccini; so insecure that he attributes his sensitivity to his talent rather than his humanity; so insecure that he treats the most ordinary questions as if they were part of an interrogation by the Secret Police. During the interview he continually clears his throat, nervously cackles, faces the other direction, folds his arms, knits his legs, leans back, leans forward, glances around, hunches, crouches, avoids giving anything approximating a direct answer and warily refers to me from behind the stalk of the beach umbrella protruding from our table. When queried too closely, he delivers jaw-shatteringly dull discourses on musicians such as David Byrne (whose function he compares to that of 'the great novelists') and the nature of art. Anthony O'Grady, publisher of *Music Network*, has known Iva for some time. 'I think,' he says, 'that Iva uses his mechanical abilities as a musician quite literally to balance his personal diffidence.'

The musician in question has decided to undergo the ignominy of this interview at Whaley's Cafe, a bright flyblown burger-and-chips establishment by Sydney's beautiful Whale Beach. It is 10 am on a glittering fragrant hot blue Friday morning, and Iva rolls up in a van. Steps out. Brisk handshake. Orders a cappuccino. Looks tense. Seats himself at the plain wooden picnic table shaded by the aforementioned beach umbrella. Hides behind its stalk. Lights a cigarette. Now forty, he is still handsome in a dead sort of way and deeply tanned. His eyes are pale and reptilian, his teeth are those of a ferret's, and he is near-lipless. His long, lovely fair hair is tied back in a ponytail. A ring punctures his right earlobe. There are dried beads of blood on his forearms ('stuck them amongst a bunch of connections and wires'). A small man, he is wearing a clean white T-shirt, black pleated trousers, a black belt decorated with chunks of silver, and Doc Martens. As I take notes on his apparel, he flashes me a patronising smirk. 'This is how *Mode* briefs you, is it?' he asks, blowing smoke. 'They've got a little technique?'

His choice of location is not the best for an interview. Over the next hour or so, our voices compete with the racket of: stereophonic doves, mating parrots, the roaring ocean, mothers berating their children, girls gossiping at neighbouring tables, passing vehicles, and a truck loaded with tropical fruit drinks which remains parked — engine running — across the road for thirty minutes. All this added to Iva's natural reluctance to reveal more than his name and date of birth to one with whom he does not surf only exacerbates the tension. 'Iva,' explains O'Grady, 'is intensely private. A lot of musicians do have communication problems, but I think he feels it more.'

The third child of a forester/ 'man of words'/ world authority on the Murray River Red gum/ 'singer' (Neville) and 'a recognised painter' (Dorothy), Iva was always considered 'introverted' and 'weird'. He takes great pains to emphasise his deep love and admiration for his parents, and breaks out in a nervous sweat at the suggestion that they were originally responsible for the cracks in his adult psyche. The most he will reveal is that they were 'artistic' (said with a toss of his chin) and had 'high standards'. He maintains that he cannot recall 'anything' of his first decade bar 'a few isolated incidents'. One of these incidents: at the age of six, Iva 'fell in love' with the bagpipes. When his parents bought him a set, the salesperson forgot to mention that they could not be played as certain pieces were missing. So, his parents went out and on their return some four hours later, discovered their son, 'lips bleeding', lying unconscious on the sofa. Shrugging, he explains: 'I was determined to get a noise out of them.'

A great adherent of the maxim that one has to know the rules to break them, Iva studied hard at the Conservatorium and has since invested much of his self-esteem in his training. 'I've often reflected on my historical perspective of music,' he says from behind the umbrella stalk. 'I've been involved in the popular music industry and never been able to take it *that* seriously, because my perspective on record companies and publishers is qualified by Mozart's patrons, and y'know — it's a bit hard to explain, but having a broad musical training and exposure can give you a kind of perspective on where you are and what that means, and what it means in the big picture of Music, Art, History and Commercialism and Exploitation and all that sort of stuff. That's the main thing.'

He speaks quickly and often nonsensically, and his gestures are abrupt. 'The thing is,' he continues with a hunted look, 'I'm very loathe to use the word "artist" — it's always been an irksome term, and to refer to music as art is always dangerous — *however*, it has always struck me as an anomaly that we can have an expression like "the music industry". Do we have an "art industry"? Do you see what I'm saying?' On one hand, he disparages his commercial work; on the other, he seems to classify it as art. He has always blamed the 'nervous breakdown' he suffered in 1988 to the inhumane demands of 'commercialism' rather than his determination to comply with inhumane demands. Although his relaxed beach lifestyle is one that many would envy, he still seems to smart at his unsuitability for fame. 'I guess where I came unstuck,' he says, 'is when I pitted myself against the machine and didn't have the absolute *arrogance* that a lot of pop stars have. They *need* that — they *need* that. I'm not equipped that way.'

A man with whom he once worked closely, comments: 'Iva could have achieved a lot more had he so desired. I think he's an immensely talented person. Also difficult, but [performers] are *all* difficult. Part of the game.' Iva sips at his cappuccino, lights a cigarette, ashes it in the soft-drink can he has plucked from the overflowing refuse bin, and contorts his body. 'Any trauma I experienced,' he says a little too quickly, 'was superimposed [sic] by the industry, and I don't know if [pop musicians who don't experience traumata] would have the *arts* basis that I do. I mean, I'm not blowing my own trumpet, but I'm watching with interest as I see people like Tori Amos emerge and go through the mill, to see if they're going to come out the other side in one *piece*.'

A thread of bitterness runs through his words. He admits to exercising 'restraint in terms of anger'; he knows that he can become 'very dark'. 'I don't scream and yell and throw punches,' he says, 'I internalise. Absolutely.' Although this internalisation of powerful emotions would seem to be a more feasible explanation for his problems with anxiety than external factors, Iva still blames 'American colonialism' and its offshoots for the ills of the world. 'It takes,' he says with an edge, 'a particular kind of person to be completely immune to the demands of fame. For example, I don't think Michael Jackson is successful at fame. On the other hand, I think Prince is. There are some people who are really equipped for stardom. They're the sorts of people who *cannot* enter a room without *having* to take control of it, y'know? I've met plenty of those. Fame requires just *arrogant* confidence ... *total* self-belief ... just *complete* self-belief. Ego the size of the Empire State Building.' He laughs tightly. 'I'm *glad* I don't have that kind of self-belief, because it doesn't make for particularly nice people.'

When he 'came unstuck', he locked himself in a room and refused to speak to anybody. 'Wouldn't come out,' he says,

'wouldn't face anything. A *complete* inability to face anything.'
Another tight little laugh. 'I didn't come out of it very well.
Physically, I was wrecked. I got up on stage when I should have
been in hospital.' The wreckage of which he speaks was not the
result of highrolling or substance abuse, but of the
unrelentingly high standards he set himself. Never a participant
in the debauchery of 'the scene', Iva only liked 'to watch'. One
of the things he watched was the mental dissolution of certain
people with whom he worked. 'A couple of people I knew were
experienced acid takers,' he says, again retreating behind the
umbrella stalk, 'and then suddenly they kind of lost it and
ended up in hospital and haven't been able to function ever
since. I was there; I saw it happen. I saw somebody flip out and
start hitting people and run off into the night. We were called
by North Ryde Psychiatric Hospital. The person spent days and
days and days there being pumped full of Valium and then
came out of it *virtually* a vegetable.'

There is no compassion or sorrow in his voice. 'I just like to
watch the whole circus,' he says. 'I guess I've always been a
voyeur.' And then, unnecessarily, he adds: 'It's partly my
classical training.' At the mention of the word 'voyeur', I am
reminded of an interview with him by Jason Romney of the *Age*:
'I have gone through periods of leather and rubber … there
aren't really many places in Australia that cater to rubber

fetishes. That disappoints me, really, and it's something I miss about England.'

His surprise is pronounced. 'What?' he asks. And then: 'I've *never* been to those sorts of clubs. Never been to those places, never participated. Fetishism isn't an interest of mine. That must be a *complete* misquote.' Jason Romney, now a solicitor, simply states: 'I stand by my story.' An industry source chuckles at my confusion. 'Many stories are made up by musicians to enhance their credibility,' he says. 'They like to pretend that they have a seamy side. Completely false stories are leaked to papers to create interest, and then everybody sits back and laughs. I've known of some *incredible* lies that have been published. Iva would have made the quote for reasons of publicity. These guys get a real thrill when they're seen as wild, whereas in reality, they're *fucking* boring.'

Press manipulation aside, Iva has a reputation for taking his commitments very seriously. Richard Wilkins, entertainment critic for Channel Nine's 'Today' show, remarks: 'I've always found that there are two sides to Iva. Professionally, very cool and talented, if aloof and unwilling to share the spotlight. Personally, he's always struck me as an affable chap.' This affability remains artfully hidden when the topic of composing a pop song is raised. 'Economy [in terms of time] is part of the medium of lyrics,' he says, at once fidgety and pompous.

'There's prose and there's poetry, and then there are lyrics. And they're kind of different ... mediums. And lyrics are probably the most refined and economic of them all. You've got four or so minutes to make a statement that means something.'

The lyric booklet to his band's most recent CD, *Big Wheel*, not only features photographs of crop circles and what appears to be the lunar surface, but many statements that could mean anything. 'Lyrics are very important,' he explains, 'but I've had managers asking me: *why do you bother labouring over these things?*' After reading *Big Wheel*'s booklet, I am inclined to pose the same question. 'I actually put priority into lyrics,' he continues, 'which is strange, because I'm actually a trained musician and not a trained writer.' One of his statements:

> *I'm watching the big wheel*
> *inside of a big wheel*
> *that's part of a big wheel*
> *turn it 'round.*

When I ask him why he enjoys writing scores for modern dance, he seems perplexed. 'Well,' he slowly says, 'I think the discipline of writing a four-minute song is a great thing, but there are other things as well.' I pause. I change the wording of the question. He stares at me. 'I don't have to write four-minute songs for the ballet,' he says, 'so it's another thing.' Again, I pause. I explain that I do not quite understand his answer. At this, he suddenly becomes testy. 'It seems to me that you're asking me to state the obvious,' he snaps. 'I mean, I grew up playing in orchestras for opera and ballet, so yes — I appreciate it as an art form, but it's not new to me, I guess.' The tinny radio from within the cafe begins blaring 'This Thing Called Love'. Iva's velociraptor eyes are now on the truck across the road. 'With contemporary dance,' he bristles, 'you're dealing with abstract things, and abstract things can be very powerful, because they leave so much open to the beholder that you can get — something like a line of dialogue can only have one meaning — can *attain* the properties of having ten meanings for ten different people. That's what I like about contemporary dance.'

Having disposed of logic and traditional sentence structure, he continues. 'My mother,' he says, again retreating behind the umbrella stalk, 'always says: *the thing about art is that if you get a reaction, you have achieved an artistic success.*' When I point out that if that were the sole criterion for art, a pie in the face could be construed as a masterpiece, he purses his lips. 'Well,' he announces in an admonishing tone, 'there've been plenty of things that have created an adverse reaction which are now recognised as art. Whenever I've put something out that's been a disaster — and there've been plenty of those — I think of the fact that *Madame Butterfly* was pulled off stage after opening night because it stiffed enormously.' He pauses for effect. 'Well?' he asks me. 'What does *that* suggest? It suggests that the people who reacted were *wrong*.'

This last word is said with all the vehemence of intellectual naiveté, and his smile is smug. I begin to ask another question and notice that his attention has strayed. Relieved at the distraction, he croaks to the tousle-haired surfer behind me: 'Howarrya? Where'dja get a wave?'

The surfer scratches his chin. 'Orr ... just down here.'

Iva nods. 'In the Wedge, yeah. Looks orright. Dja have your mal [malibu board]?'

The surfer shakes his head. 'Aw, no. No. Had m'wide board.'

Iva looks hugely surprised. 'You're *kidding*?'

'Sort of mal territory out there,' the surfer drawls, '*perfect*.'

The surfer leaves. Iva turns to me. 'That's Tom Carroll,' he says with pride, and then pauses. For the first time this morning, his glance seems to soften. 'You know what really pulled me out of my breakdown? *Water*,' he says. 'I surf. That's my great release. It's the greatest therapy there is. It's just a complete diffuse of everything. *Everything*. The Zen experience.' He clears his throat, uncomfortable with this weak show of friendliness. 'Surfing is ... the elements. Complete peace.

Personal challenge. Survival. On land, depending on where I go, I become: pop star, classical musician, next door neighbour with the big fence, son-in-law. In the water, I become part of other surfers who only understand me in the element of surfing.' The umbrella slips down to the side, and the sun is harsh against his hair. Shading his eyes, he continues. 'I couldn't go on any longer the way I was. Couldn't get up on stage again. Couldn't fulfil the commitments. I felt like a cardboard cut-out. But I've survived a lot better than most of my peers.'

He lights another cigarette, squints up at the sky and then back at me, and folds his arms. His expression makes it clear that there is nothing more to say.

Mode, 1995

RELEASING THE INNER MORON

DEAR OLD BERTRAND Russell was fond of holding regular 'squashes' in his rooms at Cambridge, to which he would invite luminaries such as Wittgenstein and Keynes. All would stand around and discuss whatever happened to be engaging their attention at the time, whether it be pure logic, mathematics, suicide, or the weather. In writing *Intimacy and Solitude*, Stephanie Dowrick has held a squash of her own, and it is strictly an A-list affair. We are treated to the musings of Jesus and Michael Leunig, Alfred Adler and Rilke, Jung and Fay Weldon, John Lennon and Krishnamurti. And all this under the aegis of 'self-help'.

The problem with this book is neither intimacy nor solitude, but the intellect which has tackled them. Just as it is inadvisable to attempt to tame a tiger with a spatula, so

Stephanie Dowrick should have avoided stepping into the ring with the two Big Philosophical Issues. Such optimistic fervour is rare, and rightly so. These are issues with which even the most muscular minds have found it impossible to wrestle. We are all familiar with the self-perpetuating nature of the questioning both intimacy and solitude hatch, but it will take a bigger brain than Dowrick's to intellectualise the shapelessness of human emotions in order to harness them.

Admittedly, juggling theory and experience is no picnic. But what must be asked is whether the personal experience offered illuminates or illustrates the theory or whether it distracts the reader and creates the impression of mindless self-exposure. Sobbing confessions of emotional inadequacy and quirky little references to childhood find happy homes in blockbusting bettering books. Their authors make no claim whatsoever to intellectual agility and their gauzy grinning dustcover portraits bear testimony to the bliss of this particular state of being. It is when the author confuses the confession with qualification that she starts running into trouble: 'Am I not the person who has studied psychoanalytic and existential literature for years?'

Dowrick feels that such rhetoric must excite in us a similar enthusiasm for self-examination. The page shivers with asinine wonder as she comes flying at us with clarifications such as,

'After all, sex *can* be a treat', 'It's okay. I am joking!', or 'The irony of these dilemmas is not lost on me!'

The great tragedy is that Dowrick has obviously milked much thought from the cow of her mind to write this book. It *squeaks* with good intentions. We do understand that she wants us all to feel better. We know in our hearts that she wants us all to smile. Unfortunately, it is not the quantity of thought that matters but the quality, which in this case is somewhat piebald. Dowrick's enquiries into the great mysteries of life ('Why is familiar sex tolerable for me only when I pitch my mind elsewhere?') are *too* nice, always delivered with a lexical smile or little frown, gassy with the crunchy granola of the Left, and argued with a noxious cuteness. Allow me: 'My constitution inclines me to a fairly high degree of anxiety, and I hate not to feel free (I am a Gemini!)'

As a Virgo with Leo rising, I have not yet decided whether it is the exclamation point or the zodiacal information which gives me the greater cramp in the leg. What is Dowrick essentially banging on about? Once the pseudo-philosophical mandala-nonsense is over and done with, what *remains*? Does *she* know? The book begins with a school excursion to 'meeting your own self' and 'remembering who you are'. From there it skips down the yellow brick road of 'leaving your self behind', hangs a right at 'intimacy — an experience of transcendence?', stops for a can of pop and a BLT at 'rage, envy, and destruction', and eventually arrives with a sigh at the 'feeling understood' motel. Flourish of trumpets, suitcase unpacked, lights out.

Yup. All of it handled with the kind of pneumatoscopic flair that gives third-rate psychoanalysis that certain Winifred Childs *je ne sais quoi*. And the fuzziness quotient just keeps rising. There are tracts of this book which make Dowrick sound like a middle-aged encyclopaedia salesman on Lithium. Witness: 'No sensible person would want to write', or, 'There is nothing essentially self-expressive about being a thug, an addict, a drop-out', or, 'Your childhood does not determine your adulthood'.

Fatuous, fatuous, fatuous. As a confirmed and critical thug, I feel the need to correct this self-styled teacher of mine. In the first case, what she *means* is that a sociable person interested in material security would not want to write for a living; in the second case, what she *means* is that there is nothing self-*cherishing* about being a thug, an addict, or a drop-out; in the third case, what she *means* is that negative childhood experiences do not preclude the creation of a happy adulthood. The book is littered with such oblique statements. And then there is the matter of Dowrick's taste for the bleeding obvious.

Bleeding Obvious I: 'I have a Mercedes Benz, *but I am not my Mercedes Benz.*'

Bleeding Obvious II: 'Your relationship with yourself is more intimate and more knowledgeable than anyone else's experience of you can ever be.'

Bleeding Obvious III: 'Many of us use the term *narcissist* to describe someone we perceive as self-absorbed.' (As opposed to those of us who use the term *narcissist* to describe someone who is partial to chocolate crackles.)

Dowrick's touch is warm but never discriminating; she fails to credibly question anything. She simply reiterates truisms and then agrees, and this Sir Pertinax MacSycophant stance begins to grate after the first ten pages. She tells us that in this age of instant communication many of us know less about ourselves and the motives of those we love than almost any other subject. Right for once, she has nevertheless produced a book which keeps it that way.

Who am I and where am I going? Only my astrologer knows for sure.

1992

LIKE A BULL OUT OF A CHUTE:

JERRY HALL

NEVER IS MESQUITE, Texas, more evident in Miss Jerry Hall than when she laughs. Where her electrodynamic husband, Mick Jagger, throws his head back and showcases his many teeth, Hall dips her chin and narrows those spectacular japanned cat's eyes of hers and snorts through her delicate nostrils. The resultant sound is that of steam released through a vibrating kettle. The resultant effect is that of a wrangler on a porch somewhere hot at violet dusk — boots kicked up, a beer in his fist, his sweat-soaked Stetson pushed right back, chewing tobacco — sly, natural, real easy like. It is a laugh which tells you that she has seen it all and done it all and at the end of the day, you know what? It's all still funny.

The fact that the Breakfast Room of Sydney's Ritz-Carlton has been cordoned off for this interview is no surprise to her. Why should it be? The fact that the waiter apologises for the distraction of the occasional staff member walking past her table is no surprise to her. Why should it be? It would take a hell of a lot more to surprise the most famous of the five abused daughters of General Patton's head sergeant and a Frederick's-of-Hollywood-loving duenna who has seen *Gone With The Wind* more than sixteen times. In Hall's blood, both battle and romance. She eases her long and slender big-boned body into the plump banquette and asks — in an improbably broad and deep nicotine-and-London-tinged Texan accent — for a 'packit' of 'Marr-boro Lahts' and a cup of English Breakfast tea. Her every request is prefaced by a dusky 'ex-*cuhse* me, please?' and concluded with a gracious '*thank* you'. When complimented, she will flutter her eyelashes and sigh: 'Whah, that's so *kahnd!*'

Shaking a cigarette from the packet, she lights it up and blows a slow blue plume of smoke. Her three children, she tells me, are visiting the 'aquay-rium' with her mother. Every place they go, her children bone up on the local culture — 'meu-seums' and the like. In a few hours, she and Jagger will be having lunch at a house loaned to them by a couple she has never met. The name of the couple? She takes a light drag of her cigarette and frowns. She can't remember. And then: 'The

Packers.' She hears they're nice people and arches a cartoon villain's eyebrow as I elaborate on their social significance. When I have finished, she dips her long manicured fingers through that jeroboam of champagne hair and wryly says: 'Ah *tease* Mick 'n call him the *macho world leader*, 'cause everywhere he goes, all these rilly important people try to be nice to him … y'know, presidents an' things, always invitin' him over for drinks. *Ooooooooooh*, ah say, *macho world leader!*'

To Jerry Hall, the world is one big Dairy Queen parlour. She is not a problemist. People are people are people, and that's all there is to it. She's as comfortable leg-wrestling for bets after too many tequilas as she is selecting antiques for her seventeenth-century chateau in the Loire Valley, her villa in Mustique, her New York brownstone, or her £2.25 million mansion in Richmond, Surrey. She has been known to treat the global press as her notepaper. Her glorious motto is that honesty is the best policy, no matter what. Her squeamish former fiancé Bryan Ferry (who was inspired by her to write the hit 'Let's Stick Together'), may have objected to her public account of being left in the room 'with the foetus still in the sink' after aborting their baby, but it was only the truth. Hall lacks the grandiosity of most celebrities.

Her professionalism is immaculate. Before the camera, she is magnificent. Much of Helmut Newton's best works features

Hall. When seated beside her during a television interview, the photographer Patrick Litchfield was reprimanded by the host for exhibiting inappropriately sexual body language. She is one of the very few (if not the only) internationally recognised models with a talent for self-deprecation. In the wake of her husband's fling with the aristocratic Italian model Carla Bruni, Hall was all mane in a US commercial for Clairol as she drawled: 'This is for you, honey. And you thought you'd be better off with a *brunette*!' One of the great original characters of our time, Hall has made an art of her life.

'Ah've noticed,' she says in a confidential tone, 'that the men are very chauvinistic here. Ah noticed that when ah was here last time. We wen' over to what's his name … that actor … Bryan *Brown*'s house. He gits Mick a beer an' everythin', an' they go out on the porch an' they start talkin' about *sports*.' With a contemptuous expression, she wrings the sibilants dry. 'We were there for *two* hours. He never *once* looked at me or made ONE sentence towards me. Drove me completely *nuts*! An Mick kept tryin' to git me into the conversation an' he didn't even *notice*. He told me where the refrigerator was an' to help mahself to a *drink*.'

To emphasise her disgust, she leans forward. Her skin is literally flawless, tallow silk. Her glossy mouth is a crimson kiss. The combination of her high forehead, straight neat nose and full upper lip is that which imparts *hauteur* to her every photograph. It is easy to see why Thierry Mugler chose her as the face of his new perfume, Angel. Thirty-nine years have tempered her ethereal beauty with a knowing sexuality. 'Thierry,' she declares, 'kind of stopped designing when the *grunge* look was out. He was really de*pressed*. Ah was, too — ah *haited* all those clothes! An' all those pitchers that [Kate Moss] did that were so kinda *victim* … like someone on *her*oin, you know? Lookin' all kinda path*etic*. Ah don't think that's at *all* sexy. So when sophis-ti-caited, glamorous clothes came back in stahle, we were *thrilled*.'

She pauses to accept her cup of tea, into which she briskly stirs a teaspoon of white sugar. 'Thierry is so much *fun!*' she exclaims. 'We went off to White Sands in Mexico to shoot the Angel campaign, and we had *such* a good time! We stayed in a mo-tel, and the only place to eat was a truck stop which was full of all these soldiers from the mili-tairy base. They were so *silly*, all the [fashion] guys! They made me laugh *so* much! Thierry is *into* sex, boy!' She snorts and snorts and takes a sip of tea. 'He's *nahce* to the models. A lot of the designers are *hor*rible. They git *mad* if you mix their skirt with someone else's *jack*it! They're, like, fee-oo-rius, y'know? So *silly*, rilly.' She snorts again, shakes her head.

Hall helped create the 'fame world' of modern high fashion by making it all seem like so much fun. 'When ah startid modellin', all the girls were rilly good *friends*,' she says with feeling. 'Nowadays, ah've bin doin' some modellin' an' *watch*in' … an' it's just so *strainge*! They are *so* competitive and *bitchy*! They don't *talk* to each other; they never have a joke; they don't have any *fun* together; they just *stare* right through each other. So *weird*!' Her eyes grow wide. 'We used to *help* other girls who didn't have their *walks* together.' Her voice loudens considerably: 'Ah mean, nowadays it's *riiiiiiiilly* weird!'

Her chin drops into her palm and she gazes lazily at me. 'Backstage at Thierry's [most recent] show, Elle MacPherson was *so* unhappy. First she had on a *red* wig that was just *so* awful, and she didn't like the way she looked, and kept *lookin'* —' here she jumps back and mimics the flustered MacPherson, all spooked eyes and outstretched hands — 'at everyone *else*. Then for the second show, she decided she wanted a *wahte* wig 'cause there were all these blonde girls. [The wig] was such a weird *shaype*!' She snorts with undisguised delight. 'Her *hair* was showin' and it was put *on* bad an' she didn't even say *hello* to me! She's *very* unfriendly! Ah was amazed, because ah was up in a dressin' room with Tippi Hedren and Patty Hearst — you know, all these *rilly* fun girls. We were havin' a *grayt* time laughin' an' carryin' on, and there were all these *sooper*models … Claudia Schiffuh an' Naomi Campbell … an' it was just ICY.'

Her brow arches. 'In between the first and second shows, three of the girls walked *out* because they didn't think they were gettin' enough star *treatment*.' She pauses for effect. 'So the clothes couldn't be *shown* — there wasn't time to get other models. They had to leave the clothes on the *rack*. Those *bee-yu-tiful* clothes!' Her voice overflows with pity. 'All that *work*! Everythin' hand*made*! Oh, it was just *so* shocking. An' then a lot of them were complainin' about how un*com*fortable the clothes were. Ah, mean, *rilly*!' She snorts with disdain. 'Ah mean, of *course*! They're not supposed to be *com*fortable — they're supposed to be *fab*ulous!'

Hall's longevity in a fickle industry, her evergreen beauty, her confidence, her marriage to one of the world's most desired men, her children and ability to sustain true friendships have made her the target of much hostile rivalry. She doesn't flinch at the topic, but merely shrugs. Drinks her tea. Blinks up. And then, in a level, creamy, deadly voice, she says: 'Couple of years ago at a show, this one model just *stared* at me with the most *hate*ful look for *hourrrrrrs*. Then she went up to Thierry and said: *Ah think Jerry should take off her ring* [her eighteenth-century diamond engagement ring] *because it doesn't look right with the clothes*. Ah think she thought ah was gonna be *stew*pid enough to put it in mah *bag*! Ah put it in the hotel safe. Ah think she was going to try to *nick* it or somethin'.' She slowly inclines her head, her eyes bristling with a gladiatorial intelligence. 'But then at the *last* show in Paris, someone put a bunch of *pahns* [pins] in mah high heels ... straight *pahns*! Ah found them an' emptied them *out*. Ah mean, can you imagine?'

Such a theatrical facility has led to many offers of acting roles. Her main problem? That accent. Hall could recite Lactantius' philosophy of religion and still come out sounding like Gomer Pyle. In an attempt to divest herself of the 'hick' in her voice, she studied at London's National Theatre for a year. She still laughs at the failure. Another problem has been that her tremendous presence is not apparent on the big screen. Her cameo as Jack Nicholson's narcissistic girlfriend in Batman was, unfortunately, wooden. In 1990, she played Cherie in the stage version of Bus Stop. The critics were unforgiving. The *Guardian*: 'Ms Hall is to the art of Thespis what Yves St Laurent is to speedway [racing].' *Punch*: 'One ought to be grateful, but it is curiously dispiriting to watch a legendary sex goddess lumbering about the set like the front end of a pantomime giraffe.' The *Independent*: 'Cherie is supposed to be a talentless singer and to this aspect of the part, Hall brings great natural gifts.'

Such *badinage* has not prevented world-class actors and directors from recruiting Hall at cocktail parties for roles. She has recently finished filming *Princess Caraboo*, *Savage Hearts* and *Vampire in Brooklyn*. The latter starred Eddie Murphy, with whom she 'got on grayyyyyyt'. 'He *loves*, you know, *a*ccents an' things,' she explains with a watermelon smile. 'Ah put on a *riiiiiiilly* hick accent with him, *real* country, 'cause he loves *mi*micking. He's a gray*t* *lookin'* guy — *amazin'* skin. *Amazin'*.' She pauses, and then — in an admiring whistle — says: 'A *bee-yu-tiful* lookin' guy.'

She may enjoy the occasional foray into acting, but blanches at the thought of relocating to Hollywood. '*No!*' she cries, one hand flat on the banquette. 'The people are rilly *a*wful! So ob*sessed*. It's all types of people, but once they git there, they're *so* single-minded and *so* competitive that they just lose all their *ma*inners, you know? They don't wanna *talk* to you unless you can *do* somethin' for them.' She makes a face. 'They're like wild *a*nimals climbin' out of a *hole* or somethin'. *Very* ugly. *Rilly* ugly. *Very* nasty. Ah can think of some [sexual] plays made in the past by some *awful* ghastly Hollywood people. An' when you git to Los Angeles, *all* everybody talks about is movies, which ah think is kind of *borin'*. Ah wouldn't want to sacrifice mah life in any *way* for mah career, you know? Because the *main* thing ah do is motherin' three *adorrable* chill-dren.'

The attention would be superfluous; her fame is as comprehensive as that of any leading actress. She has been mobbed on several occasions, her clothes have been torn by frenzied fans, her life has been invaded by the paparazzi. After ordering another cup of tea, she softly says: 'Livin' in what ah call the "fame world" destroys people all the *tahme*. They live for their coverage; they're ob*sessed* by it. It's ridiculous to git worried about it. Ah always think: *It's tomorrow's kitty litter.* Ah only buy [tabloids] 'f it's a good pitcher [of me] in it!' She snorts a while, and then her grey-green eyes gleam wickedly. 'A lot of the things they said about me in the English papers weren't *true*, so ah settled out of court. One year they kept sayin' that ah was with *this* guy an' *that* guy [Count Adam Zamoyski, Lord David Ogilvy and Lord James Neidpath] — an' *none* of it was true. Ah made *sooo* much money from those papers!' She merrily snorts. 'Ah said t' mah girlfriends: *"Make up some MORE rumours!"* ' More animated snorts. 'Lately [the tabloids] have bin very *good* 'cause ah made so much *money* out of them. They check their stories now. They're rilly *careful*.'

Hall's sense of the absurd understandably faltered in 1990 when an English tabloid 'discovered' a home video which, according to the *Daily Mail*, showed 'the quantity of sex and champagne Miss Hall actually enjoys'. With the help of her powerful husband, Hall was able to arrange an immediate High Court injunction to prevent the contents of the video appearing anywhere. Again, she shrugs. 'Ah mean, Bryan [Ferry] was *so* interested in what they said in th' papers — he *lived* it. He took it all so *hard*.' She is dismissive of Lucy Ferry's admission for drug and alcohol addiction as the 187 pound-a-day Farm Place Clinic in Surrey. 'Oh, ah think she jist made that up because it was *fashion*able,' she announces, spooning sugar into her fresh cup of tea. 'Ah saw her all the time and ah *never* saw her takin' drugs or bein' drunk or *anythin'*. It *shocked* all her friends.' She lifts the cup to her lips and eyes me over it. 'But who *knows*?' she sighs. 'Maybe she was a *secret* one, but she sure didn't *look* it. She's *very* pretty. *Ele*-gant.'

Suddenly engaged, she clicks her cup back into its saucer and moves in close, her long pale bare legs everywhere. 'An' what about that Michael Hutchence goin' out with Paula *Yaites*?' she cries, patently amazed. 'Isn't that *weird*? Bob Geldof is a rilly *rilly* nice guy. Ah *love* him. He's jist *fabulous* — very intelligent, very erudite, very witty … he's a livin' *saint*! The things he's *done*! Who else has fed a starvin' *country*? He's amazin'! An' he's bin *faith*ful to her — he *has*! Ah know that for a *fact*! Since he got married, he *has*!' Hall and her close friend Marie Helvin were recently photographed escorting the crushed Geldof from a restaurant, their antic grins reflecting their efforts to comfort the grieving musician. Hall's indignance is ferocious. 'What's Hutchence *doin'*? Why does he want to mess with someone's *wahfe*? She's got three *kids*! She's bin with Bob for eighteen *years*! Why does Hutchence want *Paula*?' Her lip curls with voluptuous contempt. 'Do you think he likes the scandal in the *pap*ers? An' now they're goin' off together ... *well!*' She stops, and her glare softens. '*Poor* Helena. An' ah feel *so* sorry for Bob.'

Her reverence for marriage is legendary. It took her something like thirteen years and one or two children to nail the aisle-shy Jagger, and there is still question as to whether the marriage was legal. Parisadha Hindu Dharma, a Hindu official, had this to say of their 1990 wedding in Bali: 'They only imitated a Hindu Balinese wedding ceremony.' When questioned of the ceremony's legality, Jagger told *Vanity Fair*: 'Depends what you call ... I *think* so.' Nevertheless, it was sufficient for Hall. 'Mick 'n ah have bin together for over eighteen years, and it's bin quite dee-fee-coolt with both of us bein' in a business where you have a lot of *op*tions,' she says with unsentimental frankness. We've managed because we love each other so much. A lot of people hold a grudge for*ev*er — they will not forget *any*thin'. Ah always take the point of view that *ah'm* not perfect and nor is anyone *else*. You have to for*give* people.'

There has been much to forgive. Jagger has been linked with numerous women — the oil heiress Pauline Stephaich, the model Peta Wilson, the model Kathy Latham, the actor Uma Thurman, and however many others. The veracity of the reports is not the question. It must be unimaginably painful to have the world gloating over these real or imagined liaisons. Hall only publicly lost her composure over one — Carla Bruni. The very name causes her eyes to spill over with tears and all of a sudden, she looks like a child. 'Ah *rilly* don't want to talk about that,' she says, trying to smile, 'that was a long time ago.' Swallowing, she lights another cigarette. 'Mick would be classified as the Bad Guy. But like mah mother, ah chose the *fun* one over the safe and predictable one.' She thoughtfully smokes for a moment. 'Ah must say, ah've had a lot of *fun* with Mick. Ah give these parties every Monday, an' he goes through the *menu* with me, he orders the *wine* — even if he's *away*! You know, the guest list — everythin'! He's very in*volved*. With the house [in Surrey], we both chose the curtains an' colours, everythin'.'

Perhaps to preserve his hellion image, Jagger contradicts his ingenuous wife at every turn. To the journalist Stephen Schiff, he roared: 'I think wine is so *boring*. There's red and there's white and I think there's pink. And they all taste good, and they all make you drunk. Nor am I interested in decorating ... in the slightest.' Hall sighs through her smoke. 'Ah don't think he rilly *likes* bein' thought of as a family man. But ah rilly *miss* him when he's away. It's *terr*ible.' She pauses a beat, and then explodes: 'But ah mean, the way he *lives* is ridiculous! It's like a *pasha*! It's like the eighteenth century — he's like Louis

Quatorze! When he comes home from his tourin', ah always make jokes about how his head's too big to git in the *door*!'

She stubs her cigarette out with alacrity. 'The minute he gets home, ah say: *Right! Back to real life!* The way everyone *treats* him, you know? Everywhere he goes it's front page *news*; everyone wants to *meet* him; they're all waitin' outside his hotel; huge bouquets of flowers arrive every *minute* … it's ri*dic*ulous!' With an exasperated expression, she reaches over for the glass of water I have just poured. 'But ah think he likes it. The Stones have made him a lot of money, but it's ridiculous what it does to his head. He can turn into a *mon*stuh! Ah make him come down to earth with a *thud*. Ah say to him: *Look* — ah've bin doin' everythin' all this whole year; ah've bin doin' the homework, ah've bin walkin' the dog, ah've bin doin' *every*thin' — now *you* can do it!'

More outraged snorts. 'But people like that need a sense of *real*ity, you know?' Her voice grows serious. 'Without me, ah think he'd be spoilt *rotten*. [Everyone needs] someone who tells them the *truth*, you know? Someone who *rilly* tells them the truth. It's not nice to have somebody who's constantly sayin' you're *old* …' she stops herself saying 'but', and clears her throat. 'Girls — you know, the groupies — don't act so bad as they did in the beginnin'. It was worse, then. In the beginnin', they all thought they had a CHAINCE!' She rolls into a wonderful chuckle. 'Ah think they've given up now, but ah still can't relax. He's just so charis*ma*tic!'

The obvious love she has for her husband and glamorous geisha image have not affected her fundamentally independent nature. 'When ah first went to Paris,' she explains, 'mah mother told me to just go and do mah ca*reer*. So ah was rilly very single*mahnd*ed. Ah wasn't rilly interested in men for a long time.' Her tone has dropped to an intimate register. 'Ah do feel ah *missed* mah childhood. Ah startid workin' when ah was eleven and worked every summer, worked every day after *school*, startid modellin' at fourteen … ah always *worked*, you know?' She pauses, her eyes vulnerable. 'Mah father was not a lot of *fun*, an' ah *never* forgave him for hittin' me. He used to beat me up with his belt pretty bad, you know. Mah sisters an' ah couldn't go to school [sometimes] an' things.' She pauses. 'Ah wasn't very *pop*ular at school, an' ah didn't rilly have any boyfriends because they didn't rilly like tall skinny girls.' She pauses again, and then says: 'Ah mean, now ah'm quite keen to have some *fun*, you know?' Her fingers drift over her short silk skirt and she looks away.

The lobby of the Ritz-Carlton is all gilt and discretion, ash-blue tapestry and pearl necklaces behind glass. Having completed the interview, Hall positions herself beside an explosion of exotic flowers, her long thin arms outstretched.

Running towards her are three unkempt blonde children —
Elizabeth Scarlett, James Leroy and Georgia May Ayeesha. Their
square-jawed orange-haired grandmother sedately follows.
Bundling them up in her arms, Hall turns to me with a radiant,
ravishing smile. 'Mah *chill*-dren!' she squeals, loud with pride.
'These are mah *chill*-dren!'

Her eyes are luminiferous.

Elle, 1995

POSTSCRIPT

Hall infuriated the paradoxically conservative Jagger by
exposing her many charms for English *Vogue* in early 1996. The
brazen shot (in which the model effectively flashes with one tug
of her diaphanous panties) made international news. In July,
'friends' of Hall allegedly hired a private detective who
compiled a bulky dossier on her errant spouse. Further reports
of Jagger's 'cavorting with two blondes in his LA home' and of
'flings' with actor Uma Thurman and Jana Rajlich, the unusually
elongated twenty-eight-year-old Czech model, caused Hall to
consult the Princess of Wales' solicitor, Anthony Julius. 'Stay
jealous,' Hall once recommended. 'If a woman stops being
jealous she's lost the flame.' Despite a pre-nuptial agreement,
divorce lawyers predicted that Hall could win up to a third of

Jagger's wealth — estimated at £110 million — if the case was fought in America. A friend remarked: 'Mick does not want a divorce. He loves Jerry and the children very much. Jerry has said before that he can have his little dalliances as long as he comes home to her. The problem is that he's had girls throwing themselves at him since he was eighteen and it's a difficult habit to break.'

Hall, famous for expressing the view that while a wife should be a maid in the parlour, a cook in the kitchen and a whore in the bedroom, the first two could be hired, was apparently enraged that Jagger's antics had upset their son, James. Keith Richard, Jagger's long-time friend and collaborator, reportedly pleaded with Jagger to book into a sex counselling clinic before his lust-problem 'wrecked his life'. In November, Hall mostly ignored her estranged husband at the Royal Court's fortieth anniversary celebration and 'pointedly offered him her cheek' before leaving. Exiled to a London hotel while Hall consulted lawyers, the contrite Jagger suddenly overwhelmed his wife with dramatically expensive gifts and Knightsbridge lingerie. By the third of December, he was permitted to return to the family home. 'You know,' Hall commented, 'we always live in hope. There is nothing more humiliating than loving someone so much that you forgive the infidelities.'

GUNS AND ROSES:
ROSE HANCOCK-PORTEOUS

ROSE HANCOCK-PORTEOUS has never known the luxury of fairness. When she was first linked to the late mining magnate, Lang Hancock, the Australian press derided her as a 'Filipino doll' in search of a 'sugar daddy', as 'the housekeeper', and it was falsely intimated that she could have been no more than a prostitute (attractive Asian female = sex toy): she was completely and ruthlessly dehumanised. This bigotry took many forms — judgment of her words, her clothes, her taste. Ordinarily intelligent people denounced her 'vulgarity'. Never for a moment was it taken into account that English was not her first language; never for a moment was it taken into account that she was the product of a violently different culture, a culture in which her style is considered enviable. Such loaded perceptions were not new to her. As a young woman in the Philippines, she was ostracised for leaving a husband she claims was abusive. As a child and adolescent, she was victimised by an emotionally unstable mother and a patriarchal social system in which women are regarded as no more than 'objects of display and objects of pleasure'. Always aware that our world is one in which victims and not perpetrators are punished, she has stifled her pain in order to promote herself as a 'winner'. Above all, Rose Hancock-Porteous is a victim of her memories.

The contradictions in her nature are also to be considered. On one hand, she keeps telethon raffle tickets in a bright red HELLO KITTY! tin box; on the other, she studies biographies of Hess, Hitler, Lawrence of Arabia, Eva Peron, Eva Braun, General Patton ('he is my dream man'). She is humble enough to talk of 'stuffing US$5000 in a [profusely lubricated] condom and [sticking] it' within herself to avoid Filipino airport currency restrictions, and so pretentious as to make remarks such as: 'You can [only] wear a dress once in the eastern states and once in the west.' Her outstanding and most admirable feature is her strength, and yet the (approximately $30 million) mansion she shares with her fourth husband, Canadian property developer Willy Porteous, is decorated with scores of rose-and-wind-machine photographic portraits of her in the manner of fragile heroines gracing the covers of romantic novelettes. Her favourite perfume is called Fracas, but her life is ordered to a degree that suggests a mortal fear of chaos — everything is filed, labelled, polished, bleached, pristine. 'It's not hygienic not to iron,' she insists, 'because when you hang clothes on the line the germs get to them, and you have to iron clothes to kill the germs, you know?' Even her underpants, she informs me, are ironed and the soles of her shoes are disinfected daily.

The Perth mansion, one of the most famous in the country, is the home of someone who has spent much time in grand international hotels — all marble and remote-controlled Austrian blinds, crystal and gold, paintings in the Romantic tradition, satiny sofas. Its overblown antebellum-meets-Louis XVI-meets-Ancient Egypt-meets-the Ritz-Carlton is to her countrymen what Lagerfeld's pad is to the French: the height of Swoonsville. Rose perches on the fatly upholstered edge of one of two sofas adjacent to each other in the 'formal sitting room'. She chain-smokes cigarettes; she drinks glass after glass of Coca Cola; her prim posture and careful enunciation are those of a convent girl. If she distorts — and has distorted — minor truths, it is only because she was taught by hard experience to equate 'whitewashing' with survival, for she is devastatingly honest about her greatest difficulties.

Her presentation is immaculate: subtle maquillage, long straight black hair, gilt-heeled KL pumps, a little navy-and-white KL sailor dress. The decolletage is eye-popping. Her breasts are bunched together like coconuts, and disproportionately large. She lightly denies surgical magic, attributing their unusually buoyant and glistening volume to a flattering 'weight gain'. On her right wrist, a diamond-heavy Piaget watch; on her right hand, the engagement ring given to her by Willy — a 6.2 carat, D-flawless, cordate diamond. It is the size of a swallow's heart. She smiles only when she speaks of Willy, but her conversation is littered with affectionate references to Lang. 'I knew when Lang saw me that the fell for me,' she says, lighting her first cigarette. 'I was standing in front of him, and said: "Good afternoon, sir — I'm your new housekeeper." And his eyes!' She mimics blatant lust. 'His eyes sussed out my face and then went *straight* into my boobs. So there I was with my very straight posture and my big boobs and my small waist, and I knew it. I thought: *here's* another one!'

Employed by his daughter Gina (with whom she has since regularly warred), Rose encountered resistance from the Australian government when she applied for permanent residency. Hancock's clout was such that all was quickly resolved. '[Prior to her involvement with Lang, Rose] worked so hard to impress him,' a former Hancock nanny was quoted as saying. 'She would get up in the middle of the night to scrub the bathroom. She even cut [his] toenails and washed his feet.' The general assumption was that Rose 'went out to get' Lang, the premises of this assumption being that a) Lang Hancock was senile and *ipso facto* a sitting duck; b) Rose was a Machiavellian robot; and c) neither of them were capable of real love or caring. Forty years her senior, Hancock photographed like a dyspeptic bullfrog, but footage of the man shows an extremely alert and humorous strategist. 'I was a recluse,' he announced at one point, 'but it's a *delight* to take Rose out at night.' The fact that she brought him great joy was ignored by most in favour of a focus upon the seeming impropriety of their union. The twin responses? Opprobrium and open mockery.

'I felt lost in Australia at first,' she says, blowing smoke. 'Suddenly here I am in this strange country, and I had this temporary job with this old man. He [would show] me videos and clippings of himself to impress me. *What do you want me to say?* I asked. You know, he would always pinch my bum, things like that. And then I began to feel so sorry for him because he was living alone like a recluse. He had all the money in the world, but he was drinking out of plastic cups. His house was in disarray, the roof and plaster were down, he had a narrow staircase that he could fall down any time ...' She pauses to stub her cigarette out in the crystal ashtray. 'And he actually ...

cared about me. I wasn't attracted to him in the beginning but later on, I saw the animal appetite in him and liked that. And he was always there for me one hundred per cent, always.'

Their relationship lasted nine years and ended with his death. During that time, her behaviour outraged the establishment. 'I enjoy coming out of the bathroom in something sexy and letting him chase me,' she cheerfully told one journalist. For her husband's eightieth birthday, she commissioned a life-sized mannequin of herself (which was delivered to him through a fog of dry ice over a swimming pool in which rose petals floated). Animatedly, she exclaims: 'Here these socialities say *darling! darling! darling! you look beautiful!*, but I know that the minute I turn my back, they stab me. I find them very cowardly because they can't say it straight to my face, you know?' Her expression becomes grim. 'They don't know where life begins and where it *ends*, you know? They can't understand. I feel sorry for them. I'm a fun person, but they hold their emotions back, they cover themselves with a plastic shroud. I was never scared of them because by the time I moved to Perth, my insides were already hardened from the past.'

In 1992, the *Sunday Times* sent two journalists to the Philippines to substantiate her many seemingly grandiose claims, one of them being that she was kidnapped by her first husband, Julian 'Jay' Teodoro. A polo player from a wealthy family and in his youth, the 'feared' lieutenant of a political warlord, Teodoro allegedly said: 'I saw her, I wanted her, I took her.' Photographs of Rose in her late adolescence show a demure and smiling girl in white, all vulnerability. This vulnerability excited Teodoro, and he arranged to be married to her in a locked church guarded by men brandishing M16 rifles. In place of a wedding march, the theme from the television series 'M.A.S.H.' — 'Suicide is Painless'. Their daughter Johanna was born in early 1972. 'I was a virgin when I met him,' she says slowly and clearly. 'He was not gentle with me. It was horrible. I was twenty-one, fresh out of college. It was like rape. I knew nothing about penetration. All I recall is … *pain*.'

On page 221 of her fluffy autobiography (*A Rose By Any Other Name*), she writes: 'The interview was straightforward. "Have you had children?" "Yes, one daughter." ' The *Sunday Times* discovered otherwise. On December 28, 1972, Rose had given birth to twin boys. The journalists did not consider that a man like Teodoro was capable of having documents falsified, and reported: '[The twins] died of a rare blood disease three days later.' Rose visibly controls herself. As she makes her allegations, her bottom teeth are in evidence and her voice rises. 'He was — he used to *hit* me,' she manages. 'One time he hit me with a .45 — a .45 Remington — he hit me here,' she repeatedly pounds the back of her skull, 'and I bled all over — I had a white gown on, I can still recall … sitting at the top of the staircase shaking and trembling; I was twenty-two years old … the blood was dripping down. It's a good thing a friend of mine came over. I was shellshocked. She brought me to the hospital.' Her hand continues pounding the back of her skull as she looks at me. 'He nearly *killed* me. He nearly *killed* me.'

She draws her hand away, lights another cigarette and pauses. 'He beat me when I was pregnant,' she says, her voice thick. 'He was responsible for the boys' deaths.' Again, she pauses. When she resumes speaking, each word has a metallic resonance. 'I wasn't … given … prenatal checkups … because … his mother stopped giving him money … and … he went gun-running … and if he didn't bring home the bacon, I had nothing to eat, so … here I am, six months' pregnant, having no lunch and no dinner … affected, of course, the twins … they were born premature … and undernourished. That is why they died. It was not a rare blood disease.'

Her features are frozen. She is staring at me steadily, her eyes moist, black, hard, sorrowful. 'I had just given birth,' she continues. 'I remember it was December 31. There were only five of us in the cemetery. I went to the funeral parlour and I saw the guy,' here her voice trembles and she sits up, still smoking, 'and I saw the guy holding one of the boys like a chicken.' She gestures as if holding a fowl by its leg. 'I rushed forward and grabbed the boy from him and cuddled him in my arms. He was … very stiff. Then I went home and got some of Johanna's diapers, and dressed the boys myself. I broke down. When my husband used to beat me up, I never cried. It was the first time I broke down, in the cemetery.'

The marriage lasted another turbulent week or so, and then she escaped with Johanna. The indifference of her family is reflected in a comment of her brother's: 'Rose outgrew [him]. She was too strong-willed. She was very impulsive, which may explain why she could not settle.' 'When I go to Manila,' she says quietly, 'I go to the graveyard and take flowers and I just sit there. I just sit there and sometimes talk to the boys and say: *I'm sorry if I failed you. I couldn't do much.*' She stubs her cigarette out, takes another swig of her cola, and lights another cigarette. 'I'm too hard to cry, you know.'

She took refuge with her daughter and nanny in the airport lounge, one of the few public places in which air-conditioning was installed. 'I just carried a paper bag and one change of clothing and I was wearing thongs,' she states. 'I left everything behind. Just survival. My focus was on Johanna. I thought: *I have got to get something for this child. She mustn't die like those boys.* I lived in the airport. I used to go to the restaurant near there and ask for hot water and sugar and shake the bottle and give it to Johanna. The paediatrician said she was not to have milk. This went on for three to five days. I ate nothing. Just water. And then the waiter gave me evaporated milk, so I drank that.'

Destitute, she began trading in the black market. 'We have no welfare in the Philippines,' she explains. 'If you go to a hospital and you don't have deposit money, you're not in.' Dragging deeply from her cigarette and still staring at me, she curls her hand into a fist. 'That's what made me strong. I *vowed* I would never go hungry again. I *vowed* that I would *never* again marry a *bastard* like my ex-husband. I used to have nightmares of starvation. Lang used to wake me up in the middle of the night and hug me and say: *it's all right, sweetheart — you'll never starve; you'll never be a waif again.* I used to scream at night, you know? I'M HUNGRY! I'M HUNGRY!' Her voice is a monotone.

During the day, she sold liquor to the airbases and American lingerie to prostitutes; at night, she sat in hotel bars with girlfriends, emotionally crushed, 'torturing men'. 'After I left that bastard,' she said, 'I had a *vendetta* on men. I'd make them fall in love with me and then scorn them. I would say: *maybe, maybe, maybe we'll spend the night together* ... After that, I'd say: *sorry — I've found out that I'm not keen on you.*' With sudden ferocity, she slashes her hand through the air. 'In those hotels, I saw the emptiness of those people's lives — people who were looking for something they couldn't find. These men had empty marriages. They didn't want to go home and have dinner with the family. They just wanted to sit in the bar and drink. All the people who live that life are full of anger. That's why I vibrated towards them as mates. Because they were angry, too. Misery loves company. And yet that lifestyle is seen as glamorous. Ironical, isn't it?'

At the age of twenty-eight she left the Philippines for Europe, where she sold Arrow shirts and knits and 'romped' in Spain, and where she modelled in Italian buying houses. She returned to Manila two years later in 1978. 'I was always proud,' she says. 'I remember I got a job in 1970 as a hostess with Cathay Pacific. I was sacked. First, I refused to cut my hair. It had to be two inches above the collarbone, so because my hair was long, I wore a wig. The instructor took a dislike to me and had a barber nick it all off.' She slowly stubs her cigarette out and lights another. 'On my initial flight, an elderly American asked me for some salt. The galley was long and on my way down, some people asked me for some water. So I walked back down the galley with tumblers of water and the salt. I knew the people who wanted the water were waiting patiently, and so I gave the American the salt. He said: "What were you doing at the back of the galley? Scratching your arsehole, you brown monkey?" I threw the water in his face. I was told I should have apologised for being busy.'

Leaving the seven-year-old Johanna in Manila, Rose travelled to Hong Kong and Malaysia in 1979. It was in Malaysia that she met her second husband, commodities broker Patrick Kuan. In 1980, they married. In 1981, they returned to the Philippines. In 1982, her second husband returned to Kuala Lumpur, where, according to the *Sunday Times*, 'he is believed to have been caught up in a credit card swindle in Hong Kong'. He did not return. Rose Lacson-Teodoro-Kuan moved to Perth in 1983.

It took Johanna Lacson until 1992 to express the rage she had been harbouring for her mother. Selling her story to '60 Minutes', she claimed her mother was a 'gold-digger' who had 'slashed her wrists' in front of her and left her alone for entire nights as a child. Earlier this year, Rose allowed photographs of her daughter (taken after she had been battered by an unnamed man) to be published in a national magazine. She acknowledges that she has been an irresponsible mother. 'I let her down,' she says softly. 'I let her down by not being there for her. I feel very guilty. It is the one part of my life I wish I could undo. My one regret. I tried to make it up to her in terms of money — she had her own car, her own chauffeur, her own maid. I used to take her to the best boutiques and say: *pick anything!* I couldn't give her much love and attention.'

Now based in London and working as a tour coordinator and French interpreter, Johanna has made peace with her mother and the two are now 'friends'. Rose's behaviour towards her daughter cannot be excused, only explained. The seventh of nine children to a formerly aristocratic family, she was severely beaten for any transgression. 'My mother and I are not very close,' she explains, nervously smoking. 'She was a cold person in the sense that if you hurt yourself because you picked up a hammer and played with it, she would whip you. She couldn't stand anything that was outside her control. She would never touch me unless I had bathed. She told me I was disgusting. There was a lot of terror.'

All nine children were regularly beaten with leather belts and guava sticks. On one occasion, Rose was pushed into a laundry bag and 'suspended for hours from a rafter'. 'If you cried,' she says, 'the more she would whip you. So I stopped crying.' She stubs her cigarette out and when she looks up, the expression in her eyes is unforgiving. 'Now that I've achieved all this, my mother thinks she can't hurt me any more. I'm not under her thumb, unlike my older sister who still lives with her — up to the last grain of rice she *eats* she has to get from my mother. I recall Lang telling her that he was *glad* that I'd been deprived of love because he was the one who was profiting from that.'

Lang Hancock's instincts had always been acute. 'We once had a grand party,' she says, brightening. 'My mother was there. Willy walked in: ROSE! ROSE! ROSE! And I told him to wait, because I was greeting the guests. And he was really drunk and said: "Who the *fuck* do you think you are? The queen of Mosman *Park*?" And he stuck his third finger at me and left. Lang asked me what had happened and after I told him, he turned to my mother and said: "He's going to be your next son-in-law." ' A close friend of Lang's throughout the marriage, Willy was the last person to speak to him before he died. He recalls the ailing Lang telling him: 'After I'm gone, there'll be a queue of men a mile long outside the house. You take care of her, Willy.' Porteous also recalls his own reaction: 'You want me to start dating your wife *now*?'

He and Rose married in 1992, five months after Lang's death. The two had known each other since 1983. 'The first time I met her,' Willy says, 'she was in a negligée and curled up on the sofa like a cat.' Having drained her glass, Rose sits back. 'I loved Langley,' she explains, 'but in a different way. This is the first time I have loved without any neediness. I feel like I'm sixteen again and dating. Sometimes we turn the music on and then we dance slow … and then we go lips-to-lips … and then we go necking … and then we go up to the bedroom … and I feel like a little girl, you know? The Catholic in me comes out. I love to do "it" because it's *evil*!' She grins delightedly.

The interview over, I am invited to join them both for dinner. At 7.30 pm, Willy — classically handsome and with an evaluative, intelligent gaze — greets me at the door. Rose, dressed in a bright orange chainstore tracksuit, knitted cardigan, starched white apron and with her hair in a topknot, is frying prawns and chicken breasts in the disinfected kitchen. I am seated at a long table, and I listen as Willy talks of merchant banks, buying buildings, cutting deals. He speaks with teasing enthusiam of his wife. 'She'll buy *any*thing as long as you let her smoke and drink Coke,' he says.

Around him, Rose becomes kittenish — coy glances, little jokes, her body language girlish. 'I've always played hard-to-get,' she says. 'You *what*?' Willy chokes on a laugh. 'You club men over the *head*, Rose.' When the (excellent) meal is finished, they offer to drive me back to the hotel. In the blue-tiled underground garage, a sign: PERVERT PARKING ONLY. ALL OTHERS WILL BE TOWED. Parked: a cream Bentley Turbo R, an indigo Porsche 928 GTS and a black Nissan Pathfinder. The Bentley (complete with customised blond wood and cream leather interior) is chosen. As he drives, Willy amiably chats about 'the ten-pound Poms who settled in Kalamunda in the 1960s' and asks me friendly questions about my life and work. Sensitive to his every sigh, Rose clucks: 'You've had a hard day. Nookie tonight.' 'Nookie tonight?' Willy drawls with interest. 'I do everything,' Rose assures him. Willy's laughter is pleasant. 'And I'll just lie back and groan at the appropriate moments?' he asks.

The Bentley pulls up outside the hotel and Willy hops out to open my door. From within the car, Rose pipes: 'I want her *lips*, Willy!' I shake his hand and reply that as mine have seen better days, I wouldn't mind a set of breasts like his wife's. 'Easily arranged,' he comments with a shrug. As it disappears down the one-way street, the Bentley's purr is feline.

Elle, 1995

ALPHA MALE:

CHARLTON HESTON

MECHANICALLY, HE PUMPS my hand at the door of Sydney's Sheraton on the Park Presidential Suite and smiles that frigid and Oscar-winning smile. The remnants of luncheon between his inauthentic-looking teeth and grey hairpiece that bristles like a badger seem to be his only flaws. His diction and his courtesy are beautifully polished. In half a century of interviews, he has managed to maintain his cool. Implied is a ferocious discipline. He is known for his austerity on set and for the grim obsessiveness with which he researches every part. To achieve a profile similar to Michelangelo's for *The Agony and the Ecstasy*, he stuffed his nostrils with plastic. By the time *Ben-Hur* was a wrap, he had become a master charioteer. He is lauded by those in his profession as one of the great interpreters of Shakespeare. A tennis champ, weight-lifter, and superb horseman, he loves raw meat and frequently refers to the 'triumph' and 'joy' of bed-wrecking sex. In the aftermath of an operation on his genitals, he wrote his wife a poem:

> I've never seen a purple cock.
> I never thought there'd be one.
> But think of this, to ease the shock:
> Be glad it's not a wee one.

His voice resonates with the authority of the Old Testament. Dressed in unbroken black, he could pass for a Monsignor. The chest he regularly bared for effect in the sheen of his youth is still absurdly broad. His pale eyes travel over that which is before him with a patrician indifference. His belief-system is blunt-mallet Republicanism; his moral framework was forged at Plymouth Rock; his defence-mechanism remains self-deprecation. The overall effect is one of pounding sincerity. One producer described him as 'so pure, he could heal the sick with a sneeze'. It can be said that Charlton Heston is the greatest role that Charlton Heston has ever played.

Exhaling heavily, he settles his 117 kg frame into the sofa, his rock-ledge face expressionless. It is difficult to picture this stern seventy-three-year-old grandfather in the flimsy g-string and gold body-paint with which he was coated for the off-Broadway production of *Cock-a-Doodle-Doo*. His fantastically entertaining autobiography, *In The Arena*, also documents his posing for life-drawing classes in a grey velour jockstrap: 'I did get an erection once. It got pretty crowded inside that jockstrap, but I never moved a muscle.' Why would he, when there was so much to admire? Although a warm, sticky and self-pleasuring vanity trickles like treacle through his anecdotes, his claims to modesty are fierce. When I comment on his remarkable beauty as a youth, he slits his eyes and archly corrects me. 'I was, perhaps, strikingly *masculine*,' he declares, straightening his back and laying one big brown hand firmly on his thigh.

He pauses warily, but the topic has intrigued him. 'Like any actor,' he says, 'I came to know *exactly* what I looked like. My looks are a work tool. I think most actors do — or should — develop a certain detachment. Civilians — actors refer to those who don't act as "civilians" — don't really know what they look like. Civilians don't know what they look like because they only look in the mirror, which is why civilians are so often disappointed with their photographs. Actors must know what they look like. And in looking at myself as an object, I would describe myself as masculine. The broken nose says a lot.'

Perhaps, but his oiled and buffed pectorals have always had the last word. Ever the 'shortest kid in class', the underweight and adolescent Heston suffered from acne and a scorifying lack of confidence. 'I wasn't aware of the power my looks had over people for a long time,' he slowly says as he pats his hair (and that of his donor). 'I don't think it ever *occurred* to me that I was physically attractive. It was only when I started to do live television and film that I realised the camera loved me.' Here he fixes me with a powerful look. 'A lot of beautiful people — *really* beautiful people — the camera does not love. The camera makes up its own mind. Once I grew up and got tall and so forth, I became aware that I had a *useful* face.'

This 'useful' face of his enchanted millions, a fact that did not seem to surprise or perturb him, or ignite in him the complexes which destroyed so many of his peers. Heston's stolid nature was never subject to such quivering neuroses. 'Acting is a precarious profession,' he explains as he glances over at his stooge (a plump young man in braces referred to only as 'pal'). 'At any time, an actor's career can end because of injury. At any time, they're thinking: *this could be the last performance!* Many actors died or were felled by drugs and alcohol. Certainly, the most outstanding example was Ava [Gardner]. Actresses who are very beautiful — well, their beauty is a great *burden* to them.'

He shakes his head. A certain pity flickers in his eyes. 'With Ava,' he continues, 'and many actresses like her, it was a case of being a better actress than she thought she was. I'm not saying she was a *great* actress, but she was perfectly competent. But she believed that the only reason she had success was because of her looks. And she knew that she was losing and would further lose her looks. Working with her on *55 Days at Peking* was appalling, you know, really *horrible*. You couldn't shoot her after 4 pm because she was [so drunk she was] *incoherent*.' He deeply breathes. 'We got any coffee left, pal?'

As the stooge waddles over to the percolator, Heston regards me with real sorrow. 'You only have to look at the *disaster* of Marilyn Monroe. I turned down a picture with her because I thought I just couldn't *stand* it. She was a *victim*; she was never the "child" a lot of people made her out to be. Not a child at all. Like [Judy] Garland, you know?' He asks me this as if I, too, were familiar with Garland, as if she had been our mutual neighbour. 'A lot of these girls were treated just *shittily* by producers and studio heads and husbands, you know? And then there was the starfuck syndrome. It was just *appalling*. Rita Hayworth is another example. They were all just terribly *abused* by the profession.'

When the percolator in the adjoining room has finished hacking, the stooge brings over two cups of coffee. 'Thanks pal,'

Heston murmurs with a nod. Looking over into my cup, he asks, 'You want some milk?' I reply yes. He turns to the stooge. 'Can we have some milk, pal?' And then, with a charming growl, he informs me, 'You can always *add* milk, but you can't *subtract* it.' His hands dwarf the white china cup as he takes a sip. 'Hollywood,' he continues after a pause, 'was very much a world of men, much more than now. And there was also a *callousness*. The "casting couch" was routine.'

The 'casting couch' was also routine for many beautiful young actors. Heston's laughter is deep and luxurious. 'I never had that problem with homosexual producers because I don't think I was *approachable*,' he chuckles. 'I think *not*. I had a pass made by an art teacher at school and accidentally kicked *him*, but that … was the end of *that*.' Heston is a man who clearly finds homosexuality bewildering, and his most famous — and long-running — row has been with the author Gore Vidal, of whom he purrs: '*Poor* Gore! A homosexual friend of mine said that Gore has turned into one of those queens who give homosexuality a bad *name*.' Vidal, in turn, has said that trying to direct Heston was like trying 'to animate an entire lumberyard'.

Heston has never been intimidated from articulating unpopular views. In 1992, he bravely challenged Time-Warner's support of the rap artist, Ice-T — in particular, the publication of the lyrics of 'KKK Bitch' (which graphically describe the sodomising of two twelve-year-old girls) and 'Cop Killer' (which celebrates the murder of police officers). Time-Warner's CEO defended the lyrics in terms of the First Amendment at the stockholders meeting. Heston then took the floor and dryly said: 'Mr Levin, Jews and homosexuals are also sometimes attacked. Let me ask you: if this piece were entitled "Fag Killer" or if the lyrics went, "Die, die, die, kike, die!" would you still peddle it?' Ice-T was magically dropped from the label.

His stance is not one of bigotry. In his youth, Heston was one of the world's most visible proponents of civil rights, and his actions substantially altered public opinion. 'Marlon [Brando] and I were both involved in the civil rights movement,' he casually says. 'Marlon behaved like ... Marlon. Marlon saw the whole civil rights issue as a theatre, you know? He wanted us to chain ourselves to the Lincoln Monument. We hardly had any contact except in that context.' Smiling, he takes another long sip of his coffee. 'Marlon, as you know, is a very strange package. He *really* is. What a waste of a *huge* talent,' he sighs.

The physical, spiritual, emotional, and mental collapses of those around him were and are saddening to the straightforward Heston, whose sense of purpose has never wavered. A virgin when he married at the age of nineteen and now the radiant father of two grown children, he has never known the breath of scandal. 'I don't know if, in the words of Jimmy Carter, I ever experienced lust in my heart for other women,' he says with enormous amusement, 'but one would be *stirred*. Yeah, of course. When I was younger, that is. Not now. That's why I'm a little bemused by older men — say, anyone over forty — being attracted to *very* young women, as some of them are, you know? It's *ridiculous*!'

He stops to regard me, his look profound. 'One is aware that in my profession and position it would be very *easy* to establish even the most *casual* relationship with a woman,' he remarks. 'And I think that's kind of *mean* to do. It's mean-*spirited*. Maybe if I'd been a welder or something, I'd feel differently. The one actress I thought really *stunning* —' his brow furrows with emphasis — 'was Jennifer Jones. She's the only actress I've ever worked with who worked without makeup. She was a rather *skittish* girl, but stunning.'

His parents' early — and bitter — divorce left him a legacy of guilt and shame, a legacy which may have shaped his determination to help create a seaworthy marriage. Throughout his autobiography and in conversation, he refers to Lydia as 'my girl' and always with a deeply protective tenderness. 'I think men and women fall in love very differently,' he says, allowing a warm smile to thaw the frost. 'Men think: WOW!

OOOOOOOOOOH BOY! ISN'T THIS FANTASTIC? And women think: *Mmmmmmn* ... I don't know ... maybe with a bit of work ...' He looks down at the floor and shakes his head. 'Love is an enormously *stablising* factor. You have someone that you want *desperately* to please. You want to *share* things with them; you have someone you want to do *well* for, to have *admire* you; you begin to think of your life in terms of making a life to *produce* that result.'

Like any other, the marriage has not been without its difficulties. Heston acknowledges that in his thirties and forties he 'drank more than [he] should', but when his wife developed a severe drinking problem to ease the pain of migraine headaches, he was disturbed enough to insist that she enter an alcohol rehabilitation centre. 'It's kind of awful to see someone who's *really* drunk,' he says with uncharacteristic awkwardness. 'It's embarrassing. The dreadful life of Richard Burton, who was an alcoholic — one became aware of it. As for Lydia, well ... I *loved* her.' The way in which he articulates these last three words is almost painfully childlike. 'She displayed an extraordinary capacity to overcome the problem. We recently saw *Leaving Las Vegas*, but I felt no sympathy for that. We, uh, saw about a third of it and I said to Lydia: *d'you want to go now?* And she shook her head. Another thirty minutes passed. I said: *honey — come on!* and she said: naw — *I wanna see him DIE.*'

Heston has only ever really trusted his family, outside of which for him, there has been only work. 'Great men,' he says, 'tend to be separate because they're burdened with what they're *doing* — discovering a new world or being elected president or painting the Sistine Chapel or saving the Sudan from Muslim hordes. They don't really have much *time*.' Standing with difficulty, he is a pure pillar of black. 'You know,' he adds, 'in the beginning, an actor attracts us with his looks; then he enchants us with his voice; then, it's his capacity to create people ... but in the very end, he impresses us with who he *is*.'

There is a pause fit for a drumroll and I stand to shake his hand. Suddenly fidgety, he inclines his head and confided, 'This has all been rather ... *deep*, don't you think? Not quite what I'm used to.'

Elle, 1997

BIG SWINGING DICTUMS

I HAVE HEARD that states other than perpetual aesthetic and intellectual arousal exist, but have yet to experience them. The stressing of a white instep with a black velvet slipper is sensual if only because contrast is a form of unity in that it brings together the disparate for a comparison and in such unity we find release, relief, a certain truth. Consider for a moment the impact of knowledge on the curious, the depth-pleasures of discovery, ecstatic and throat-catching thought. Consider for a moment calculus, the concepts of which apply themselves to curves. Eloquent mouths understand language as others understand a kiss, and in this, an eroticism known only to a few.

With his fear of spiritual revelation and authority, the rationalist seeks to strip himself and his world of such meaning beyond purposes consigned by the rationalist mind-set. All becomes a matter of action — the profound relationship between the agent and his act is ignored, as is the agent's attachment to the philosophical origin and outcome of the act, as is the passion of the agent to fulfil the requirements of his philosophy and that wish or need to impress those whom he values. Rationalism does not acknowledge vulnerability to higher ideals. The value inherent in the *desire* to will, in the *desire* to act, is threatening to all that which is held. Without questioning why, the rationalist reasons that reason is reason enough.

Michael Stocker, Guttag Professor of Ethics and Political Philosophy at Syracuse University, takes Daniel Goleman's bestselling argument about that which constitutes intelligence one step further. Stocker is an academic emissary of unification: the premise of objectivity, he holds, can only be subjective. His beautiful analysis, *Valuing Emotions*, promotes the understanding that like all idealisations, the idealisation of reason involves 'serious interrelated misunderstandings' about that which is idealised (in this case, rationality) and that which is, as a consequence, split-off and demonised (in this case, emotions). He and his co-author, Elizabeth Hegeman, Associate Professor of Anthropology at the John Jay College of Criminal Justice, City University of New York, have produced a book which should be mandatory reading for all those in the fields of law, medicine, psychology, and philosophy — a profound examination of the way in which our culture's seers have excised their work of its debt and relevance to the human heart.

Ignored, denied, or 'only equivocally and vacillatingly accepted', emotions have come to be perceived as a subset of psychopathology and as such, irrelevant to other academic disciplines. Here Stocker's argument is straightforward: that there are not only crucial constitutive and epistemological connections between emotions and values, but that there is absolute centrality in subjective experience. Holding that emotions are inseparable from value, he concludes by explaining emotions as evaluative knowledge in themselves.

The fact that ethicists have ignored emotions or thought them evaluatively and ethically unimportant is a form of prejudice (a stance, as Stocker reminds us, that involves a very significant power relation of correlative superiority and inferiority). This prejudice is based on our fear of our extreme perceptions of emotions and their role in human life. Page 5: 'If emotions are thought of in terms of emotional mountains and canyons, it is natural to see them as abnormal, overwhelming, misleading, and disruptive, and certainly lacking secure and respectable connections with value.' Admonitions against emotion — with the exception of what Stocker calls 'intellectual interest and excitement' — are a Western tradition: emotion is to philosophers as Asian integration is to Pauline Hanson. The belief system? That which is not part of or does not contribute to rationality is unimportant, if not harmful to us. And yet the conceptual interconnections between attention and interest are indivisible. Cathexis is that process by which we solipsize the world.

Those who reject affectivity by citing its 'corrosive' effect on logic and those who reject logic by citing its 'corrosive' effect on affectivity flounder in darkness. One has only to plunge into Professor Simon Schama's masterpiece, *Landscape and Memory*, to know passion; one has only to reach through black lexical bars to apprehend Bellow's greed for being, Schopenhauer's sexualised intensity, Nabokov's responsiveness. To these giants, the intellect is that which constitutes affectivity. Their love is immortal. The tone and colour, the affective taste and feel of activities, relations, and experiences is decided by emotion; it is the axis upon which the world and its interpretations turn.

Whilst this may seem evident to many, the preconscious or unconscious nature of most ego processes blinds some. The rationalist does not recognise that in adhering to his law, he reduces himself to a system or instrument of duty. Nor does he recognise that psychic feelings of which one is aware only in part, feelings from which one has dissociated oneself or blocked or repressed, *remain* feelings. If this information is added to the fact that those who are unaware of their emotions or of their emotional lacks will be ill placed to see which values they hold and deploy, and how they hold and deploy these values in their judgments and decisions, the result is a negation of the moral and ethical validity of the rationalist's conclusions. How can the work of any philosopher be relevant if the philosopher does not consider the needs of the self relevant?

In order to be relevant, moral and ethical theories must pass through the filter of wisdom, and at the heart of wisdom is deep empathy. Page 188: 'By engaging emotionally with others, we learn emotions — how and when to have them, how to recognise our own and those of others, and the significance of each.' Fellow feeling establishes a fellowship, and it is only fellowship that bestows entitlement to respect, to care, to mercy rather than a detached equity. Emotions, as the philosopher Ronald DeSousa holds, also embody scenarios and patterns of salience which allow us to move from one set of facts to another when we do not have sufficient time or evidence to do this by non-emotional inferences. Identification is the core of understanding as understanding is the core of identification: they are irreducible. Without emotion, there is no *interest* in understanding. Without emotion, there is no motivation to be interested.

Many years ago, the philosopher George Santayana spoke of the prejudice man has against himself: 'We are satisfied only when we fancy ourselves surrounded by laws independent of our nature. We still have to recognise in practice the truth that from these despised feelings of ours the great world of perception derives all its value, if not also its existence.' Had our perception no connection with our pleasures, what value could a kiss or word or gesture have to any man?

The Sydney Morning Herald, 1997

TAKING IT LIKE A MAN:
PORNOGRAPHY AND ITS EFFECTS

AT THE AGE of seven, I was conservative as most children are conservative, and inherent in this traditional outlook was the 'best friend' with whom I played traditional girlhood games — mummies and daddies, dolls, horses, skippings. Late one afternoon (I believe we had been paddling in her pool), she told me that she had something to show me. And so I followed her into her parents' bedroom. From beneath a pile of woollens in the wardrobe, she pulled out a black-and-white leaflet. On the cover of this leaflet was a photograph of a naked woman with her legs spread and in between them, a kneeling man performing cunnilingus. I can still remember the intense impact of this image: a certain shock, fascination, multi-layered disturbance.

PORNOGRAPHY AND ITS EFFECTS

On arriving home, I took my younger brother by the hand, led him into my bedroom, took off my pants, spread my legs and blithely asked him to perform the act I had seen depicted on the cover of that leaflet. I was curious as most children are curious, and inherent in this curiosity was a desire to experiment with behaviour condoned by adults I trusted. My brother refused; he left the room to tell our mother. Her response was measured. I was discouraged from visiting my friend's house and told not to repeat my actions. Nevertheless, that image haunted and confused me. I had been given a particular understanding of adult sexuality, an understanding which distorted the way in which I viewed both adults and myself. In retrospect, I feel that I was poisoned.

Beatrice Faust, co-founder of the Victorian Council for Civil Liberties and author of *Balderdash Backlash: Where Feminism is Going Right*, believes that there is no correlation between pornography and actions such as the aforementioned. 'Numerous commissions and committees of inquiry,' she wrote in the *Australian*, 'have failed to demonstrate a causal or even permissive relationship between pornography and social harm. This plethora of evidence is all very unsatisfactory for those who want to ban pornography and tragic for feminists seeking a quick fix for rape and violence against women.' Had my brother responded differently, I wonder what the consequences would have been and whether they would have been classified by Faust as 'social harm'.

Melbourne, 1991: a six-year-old girl met a ten-year-old boy after school and was by him led — without coercion or violence — to 'the back of a vacant flat'. She later explained to police that the boy had 'rooted' her, inserted his 'dick' into her mouth, and then sodomised her. The boy did not contest her account. Police gave evidence that in his home were 'about fifty pornographic magazines'. An education comes in many guises. The Crown Prosecutor commented: 'Each of the sexual acts the boy inflicted on his tiny victim were graphically depicted in close-up colour … in those magazines.'

The impact of photographs and televisual images on viewers is profound in that those whom the pictures record can act as behavioural role models. 'Pictures are a form of communication and *highly* effective,' remarks Doug Watson, creative director of Mojo Advertising. 'The impact they have is emotional, not logical.' After seeing an advertisement, we may find ourselves selecting the product it promoted without even knowing why; all that matters to the producers of the product and its advertisers is that we do, and their persuasiveness hinges on the emotional appeal of their imagery. The ability to absorb text and subtext is the crucible of our psychological development, and when presented with an effective image — that is to say, one that on some level startles or gratifies — we learn to link all that the image represents with the response elicited.

'It's all about the association of having a wonderful time with something that isn't necessarily good for you,' explains Ross Renwick, creative director of Billy Blue Advertising. 'Our advertising industry and educational system are based on rote-learning, on the acceptance of images and ideas you wouldn't have accepted unless they had been pounded into your brain.' As seven-year-old children, we sit in classrooms chanting multiplication tables, copying the alphabet, mimicking the pronunciation of our elders, absorbing the behaviour of our guardians as that which is appropriate and acceptable. As adults, we retain this 'parrot' methodology. In 1994, Dr Hugh Potter, sociology lecturer at the University of New England, conducted a study of the 'X-rated client' and discovered that fifty-four per cent of those surveyed watched one or more pornographic videos a week. Exposure and repetition, the technology of fixation.

Imagine, then, the psychological and behavioural returns of pornography, the text and subtext of which are absorbed when our ability to filter out the inappropriate is at its weakest. Firstly, pornography not only validates but promotes the linkage of sexuality and commerce. Within the industry, footage of ejaculation is known as 'the money shot'. In five-star international hotels, hard-core pornography is prominently listed on the 'in-house' videotape 'menu'. The newly-mainstream veteran of 150 pornographic movies, Annie Sprinkle, encourages all women to think of sex as '[a way] to make money' and as a tool for barter — 'trade it for all kinds of things'. The pornographic equation is simple: sex = money = more sex. Our cinematic heroines reflect the social acceptability of this equation. Reporting on the 1996 Academy Awards, Mike O'Connor wrote: 'Susan Sarandon, Best Actress, [played] a lone nun in a category ... filled with prostitutes.' And why *shouldn't* prostitutes represent womankind in the films of men to whom womankind's dominant representation is pornographic?

'We know that eighty-one per cent of American students use pornos,' Alex Katz, a pornographic director, commented. 'Sixty-three per cent of American singles masturbate three times a week or more and buy our movies as fantasy ideals.' The 'fantasy ideals' of which Katz speaks are imposed — however indirectly — on all of us: men, women and children. The advent of mainstream pornography has created a new consciousness and with this new consciousness, dangerous new definitions.

Let us shelve the issues of violent and 'bizarre' pornography and instead focus upon the portrayal of human beings in 'non-violent adult erotica' (that Disney phrase so loved by pro-porn lobbyists). Every verbal exchange, every gesture, every look, every sentiment in these magazines and films is directed at one goal, and that goal is copulation. In pornography, there is never the suggestion of either sex being valuable for reasons other than its ability to penetrate or to be penetrated. There is no consideration for intellectual, emotional or spiritual complexity. There is never the suggestion that expressions of sexuality are significant beyond their relief-value (orgasm) or their enhancing of status (conquest). There is never the suggestion that sexual expression is based on any perception of our fellow human beings as anything other than autonomous sex-aids.

This perceptual dislocation is reflected in modern slang — 'ho' (whore), 'cunt' and 'slut' denoting a girl; 'motherfucker', 'cocksucker' and 'prick' denoting a boy: the verbal reduction of human beings to their sexual organs and sexual functions. Pornography is a culture of reductionism and destruction. Its target? Our ability to enjoy sexual expression without it. This remarkably sound economic principle is ignored by those who would redeem pornographers as defenders of the First Amendment. The sad fact is that pornography is not created to help us enjoy sex; pornography is created to help us enjoy pornography. The aim of pornographers is to sell wares, wares which demote sex to a subset of financial enterprise. Rejected as a form of powerful emotional communication, sex is depicted by pornographers as a system of exchange. And to remain a major player in the market of our consciousness, pornography must condition, and in this respect, it is fantastically effective.

Those who view pornography do not do so in a public place or where they can be easily distracted. The material is viewed in private and with intense concentration. These and other factors facilitate absorption of the pornographic ethos. Dr Freda Morris, former professor of medical psychology at UCLA, has stated that to be hypnotised, the subject must be kept still and quiet in order that a 'new focus' can be created. 'And at a certain point,' she told Jerry Mander, author of *Four Arguments Against The Elimination Of Television*, '[you] get them to follow your mind.' Dr Charles Tart, Professor Emeritus of psychology at the University of California, Davis, explains hypnosis as 'a state where you destabilise the ordinary state and then eventually get people into an altered state where they will follow a particular stimulus input much more strongly and with *much less critical reflection* [my italics] than they would normally'.

It can be said that human powers of discrimination are not at their most acute in the build-up to orgasm. 'We rehearse sexual roles in fantasy,' says Dr Iain Montgomery, senior lecturer in psychology at the University of Tasmania, 'and if the fantasies are of a particular nature, then that is the image of ourselves and others we develop. It becomes conditioning. Over the course of a number of years, there are thousands of "trials" and repetitions of this fantasy and in turn, these help create the sexual identity and sexual behaviour.'

Regular viewers of pornography are conditoned to respond sexually to objects and to objectification, rather than to subjects and to the subjectification by which individuality is defined. Regular viewers of pornography are conditioned to respond sexually to that which they can see, rather than to that which they can feel or touch or smell or hear, thereby dulling emotional intelligence and coarsening emotional response. Regular viewers of pornography are also conditioned to develop particular expectations of themselves and of their sexual partners. Once the mechanisms have been activated (by high heels, pigtails, et cetera), the expectations follow. 'The width of the span within which two stimuli are perceived as "the same thing",' Arthur Koestler wrote, 'depends on the precision of the analyser — the gauge of the sieve through which they must pass.'

The gauge of the sieve has been damaged. English *GQ* magazine recently ran a 'special' on seduction (that is to say, the pornographic definition of seduction). One of the pull-out quotes ran as follows: 'The two women who have invited us back for coffee genuinely mean coffee — maybe with milk, but certainly not with fellatio.' There is a tone of surprise in the writer's voice. *Maybe with milk, but certainly not with fellatio.* What can the world be coming to? These are very modern sensibilities, sensibilities appropriate to our new consciousness. In 1996, it may be assumed in the pages of a highly respected upmarket magazine that coffee is a synonym for fellatio. In 1996, it only seems logical that a national study conducted by the Office For The Status Of Women discovered that one in ten Australians surveyed believe that women are 'often asking' to be raped. Given the proliferation of pornography and its associative ramifications, why *wouldn't* one in ten Australians hold such a belief?

We are living in a society in which the dominant representation of our sexuality is divorced from those qualities we are as children taught to believe our finest. As a society, we are growing to understand sexual expression as devoid of context, as distinct from our emotions, as a commodity, as the end and not a part of a vital continuum. In its ruthless promotion of orgasm as the ultimate reward of any human interaction, pornography dehumanises, and when we buy or sell pornography we are, in effect, condoning this dehumanisation and incorporating it into our psychosexual vocabulary. And above all, pornography teaches us that we are the sum of our genitals and therein lies our meaning and our appeal.

The social harm resulting from these lessons is the real price of pornography and understandably, not acknowledged or advertised by its producers.

✦

When visual material is used as a source of arousal, repeated exposure to it inevitably results in lower levels of sensitivity. This process is known as 'desensitisation' and is used internationally in psychiatric departments to help cure phobias and anxiety disorders. Once desensitisation takes place, more extreme levels of the material are tolerated. Allied to this is disinhibition. If the viewer originally felt inhibited by social constraints about certain acts — rape, say — then repeated exposure to the material in which these acts are successfully depicted serves to reduce inhibitions. The acts become increasingly less troubling to the viewer. They can become acceptable.

Prior to his execution, the highly intelligent serial killer, Ted Bundy, said that 'without exception', every sexually violent man he had encounted in prison was 'deeply involved' — as he was — with pornography. A Michigan police study of over 35,000 sexual offenders revealed that in forty-one per cent of sexual assaults, 'pornography was involved just prior to ... or during the act'. Isabel Koprowski, a member of Feminists Against

Censorship and self-described 'hardened, jaded pornographer', begs to disagree. 'No causal link [between rape and pornography] has ever been established,' she confidently told the *Age*. 'I know a woman who has worked with sex offenders for ten years, and not one of them has ever blamed pornography.'

Koprowski was clever in using the verb 'blamed'. The issues she does not address are whether pornography triggers, encourages or *teaches* rape and its allied sexual crimes. Dorothy Ginn, director of the Child Abuse Prevention Service, does not produce or sell pornography. She merely works with its results. 'However outwardly respectable,' Ginn states, 'people who regularly watch pornography *inevitably* adjust their perceptions of their own children. Most of this is subconscious. What we're talking here is a perversion of context, wherein inappropriate sexualisation is validated. Pornography *triggers* abuse. We see the damage wreaked by this stuff; we work with the offenders; *we* are the ones who pick up the pieces.'

Robert Manne, associate professor of politics at La Trobe University and editor of Quadrant, has argued the point for many years. In a lucid essay for the *Age*, he wrote: 'Most liberals believed that pornography was a product of puritanism. How wrong they all were. Pornography once existed on the margins of society. It is now ... larger than the film and record industries combined.' Interestingly enough, there has also been a sharp increase in the number of recorded sexual assaults. The number of victims presented to the NSW Department of Health Sexual Assault Services has increased by over thirty per cent since 1989. The incidence of child sexual assault has increased by fifty per cent. Susan Kendall, coordinator of the sexual assault department of Sydney's Royal North Shore Hospital, believes pornography to be 'an anathema'. 'My observation is that rapes are becoming more violent,' she says. 'The injuries are worse, they are *increasingly* horrific. As someone who works in the field day in and day out, I believe that pornography of *any* description inspires violence, whether actual or ideological.'

Pro-porn lobbyists would have the public believe that pornography celebrates 'freedom of expression', rather than the freedom to be abused with true ingenuity; its 'freedom of expression' is that of the Holocaust. Victorian Crown Prosecutor, Richard Read, is a professional witness to the results of such liberal creativity. 'The nature of rape has changed in recent years,' he stated. 'Where thirty or forty years ago most rapes were forced vaginal intercourse, today they often include anal or oral rape, or the insertion of bottles and other instruments into the vagina.' Connoisseurs of 'non-violent adult erotica' will (perhaps with an indulgent smile) consider the many times they have reviewed those routine pornographic films in which a woman is happily 'bottled'.

Beatrice Faust, now fifty-eight, is proud of her 'modest' collection of pornographic photographs depicting objects inserted into the vagina. 'There are ones with lighted cigarettes,' she affably explains, 'Coca-Cola bottles, saveloys … in one case, a broomstick! The thing about these women is that they're *comfortable*. It's a party trick!' Faust, whose saveloys I shall ever courteously refuse, has been defending the right to be 'bottled' for posterity — without violence and between consenting adults within an appropriate sociopolitical visual context, it must be said — on the condition that the bottle is 'well-greased'. 'Irrational responses in adulthood,' she opined in the *Bulletin*, 'are assumed to derive from anxieties originating in childhood; distress over sexual explicitness is basically a gut-reaction called "visceral clutch".'

Some 'visceral clutch' was undoubtedly experienced by the boys sexually abused by those exposed by Justice Wood's Royal Commission. It is possible that these boys — that is to say, those of them who did not commit suicide — will or do, as adults, exhibit irrational responses deriving from anxieties originating in their childhoods. Paedophile T7, a trader in pornographic photographs of young boys, told Justice Wood that 'without appearing vain, I wanted some acknowledgment or recognition for my sort of artistry'. Three years ago, Faust dismissed public concern over such matters as 'the "kiddie porn" panic'.

'Visceral clutch' may also have been experienced by the eleven-year-old girl who was shown a 'non-violent' pornographic video cartoon by her stepfather before he raped her. Distress over sexual explicitness may have been one of the responses of the thirty-one-year-old photographer to her rape (after which she was slashed with a knife and had her nipple 'sliced off' by a fan of *Bondage Love*, a pornographic video Justice McGarvie of the Supreme Court described as 'almost a blueprint of what actually occurred').

The causal relationship between *Bondage Love* and the photographer's rape has, as yet, to be established by Faust and Koprowski.

But let us not gag those who celebrate post-modernist expressions of sexuality. 'Pornography,' gushed author Sallie Tisale in the *Independent Monthly*, 'tells me that none of my thoughts are bad, that anything goes.' Pornography told Fred and Rosemary West exactly the same thing. It has to be said that unlike many of us, pornography is, at least, consistent. Tisdale expressed her (few) reservations about her passion to the *Sun-Herald*: 'What disturbs me the most about pornography ... is the narrowness of the images ... It's limited to young, good-looking white women — where are the old women, the fat women, the average women?' A visit to any sex-shop will confirm an abundance of pornographic material in which obese and unarguably 'average' women feature. As for the 'old' women, well — we can only hope that as Paedophile T7 exists, so must Gerontophile T7 (in which case all women — and not just we 'young, good-looking white' sterotypes — can be inappropriately sexualised for Tisdale's delectation).

✦

Annie Sprinkle, 'fat' and 'average' prostitute and a 'performance artist' who, in her biography, lists her favourite films as being those in which 'people [have] sex with animals', is a figurehead of the pro-porn movement. During her show, *Post-Porn Modernist*, Sprinkle (ingenuous baby voice, corkscrew curls) announces: 'You know, if you've got to work to make a living, this is not a bad job.' Sally-Anne Huckstepp, the prostitute whose strangled corpse was dragged by police from a Sydney pond, may not have agreed. The average American woman, Sprinkle informs her audiences, earns $230 a week; in her heyday, Sprinkle could make $4000. The average American woman, Sprinkle informs her audiences, works forty hours a week; in her heyday, Sprinkle only worked seventeen.

Sprinkle conveniently omits to mention the spectacular rates of battering, suicide, drug-abuse and mental instability in her 'profession'. Justice McGarvie expressed his opinion of Sprinkle and her fellow ideologues in 1991: 'It is a despicable thing that people in this community make profit by carrying such [a] trade as the sale of [pornographic] magazines. The message which is strongly made in those magazines is that it is socially acceptable for a man to engage sexually in cruel, degrading and humiliating conduct towards women.'

'Cruel', 'degrading' and 'humiliating' are not adjectives that interest Sprinkle, who on stage shows numerous slides of herself in action: Annie holding her labia majora apart in order that we fully see the process of her urinating on a man's face; Annie chortling as a man inserts his foot into her vagina; Annie rapturously smiling as an amputee penetrates her vaginally with his truncated limb; Annie's mouth bulging with the penis of a man she introduces as 'Mark'. 'Mark,' she purrs after a beat, 'was like a *brother* to me.' Given that most children are unlikely to report sexual assault and that of reported cases, 27.4 per cent of children were sexually abused by members of their families, Sprinkle's commentary is, of course, hilarious.

The venerable Faust will undoubtedly be pondering the causal relationship between these Health Department incest statistics and the offenders' socio-economic status. 'Whereas the link between pornography and harm is disproven,' she wrote in the *Bulletin*, 'or, at worst, weak and indirect, the crucial relationship between poverty and all forms of social casualty is well established.' Susan Kendall, who actually works in the field of 'social casualty' rather than promoting herself by merely discussing it, disagrees. 'Nice, middle-class people do rape,' she emphatically says. 'Rape and violence statistics on Sydney's [A1] North Shore are the same as they are anywhere else. What you find, though, is that highly-paid and educated people have the werewithal to *protect* themselves.'

If, as the pro-porn lobby believes, there is no causal relationship between pornography and social harm, why do they bother drawing distinctions between 'non-violent adult erotica' and those magazines and videos known in the trade as 'nasties'? If, as the pro-porn lobby believes, pornography has no deleterious effects on behaviour, why *not* legalise *faux* 'snuff' films and publications celebrating the infinite scope of sexual brutality? After all, as Faust says, the link between pornography and social harm is disproven or, at worst, weak and indirect. In fact, why regulate pornography at all when most children can access it on the Internet or in their parents' bedrooms or the bedrooms of their friends' parents? Why not just cut out the middleman and put *Bondage Love* on the school curriculum?

An advertisement placed by the Citizens Against Unnecessary Government Censorship amply exhibits the immaculate reason of those who defend pornography. In large black typeface next to two photographs of Hitler and Stalin is the information: 'THE EXPERTS AGREE THAT CENSORSHIP WORKS ... AND LIKE ALL GOOD CENSORS THEY BOTH PLAYED THE MORAL GUARDIAN AND BANNED NON-VIOLENT ADULT EROTICA.'

Both Hitler and Stalin also sported distinctive moustaches. Given that this is the case, should Albert Einstein and Groucho Marx have been tried for crimes against humanity?

Elle, 1997

THE NAKED AND THE DERRYN:
DERRYN HINCH

THE MOTHER OF all television hosts, he sits: a tense squab man during commercial breaks, surprisingly cute in his cuban-heeled R.M. Williams riding boots, 'lucky' hearts and flowers tie, and pimento olive suit. His geometric beard is neatly clipped, his hair shines like a centurion's helmet, and he anxiously licks his lips as he studies the proferred schedule. For Derryn Hinch, Channel Nine's 'Midday' show is still too new. Unlike his other televisual vehicles, it was not tailored for him; this time he's had to be the malleable one, adjusting his attitude to the timeslot. His testosterone-fuelled primetime energy has simmered to an avuncular affection. The days when he told his staff that it was 'time to eat raw babies' are over. One of his former senior reporters comments, 'The personality he shows on "Midday" is consistent with the way he has always treated his staff, both socially and professionally. The unfortunate aspect of his current affairs persona was that the format of an MCU [medium close-up] gave him little or no scope to be anything more than a barking beard.'

The ON AIR signs suddenly flash and the band strikes up a tune. Hinch turns to the camera to interview his satellite-linked guest, a lichen-faced Norwegian who condones the murder of whales. This is the heart-tugging stuff of daytime television, watched by sentimental pensioners and housewives, shiftworkers and mental patients, prisoners and the unemployed. Slasher Oslo hasn't got a chance. As his tinny modulations drift across the airwaves, footage of gutted whales and whale sushi is run, followed by Hinch's earnest face.

This, above all, is his signature style — that direct emotional hit, right between the eyes. The Shame File. The Sludge File. The Law of the Land. Lies, lies, lies. Hinch's flat Irish face fulminating into the camera, and that voice of his — gruff with emotion, all choked up, grandfather stern, breast-beatingly moral. None of this has empowered him with any intellectual credibility. 'Guys like Nixon and Kissinger didn't show their emotions in public,' he'll tell you. 'They just got their jollies bombing Laos and Cambodia.' His motto of NO GUTS, NO GLORY is shared by those who work in abattoirs.

Hinch's demonstrativeness is unusual in the zombie-ward of television presenterdom, and it has brought him great notoriety and many fine material rewards. It has also brought him death threats, pigs' heads, and faeces in the post. After the show, he grabs the microphone and blurts out a speech about the Recession and The Need For Hope. The studio audience cheers. His eyes mist over and his chest puffs out. It wouldn't surprise anyone if he burst into hot tears or a few bars of 'My Way'. After all, Hinch is an openly emotional kind of guy.

We are driven to the chic Suntory restaurant in Sydney's CBD by his affable chauffeur. The stretch limousine attracts stares from pedestrians. Hinch hands me a comment-sheet culled from the day's viewers. The opinions range from 'Derryn is so sleezy [sic]' to the more predictable, 'Whale-killing is the cruellest thing in the world'. Hinch is comforted by the strength of these criticisms, and snuggles up to his mobile phone.

He is guarded and polite to me, and makes a minimum of eye-contact. At the restaurant, there is a brief moment of belligerence between us. Neither of us wants to sit with our back to the door. I won't because I'm taking notes on the reactions of others to my stellar lunching partner (surprise, supplication, animal awe), and he won't because he is scared of being shot through the back of the head. We eventually reach a compromise and sit beside each other.

At close range, he is ruddy-cheeked and boyish, bashful and brash, sometimes crude. He frequently giggles, a tickled giggle; he says he likes to have his 'tummy rubbed'. It is only his eyes that are disturbing — vacant and grey and a little rheumy, they are the eyes of a heavy drinker, which Hinch has always been. Today he will order two medium-sized bottles of beer and a bottle of wine, his 'usual' lunchtime ration. 'Alcohol abuse,' remarks one television journalist, 'is, and always has been, a terrible problem in this industry. It comes with the turf.'

It also came with the turf of Hinch's smalltown New Zealand upbringing. He was conceived when his father, a member of the WWII infantry, was on leave, and recalls his father telling him that on one wartime occasion, he dodged bullets by jumping behind a truck. When the bullets come for Hinch, he jumps behind the truck of his personality.

'My father was not a good drunk,' he concedes, beginning on his beer. 'I think that like a lot of people of his generation, the war was something he'd put in a black box somewhere.' He pauses, and then continues with difficulty. 'My parents had violent ... verbal arguments. Occasionally, plates would be thrown. Really *violent* arguments, but I have no memory of ever seeing my mother with a — with a — with a — with a — with a bruise. Whenever the drinking would become really bad, she'd say: I'm out of here. I'm taking the kids and I'm out of here.'

Despite witnessing these violent alcoholic rows and being sexually molested at the age of eleven by a thirty-year-old acquaintance of the family's, Hinch — committed crusader against drink driving, domestic violence, and child abuse — insists that he had a 'ball' as a child. He stresses that he left home as soon as humanly possible only because 'it looked good out there'. He also insists that his father, who seemed to have trouble holding down a job for any serious length of time (at different stages he worked as a farmer, baker, bus driver, shopkeeper, cab driver, and milkman) and who would not control his temper, had not been psychologically damaged by his experience of war. The idealistic cloud through which Hinch sees his parents is still like that of a child. 'My father would never say if he'd killed anybody,' he says, drinking more beer, 'but he once handed me a knife that he had, a knife made from part of a bayonet. Part of the leather inlay on the handle was from a Japanese soldier's *boot*.'

The Japanese waitress, whose relatives may or may not have been sacrificed to the same war, bows and takes our order.

Young Hinch was a voracious reader of Champion comics. 'Dan Dare, the first astronaut!' he enthuses. 'He had an exciting time, he went up everywhere, he fought the evil Mekon who's this big green melon-headed creature! Even at fifty — and I shouldn't tell you this — I read Torkan. Torkan's *out there*: he looks like Michael Bolton, he has this sword and slashes it around … it's preposterous, but it does appeal to me.'

Those who have followed his turbulent row-and-sacking-strewn career may have noticed some similarities between Hinch and his cartoon heroes. In 1987, Hinch spent twelve days in jail over the naming of a priest in a child-molesting case. His comments on radio about 'a poacher in the sanctuary' were declared by the courts to be blatantly prejudiced and as a consequence, the case was dropped. 'The wretched result of Hinch's contempts is that the stream of justice has been permanently polluted by them,' Justice Nathan of the Supreme Court later said.

In 1991, Father Glennon (the 'poacher' in question) was convicted on charges of buggery with violence, attempted buggery, and three counts of indecent assault on three boys and a girl aged between thirteen and sixteen. After the ruling, Hinch angrily told the press: *'I did everything I could to stop it.'* This passionate interference with what he respectfully calls 'the law of the land' has been the hallmark of his career. In 1988, he was ordered to perform 250 hours of community service for naming a judge in a rape-in-marriage case. In February 1991, he was fined $2000 for broadcasting the name of a sex-attack victim. In April 1991, a judge ruled that Hinch was not to air a tape of a conversation between a solicitor and one of the men acquitted of the Walsh Street police murders. On another occasion, he aired information police had asked him specifically not to disclose.

His press release lists some of these troubles under the title 'Hinch Highlights', as if his legally questionable activities were somehow glamorous or indicative of his bravura or intelligence. One of his more infamous views is that capital punishment is an expression of 'justice' and not of hatred. On one hand, Hinch gets misty over abused children; on the other, he wants the government to execute the adults that these children often become. He is a man of symptoms and not causes, a man who will — without the slightest flutter of his conscience — expound on the 'right' to exist. Hinch will even quickly suggest contenders for his death-chamber of 'justice': 'Repeat offenders, cop-killers, people who abduct or murder a nurse or a child.'

A nurse or a child? What about prostitutes and garbagemen? What about people who murder *accountants*? Do they also deserve to be fried in the name of 'justice' or should they be granted clemency on the grounds of their victims' cuteness-deficiency? It is precisely this kind of sentiment-pickled reasoning that so enrages many of his detractors.

A: Given your belief in the death penalty, would you press the button?

D: I wouldn't want to, no.

A: Why wouldn't *you* want to be responsible for another's death?

D: Presumably you'd have a professional person … a … a … a … a … a *doctor*.

A: A doctor who kills people?

D: A lot of them [do]!

With Hinch, it's a case of what's on the lung is on the tongue. He doesn't devote too much time to thinking about the repercussions of his words. 'I'm not an introvert — oh, *shit*, no!' he laughs over his second or third or fourth glass of alcohol. 'I don't examine my life. Not really. Naaaaah.' This readiness to speak his (unexamined) mind combined with his old warning to his staff — '*never* over-research' — makes his grass-roots impact potentially dangerous. 'Fifteen years ago,' he says, 'I would have argued that the media doesn't influence people, and that is bullshit. We can influence public opinion *incredibly*.'

Given that he is aware of the hatred that some of his views could incite, it seems surprising that he should continue airing them. 'I have no bloody font of knowledge and I've never said I do,' he barks as he is served his *shabu-shabu*. As he begins to delicately dip the strips of beef into the boiling pot, he shrugs and says that four of the people involved in the crossfire of his investigative journalism have suicided. It seems odd that this should not even prick at his conscience. Of one of the four, a child molester, Hinch comments: 'My immediate reaction was that if he'd jumped off the roof ten years earlier, he may have saved the kids.'

He admits that he can be 'very hard professionally'. 'I've given people *terrible* kickings in my editorials,' he says, 'and then asked my producer to get them in for a talk. She would say: *but you called him a sleazebag and a wife-basher!* And I'd reply that I don't hold grudges.' The latter comment is not strictly accurate. According to one producer, Hinch is 'a petty-minded little turkey', professionally envious, and can hold a grudge 'as well as anyone'. Hinch was outraged when one journalist publicly referred to him as a 'bad apple', and hunted down a videotape of a Christmas party in which this journalist had sworn and brawled with another man. Despite pleas from his staff, Hinch aired the videotape on national television and then announced: 'And he called *me* a bad apple.' It was, at best, a playground response. 'I've hated the times when I've had a friend I've had to kick,' he shrugs as he sips his wine, 'but you can't as a journalist only attack people you don't know. I mean, I call that shooting fish in a bucket. I don't have a special rule for mates.'

The cause of most of the criticism levelled at him is, Hinch thinks, 'E-N-V-Y'. I put to him that another possibility is that his analyses of situations leave something to be desired. 'Nicely put,' he muses, 'but I'm Irish. Jacki [Weaver] always said she knew I was Irish because I'm so illogical.'

By all accounts, Hinch and his actor-wife are still deliriously in love with each other. An industry source relates Hinch's traditional response to what he thought was a bad story: 'He'd wait until he got home to Jacki and if she said it was good, he'd come back the next day and agree it was good. He listened to Jacki as if she were the ultimate authority. Great loyalty.' A friend of Jacki's comments: 'She *adores* him. Worships the ground he walks on.' And indeed, in every photograph of the couple, Jacki lovingly leans against her man, her expression that of a startled hamster. It is the third marriage for them both, an eleven-year triumph of hope over experience.

'Jacki was in Minsk,' Hinch recalls, 'and sat bolt upright in her bed whilst reading *Death in Newport*. That was my first novel, and there was an awful rape scene in it, a terrible rape. She got this jolt and thought: *how did he know this?*' He smugly smiles. 'I told her that it was this thing called *imagination*.'

This thing called Hinch's imagination is responsible for the following excerpt: 'Hunter noticed that the cool September air coming in off the water and over the lawn had stiffened her right nipple. He couldn't see her left one, which was hidden in the tie-dye pattern. At that moment … Jim Hardy walked past … he looked first at Hunter, then at Dee Dee, and also noticed the errant nipple.'

He has been known to produce 50,000 words a month. Whether these 50,000 words are well-chosen is a matter open to debate. Hinch has written a Q&A book on AIDS, his autobiography *That's Life*, a book on Scrabble tactics, and two novels with the word 'death' in the titles. Without hesitation, he says: 'I do think I'm a good writer. I love writing novels! I love creating dialogue in the shower. I think I write dialogue very well.' Mildly drunk and nodding, he finishes his glass of wine.

Alcohol has been Hinch's most constant partner in life. In his autobiography, he wrote: 'I have been around for about 11,000 days of adult life and have gone without alcohol for less than 100 of them.' He jovially rechristened his soup-and-wine diet the 'drunk-for-life diet'. His wife calls one of his favourite restaurants in Melbourne 'the creche'. She has said, 'I park him there and the boys give him his bottle.'

Hinch really *enjoys* the effects of alcohol. He used to enjoy them to the extent that he'd drink four bottles of wine a night. These days he sticks to a mere two bottles in the evening. 'Nothing happens with the first glass,' he giggles. 'The *first* glass is a thirst quencher.' He says that he cannot *conceive* of a meal without wine. He says that he doesn't use it as a crutch although 'people who don't drink would say that anyone who drinks does use it as a crutch'.

The black lacquered table has been cleared of bottles and bowls, and Hinch is looking weary. 'When I was in jail,' he says, 'I looked at Hinch in the third person. I wrote him in the third person. I saw Hinch go to jail, and I watched what happened to him. Journalists step back and observe everything. In conversation, I often adopt the third person approach. It shouldn't be like that, because it's the same person — the opinions are the same, the behaviour's the same, *I am the same.*'

But is he? Hinch realises that he is, in essence, a product. 'I am being sold,' he agrees. 'But the thing is to be a *real* product and not a synthetic product; not a made-up product, and a product you make yourself. I used to tell a joke that is not as silly as it seems. I used to say that everybody in the world has a silver box in their heads. There's this little silver box and it's very precious, and it's very personal, and *nobody* — no lover, no husband, no wife, no father, no mother — is *ever* allowed to look into this silver box. The irony? You finally get to open it and there's *nothing* in it. *Absolutely* empty.'

Standing up to leave, he grins, his eyes a mild blur. 'I'm sorry you rang the bell and there was nobody home,' he says, 'but that's the way it is with me.'

Mode, 1995

POSTSCRIPT

Hinch continues to be the stuff of which headlines are made. On the sixth of August 1994, the *Age* reported that Hinch would face sentencing in the Magistrate's Court for publishing the name of an eight-year-old victim of sexual assault after seeking permission from the boy's parents. Hinch said in a prepared statement: 'I have no comment to make except to say that all legal avenues are being considered. I am upset and disappointed for myself, but more so for the family.' A mere month later, Hinch reached an out-of-court settlement in a damages case against the Seven Television Network in which he claimed A$3,998,640 over the axing of his current affairs programme in 1991. Two months later, Hinch was again out of a job. The *Sydney Morning Herald* quoted Channel Nine's chief executive, Mr David Leckie: 'I don't believe that ['Midday'] is the program to take us through the next decade.'

On New Year's Day, the *Age* included the following in its 'Under Achievements of 1994': 'TV executives almost get repetitive strain injury sacking Derryn Hinch.' Possibly aware of the truism that God hates a quitter, Hinch loudly decided to return to Radio 2GB in a 'head-to-head contest with top-rating John Laws'.

Forced to wait a number of weeks for new headlines, Hinch was, some have suggested, suffering acute drama withdrawal. This unhappy state of affairs was not to last. 'To say I identified the victim of a sexual assault makes me sound like the most callous, insensitive dickhead in the world. I was trying to help the father of this kid on his insistence,' he told the *Sydney Morning Herald* on the first of February 1996. The Victorian Court of Appeal upheld a judge's findings that he and Channel Ten breached the Judicial Proceedings Reports Act, which prevents the publication of the identity of sexual assault victims without consent by them or a court. Seven days passed. The *Sydney Morning Herald* then reported that the Reverend Dr Gordon Moyes, chairman of Radio 2GB and superintendent of the Wesley Mission (which owns 87.25 per cent of the station) called Hinch 'immature' and said that he needed to control himself following 'gratuitous' statements on air. Four days later, the humbled Hinch announced his marital separation on air: 'There have been a lot of rumours about me lately. Sadly, some of those rumours are now true. Jacki and I are taking time out. We are not getting divorced, but we will go our own way for a while.'

A fortnight later, the *Sun-Herald* reported that 'according to friends, Weaver has been hitting the dinner-party circuit with another man on her arm, freelance lighting designer, Peter Neufeld'. On the twenty-fifth of March, *Woman's Day* quoted the loyal Hinch on his well-lit ex: 'She is still my best friend. We still love each other ... it might sound corny or weird ... there's not anyone else out there for me.' On April Fool's Day, the *Sydney Morning Herald* published a report on the opening night of the Sydney Theatre Company's production of *The Heretic*: 'While the passing theory in the David Williamson play that all men want to marry their mothers had many in the audience mentally casting a sideways look at their partners, perhaps Jacki Weaver knew what they were talking about.'

Three weeks without headlines can seem like an eternity to some. The *Age* heroically came to the rescue with a report that Hinch 'was relieved and grateful yesterday to receive a $2000 fine for naming an eight-year-old sexual assault victim, instead of the three-week jail sentence he had expected. "I still believe that I was morally right, but I've now been proven legally wrong," he said.' Hinch was convicted and fined $2000, but not without the magistrate's stirring character reference: 'I have [here] a man who is clearly passionately concerned with the welfare of children.'

It would be months before Hinch and/or his estranged spouse would again penetrate the national consciousness. On the ninth of September, *Woman's Day* glowingly reported that at the 'elegantly refurbished Regent Theatre in Melbourne,' the two, 'looked like a couple courting. Derryn Hinch and Jacki Weaver sat together on the floor, giggling and exchanging looks of love … [they] arrived separately, but after spending most of the evening clearly enjoying each other's company, they left together. Just six months after their highly public split, Derryn is dating his wife again.'

Why the two were seated on the floor remains unknown.

Possibly peturbed by this eccentric behaviour, Radio 2GB owner John Singleton told the *Sydney Morning Herald* on the fifteenth of October that he had 'urged, cajoled and pleaded' with Hinch to change his programme, but that his advice had been ignored. Hinch duly informed his listeners that he had resigned.

Much sadness ensued. And then in February 1997, the *Australian Women's Weekly* reported that Hinch was 'almost broke'. The many millions he was reputed to have earned during his extraordinary career had seemingly vanished. Threats of financial ruin were not sufficient to deter the romantic Hinch from grasping the opportunity to express his eternal affection and respect for Weaver (whilst reassuring those of us who may have churlishly started doubting his pulling ability): 'He still phones her daily for advice and support … yet both have found new partners since their split last year. Derryn's is "lovely, charming. Suzie is a photographer and no one knows anything about her, because I have kept her out of it deliberately." He and Jacki have no plans to divorce or to reconcile.'

It must be remembered even in such circumstances that for the inimitable Derryn Hinch, tomorrow is another day.

PARTING THE PAINTED VEILS: HRH PRINCESS HAYA BINT AL-HUSSEIN

SHE IS THE most visible of all the Middle Eastern princesses, caught between purdah and the call of the First World, the only unmarried daughter of the man whose efforts to create lasting political harmony between the Islamic and Christian cultures have fascinated those sceptical of compromise. Whilst the Taleban mullahs of Afghanistan have declared the education of girls blasphemous and wrested all rights from their women, King Hussein of Jordan has been denouncing fundamentalism and achieving his objective of increasing understanding through humanitarian exchange. And HRH Princess Haya bint al-

Hussein is, in every sense, her father's daughter — conscious of her role between the two belief-systems and conscientious in respecting both of them. It is an onerous, if rewarding responsibility: through her cultural cross-pollination, she is a symbol of that 'comprehensive peace' of which her father dreams.

Her preternatural maturity allows her to perform a behavioural balancing-act that would destroy a weaker individual. Effectively an instrument of reform, she will never be permitted the liberties of ordinary womanhood. It is impossible to separate her life from international politics; her position, her privileges, her responsibilities, the very fact that she agreed to an interview — all are political statements. She has suffered through attempted *coups d'état*, heard her father criticised by the world's leaders for his friendship with (the unrelated) Saddam Hussein, feared for the safety of her family members at the hands of extremists, sacrificed her own freedom to duty, and through all this, had no mother to whom she could turn. Haya's experience of life has been extraordinary and in that, profoundly isolating. Her father's insistence that she 'keep [her] feet on the ground' has enabled her to cope, to survive. She rationalises the situation, understanding herself to be a means to philosophical progress. She also knows how gratifying it can be to supply comfort to others — during Jordan's civil war in the 1970s, for example, photographs of Haya and her siblings adorned Palestinian refugee camps, and her work with charities is comprehensive.

She is under surveillance twenty-four hours a day, every day, every week, every year. During public appearances, she is shadowed by her bodyguard and several Jordanian policemen. At Sydney's Sheraton on the Park, her suite — the presidential — is permanently guarded. My umbrella is taken from me at the door by an unsmiling guard and when it is returned after the interview, I find that the wooden tip has been removed in the search for weapons. This consciousness of threat is unpleasant but necessary; there have been too many assassination attempts on her father's life to allow for any risks. As a result, she has been taught to be wary of both crowds and solitude. Fear is a constant. Hotel rooms, in particular, terrify her — the shadows, the echoes, the dark possibilities.

Instances of marginalia. The politicising runs much deeper.

There are topics she will not discuss as she does not wish to jeopardise her father's delicate negotiations for peace. As the mediator between the Arab States and the West, Jordan's current role in the Middle East process in progress in Washington is crucial. This places Haya in a difficult position. The subject of fundamentalism, in particular, elicits from her a searching and intelligent gaze, but she chooses only to remark that she will not judge, she will not judge. Jordan is the least militant of all the Islamic countries, but the stereotypes are still abundant — the aristocratic wife, who, as Sandra Mackey writes in *The Saudis*, wears lingerie 'that belongs in a Paris brothel' beneath her chador; the lower-class girl whose marriage is arranged for 'the good of the group' rather than her personal fulfilment; the daughter of extremists who is subjected to excision (the removal of the clitoris and all or part of the vaginal lips) or infibulation (the removal of all genital parts and stitching of the two sides of the vulva, leaving only an aperture for blood and urine).

She makes a point of challenging these stereotypes in her everyday life. The impact is subtle but far-reaching. A professional showjumper, she dreams of winning gold at the Sydney 2000 Olympic Games; this ambition is in itself a flouting of Sharia, or Islamic law. Rather than relying on her father, she arranged for Rolex to sponsor her team. She wears no veil, her couture skirts are smartly above the knee and although she displays remarkable tact, she pursues her ambitions with an application unknown to many of her Western counterparts. Whilst oppression and terrorism — both political or psychological — are realities, they are not the only realities; the perception of Islamic culture, she gently makes clear, has been much distorted by the fundamentalists.

Curled on a voluptuous white sofa before an activated television screen, she is barefoot in jeans, her hair loosened, her diminutive torso lost in a voluminous fawn Georges Rech sweater. Cautious in public, her gestures in private are dramatic, and that Persian mouth easily lifts its corners to a smile. By her left hand, a tall glass of water in a pool of lamplight; behind her, a wide window and a darkening sky in which few stars are visible. 'The Middle East *is* a very violent part of the world,' she gravely says, 'and as a consequence, it is not somewhere you would choose as a holiday destination. I've heard that the mountains in Iran and Iraq are fantastic for skiing, but they're not places you would go on a package tour, you know? But not being able to see it and speak about it is what makes it scary. The not-*knowing*.' She is diplomatic in not elaborating on the problem of the militant Muslim factions, who have never approved of her father's moderate hashemite monarchy or his distaste for their efforts to convert Jordan into an Iranian-style theocratic state.

Fluent in five languages and with a 2:1 degree in politics, economics and philosophy from St Hilda's College, Oxford, she speaks English with a lilting Irish accent acquired from Paul Darragh at his Waterside Stud in Tara, County Meath, where she will be training for the next three years. In her mouth, 'horses' becomes 'horshes'; 'really', 'raelly'; 'sports', 'sportsh'. She is silent in observation, candid when questioned about herself, and discreet when discussing others. No, she says, unlike every other member of her family she has never met Saddam Hussein; she was never in 'the right place at the right time'. Yes, she says, she knows Queen Elizabeth II, and thinks her very graceful and gracious. No, she says, she remembers little of Baroness Thatcher, only her exemplary courage and that unforgettable ejaculation of *'Poppycock!'* during an interview. And her friend Princess Anne? Well, Princess Anne is a 'fantastic' woman. The sound levels of the television are turned down; all that is left is Fran Drescher — teased wig, black slacks, and silver-sequinned waistcoat — mugging and noiselessly howling on the screen.

There is nothing imperious about her. The people whose company she prefers are 'straight-shooters' and not those who are 'kind of slimy and tell you all the time nice things'. Her eyes are large and tender, eloquent, steadily rimmed with black liquid eyeliner that tapers to a feline point. *'Spectacular* eyes,' George Sanna, a fellow rider, former Olympian and friend, appreciatively remarks. She is captivatingly attractive. An oval face. Long glossy hair, its jet sunburnt. 'As a child,' she softly says, 'I thought I was *lucky* a lot. In our religion there is no reincarnation, but I used to wonder whether reincarnation existed as I couldn't understand how it got to be *me*. Why *me*?' Her tone is almost plaintive. 'What have I done to kind of deserve all *this*? As I got older, I started to think of it maybe sometimes as a pain in the neck. And then I wasn't so grateful. But I do remember consciously wondering whether I was part of the wrong religion, whether reincarnation was possible or whether it was a matter of chance. I mean, there must be a *reason* for this!'

It is only normal to enjoy attention, but the constancy and singularity of the attention she receives is enervating. Whilst she has successfully managed to maintain a 'private life', she is still horrified by the possibility of scandal, of misinterpretation, of intrusion, of the impact such things would have on her family. 'It's not that I *envy* the freedom of other people,' she explains with a forlorn look, 'it's just that I wish *they* had the same level of attention sometimes.' Her title is a stumbling block for the 'right sort' of men. This is something she understands as she, too, is intimidated by those with whom she feels she has little in common. Bankers, for example. Those squeaky shoes they wear! She grins. And economics students — people who are so 'into a role that they could almost impersonate themselves'.

Raised in a palace ('just a big house,' she insists), she has socialised with princes, presidents, prime ministers and the luminaries of every sphere. She rises late, has never known want for the material, and her advisers and instructors are elite. Nevertheless, she tires of seeing the world through the tinted glass windows of limousines. Twenty-three years of royal protocol have not accustomed her to being treated like 'a zoo animal' at public functions. In such situations, people do not talk normally to her, they just continue staring. The boredom she experiences is intense. The awkwardness is worse. She never knows what to do with her *hands* when performing her duties. Looping them behind her back does not feel right and nor does linking them. She cannot cross her arms for fear of conveying disapproval or place her hands on her hips for fear of looking like a fishwife. This causes her to feel self-conscious; she has tried to solve the problem by carrying a handbag, a thing she hates. Sanna remarks: 'She has a very distinct sense of duty. I mean, how *else* would you put up with that kind of thing?'

She says that few fully apprehend the extent of her sheltering. They find it bizarre or funny or touching. Her vulnerability coaxes protective instincts from the most unlikely people. Even at Oxford, 'one of the … universities with the [highest incidence] of drug use', she found herself 'protected' from the uglier realities of privileged youth by girlfriends. 'Maybe I just look like the kind of person you don't tell,' she says, sadly smiling. 'I'm not sure.' Parties and nightclubs 'intimidate' her as she does not understand the 'code of conduct'. Codes of conduct are, to her, serious concerns; she is solicitous of others' needs to the point of self-effacement. There was a time when she felt she was an astute judge of character and knew precisely whom to trust; now she's not so sure. 'I think,' she says, 'that as you grow up, the more you realise the less you know.' Sanna comments: 'She is a very appealing mixture of naiveté and sophistication. On one hand, she is extraordinarily cultured; on the other, she is so innocent, a child.'

Her name means 'female falcon'. *'Bird!'* she chortles, her intonation shared by Bambi. A tomboy whose three older sisters were already in school, Haya was raised with seven brothers with whom she 'played football and wrestled and had pillow fights'. Her fantasies were straightforward: she wanted only to be a boy. Subconsciously, she may have felt that males were survivors. Queen Alia, her Palestinian mother and King Hussein's third wife, and after whom Amman's international airport is named, was killed in a helicopter accident when Haya was three. She feels 'guarded' by her — a near-fatal car accident from which she escaped unharmed, perilous situations circumvented. When she speaks of her mother, her voice grows firm, as if to rein unmanageable emotions. 'I feel her absence strongly,' she admits. 'Not so much in serious issues, because if I had a serious career move to think about then I would have lots of people to talk to, but really *stupid* stuff like — um, I don't know — if a friend upset me or I wanted to have a conversation about principles ... really just girls-growing-up problems. Asking about boys, wanting to know about make-up. That would be more when I really miss her, because there is no one I could discuss something that trivial with.'

One of the effects of losing her mother is a reluctance to openly emote. 'Being out of control,' she muses, 'is something that frightens me.' As a result, she has never 'truly' been in love and is repelled by the concept of drunkenness. She *thinks* she can recall her mother — her fragrance, perhaps, or the way she moved — but is unsure as she has seen so much documentary footage and so many photographs that her fantasy seems to have acquired the sheen of reality. Reluctant to call the articulate American-born Queen Nor her 'stepmother', she prefers to regard her as her 'father's wife' and as 'a really good friend'. 'I think,' she says thoughtfully, 'she gave us every chance to hold on to our mother and at the same time, was always there to help with anything she could. I think she did it very, very well. The "Evil Stepmother" scenario never really happened to me. It is very different, though, when the mother has died; a lot of girls have stepmothers as a result of a divorce case and that's another issue altogether.'

The women of her family have always been powerful. Her formidable and striking grandmother, the late Queen Zein, was renowned for wielding considerable influence whilst respecting traditional public constraints. And Haya's temper, something she monitors, is 'frightening' when it erupts. 'You can push me and push me and push me and I'll take it,' she says, her eyes darkening, 'until it just gets too much and then I will explode. People don't get a second chance. That's the way I am. I've lost my temper twice in my life. I didn't do anything; I just got very quiet, and then spoke in a very low voice. I didn't say very much, but just *went* for the jugular. I don't take prisoners.'

Her Harrow and Sandhurst educated father — who recently spent over $100,000 buying Harley Davidson motorcycles — has always encouraged an elegant universalism in his children. When Haya was eleven, he enrolled her at Badminton Boarding School in England, where she passed fifteen GCSE examinations, and then at Bryanston. Flopping back onto a pile of cushions, she grimaces. 'I *hated* it!' she cries. 'I absolutely hated it! There was a *huge* difference in family values. I just couldn't understand why people were so comfortable with the idea of their grandparents in old peoples' homes or why they had big arguments with their mothers and fathers — you know, just being *angry* with them for not bringing them up the way *they* thought they should have been raised. I just kept wishing that my parents had brought me up *themselves*. I was envious of their closeness. *We* had nannies. My parents spared a lot of time for us, but obviously only as much as they had — it wasn't full-time. I *certainly* didn't spend enough time with them to argue about trivial things.'

At the mention of her father's name, her eyes fill with light. He is the person she most loves, the person she most respects, and although the possibility of another assassination attempt is always in her thoughts, a native stoicism prevails. 'I believe that when your time comes, there's nothing you can do,' she quietly says. 'If someone doesn't shoot you, then maybe you'll get killed in a car or you will die of pneumonia or fall off a *toilet* seat, you know?' She quickly laughs as if to dispel her fears. 'Something as ridiculous as that.'

The Assistant Chief of Protocol clears his throat in the background, an indication that the interview should stop. Dismissing his concerns with a glance, Haya then sits up, her expression one of incredulity. 'I remember doing a television interview in Jordan,' she says, 'and in referring to my father, said: "My daddy — I mean, *His Majesty*" — I was trying to be respectful, but the guy who was interviewing me said: "You know, he's not only your daddy, he's the father of everyone in this nation!" And that really annoyed me! I thought: "No, he's not! He's *my* daddy! *You* can't have him!" ' Scowling, she sits back and further tucks her legs beneath her. 'The thing that keeps me sane is this perspective: when I look at my father, I see two people. I see the king — the king is the guy in pictures in supermarkets and in people's houses, the guy people admire and talk about and debate and argue over, and he's *their* daddy in the way that he's our king. That way I share him with anyone, but he's really *my* dad and not anybody else's. It's not fair to say otherwise.' A judicious pause. And then: 'We don't see him enough to share him!'

Secretly taking the Oxford entrance exam under another name, Haya was able to surprise him with news of her success. She applied herself to dual tasks with customary diligence: whilst completing her degree, she rode her horses daily. Her love of the equestrian began when her father bought her a horse at the age of six; from there on in, all her unallocated time was spent at the Royal Jordanian State Stud. The self-reliance and control implicit in horse-riding were, to a girl who had always been forced to consider the opinions of others, intoxicating. At the age of twelve, she organised the first horse show to be held in Jordan — a landmark gesture of unification between Iraq, Syria and Jordan. In 1994, she was voted BBC Arab Athlete Of The Year.

She acknowledges that the demands of showjumping are probably an escape from troubling feelings. 'Certainly,' she says, 'the kind of goal I've set myself has meant that these four years — which would, in a normal girl's life, be four years of going out and having a social life and making friends and thinking about boyfriends — are dedicated to work. I've managed *totally* to shut myself *off* from that other stuff and in a way, to erase the problem of not having anyone to *ask* about it. I also can't do that and ride the tour at the same time. I mean, I really need every ounce of concentration and more or less to go to bed early and stick to people I know.' Most of the trainers with whom she worked initially presumed her to be an indulged anachronism who would never emerge as a serious talent: what she calls her 'breeding' was seen as disability. Such prejudice reacted with her fixed nature, making her determined to 'put in 120 per cent'. 'I think people kept saying: *she's gonna quit! She's gonna quit!*' she chuckles. 'I suppose people don't expect you to be hungry enough to want to excel, you know? You have to prove yourself because you've already *got* the position.'

After competing in her first international competitions, she implored her father to arrange 'much lower-key' security; the pressures of being conspicuously guarded had become overwhelming. 'Every time I fell off [a horse], *fifteen* of them would run into the ring and pick me *up*! It was *so* embarrassing!' Her mirth becomes parodic. 'There I was, trying to act like a serious professional with a professional attitude, sitting on my *arse* on the ground and everyone would be running in and dusting me off! So they actually only travel with me now on official stuff like this.' Constant observation has instilled in her an automatic behavioural-modification mechanism; Haya knows that she cannot be impulsive, that spontaneity is too dangerous on too many levels.

'They've worked it out so I don't really know and can't notice,' she says, clearing her throat. 'I just tell them what I'm doing. I guess I'm *watched* all the time, but if I want to do anything — if want to have a boyfriend or go out to dinner or dancing, I ask my dad. If he has a problem with it, he doesn't just say no — he gives me a reason, and that reason will always be good enough for me. The whole world can watch if my dad says it's okay. A few bodyguards wouldn't make any difference.'

She deeply misses her father; she misses Jordan — that desert kingdom peopled by descendants of the Bedouin; she misses its turquoise blue and 'shocking green' grass, the smell of baking bread, the honeysuckle, gardenia flowers. 'There's a very special light there,' she dreamily says, 'almost luminous. There's just a special kind of hue over everything.' When she speaks English, part of her heart remains veiled; it is only when she talks in Arabic to the Assistant Chief of Protocol that a powerful passion informs her words and her laughter is throaty. 'People are *totally* driven by emotion in Jordan,' she explains. 'They're highly romantic and highly extreme in their feelings and I really like that. I don't think they're afraid. They're not afraid to hate

— which I don't think is a good thing — but they're not afraid to love. They're also not afraid to *give*, and when they give, they don't expect to have to *take*. A lot of times in other places I find that everything's a trade-off. *I'll give you this, but what will you give me in return?* And that,' she adds, 'is not nice.'

Her ultimate concern is the cultural revolution currently taking place in Jordan, a revolution fundamental to global peace. 'In the span of a single generation,' the *Los Angeles Times* reported in 1995, 'tens of thousands of Jordanians have been educated [in Europe and America], and have been exposed to a way of life radically different from traditional Arab culture.' These radical differences in perception have led to a new consciousness of human rights, an increasing demand for birth control among Jordanian women, and to the election of the country's first female MP, Toujan al-Faisal. Other attempts to create a working partnership with the rest of the world include the $500 million Dead Sea Tourism Project, the decision to ease controls on foreign currency deposits, the celebration of the first air route between Tel Aviv and Amman, and the new code-share service between TransWorld Airlines and Royal Jordanian Airline. The fact that forty-three per cent of Jordan's total population is under the age of fifteen also augurs real receptiveness to change.

Typical of this new 'moderate' generation, Haya is one of the best ambassadors for which the Middle East could hope —

sufficiently respectful to please the Muslim community, and sufficiently intelligent and cultivated to make her culture seem plausible to the West. 'What many people don't know,' she says, 'is that while Europe and the rest of the world was living in the Dark Ages there was enlightenment in the Middle East. The Arabs believed that enlightenment was defined by the evolution from the scientific to God, whereas the West went the other way — from God to science. That is, I believe, the only real difference between the two regions.'

She pauses to glance at the credits on the screen, and then fixes me with a look that tells of nothing but the desire to connect. 'I want to have more to do with people, to have a cause — not to be a Mother Teresa, but to have a cause to fight for that will make a difference to the world. I haven't found it yet. Perhaps showjumping is a way of treading water until I do.' Resting her chin in her hands, she smiles. Her warmth envelops.

Elle, 1997

LIVING WITH DREADS:

LINDA JAIVIN

It is a dark and dilapidated Tuesday night, and the Sandringham Hotel in the inner-Sydney suburb of Newtown is only partially full. Linda Jaivin, Sinologist, journalist, and author of the controversial and bestselling *Eat Me*, is waiting at the foot of the tiny makeshift stage to fulfil one of her greatest fantasies. She is a violent spray of colour against the dim, beery tableau. Her black patent-leather Mary Janes have glittery perspex heels; her muscular thighs are uncomfortably revealed by a scarlet lurex micro-mini; vermilion dreadlocks emerge at right angles from her head in the manner of the ears of the Goofy cartoon prototype: she is electric — sparkling bomber jacket, diamond-shaped spectacles, grass-green fingernails, lightning-bolt earrings, performance anxiety. The barely post-adolescent drummer, bass player, and lead guitarist from the Melbourne band Hum step up on stage. To their backing music, the forty-two-year-old Jaivin will 'perform' the first chapter of her most recent novel, *Rock N Roll Babes From Outer Space*. 'Ready to rock and *rollllllllll*?' she shrieks, and launches into her grotesquely lascivious and comic act.

Age has not wearied her, nor success condemned. Jaivin is a woman of principle — a liberal humanist who has resigned from senior positions to protect the interests of her friends, who volubly defends that in which she believes, who has no interest in material reward beyond funding her fiction. 'As a writer,' comments Michael Heyward, her publisher at Text, 'she is extremely professional. She works very hard and is very organised.' The unexpected splash of her first novel in 1995 — *Eat Me* sold 27,000 copies locally and 20,000 in Italy — has had little effect on her lifestyle. She stresses that whilst the advance was 'broadcast as being six figures', it was a two-book deal and that the money is paid to her in unimpressive allotments. The Australian-Hungarian producer, Reszo Bodonyi, bought the film option and is in the process of 'talking to funding bodies'. Jaivin's role will be that of script consultant. In June, the novel is to be published by Broadway Books in the United States. The British have been less enthusiastic.

Dismissed as 'dismal fare' by the *Times* and as 'right-on Australian feminist pornographic revisionism' by the *Guardian*, it sold only 2,000 copies in the UK.

Rock N Roll Babes has done markedly less well than its predecessor, although the film option has been purchased by Sullivan Entertainment, a Canadian-based company which, ironically enough, has produced the award-winning 'Anne of Green Gables'. It is said that the sale of the book will net Jaivin six figures. Rose Creswell, Jaivin's agent, remarks: 'I can't see how you could make the film for less than ten million because of all the special effects, and Linda is on a percentage of the budget.'

Jaivin's writing can be amusing, but with its celebration of tribal — rather than individual — consciousness and undergraduate tilt on existence, the book is unlikely to appeal to the more discerning market. Her fictional world is one of schoolyard puns and neologisms, a world in which eyes are 'ice-blue', lips are 'blood-red', thrusts are 'well-timed', and any 'young executive type' with an 'Armani suit' is a 'wanker'. Writing apart, her greatest strengths are her vibrant energy, application, and eagerness to promote her work. Jonathan Nix, bass player with The Gadflys, laughs as he comments on his eccentric flatmate: 'We were performing a passage from *Eat Me*. I was badly dressed as a detective and bent over my double bass, providing a soundtrack to Linda's dialogue whilst she simulated the insertion and removal of a Lebanese cucumber from my backside.' Jaivin agrees. 'I am *totally* happy to play the dippy, wacky writer,' she says. 'I am accused of being superficial, but people *like* it.'

The afternoon after the night before, she describes herself as 'trashed'. She and Hum were up in her rented Elizabeth Bay apartment talking about life, the universe, and everything until dawn. When there is a knock at the door, she freezes; she is palpably terrified that her neighbours will come and berate her for 'dragging amps up the stairs' at 3 am. She then throws herself onto one of the futons on the floor. The gesture showcases her naked buttocks; she quickly tweaks and readjusts her purple and silver lurex mini skirt. Jaivin's wide-eyed disregard of postural and behavioural conventions is both charming and awful. She extends her milk-white calves and then retracts them, hugs her knees to her breasts, sits cross-legged, unselfconsciously bares her black cotton crotch, scratches, laughs madly with a gaping mouth. At one point, she removes the blue-and-white sneakers she has been wearing with no socks. The smell is asphyxiating. She doesn't notice.

There is something of the frightened animal about her; a belly-exposing quality created to deflect attack. She is girlish, clever, nervous, neurotic. When she answers the telephone, her trilling greeting sounds as if it has been fuelled by Prozac. Her undulating American/Australian inflection ranges from a sweetly giggling word-choked whisper to a Norman Gunston roar (shoulders lifted, chin dropped, machine-gun blast of mirth). Under the pink, her thin hair is completely grey. At the age of twenty-five, she dyed her hair black so as not to be too conspicuous in China; she has now dyed it vermilion, waxes it with Murray's Superior Hair Pomade, and rolls it between two furious fingers to create dreadlocks. From a distance, the result is something like Tinkerbell on acid; at close range, deforested patches of white scalp are visible. Mary McCarthy, a close friend and word-processor operator, chuckles. 'Linda,' she explains, 'finds *everything* fascinating and in that way, she is like a child. She has an incredible naiveté about her.'

Earlier this year, Jaivin was quoted as saying that 'despite the many excellent adventures and extreme pleasures that came with growing up, it was going to be hard to come up with a year that could, in its entirety, match my halcyon ninth'. Appropriately, the fictional character with whom she most identifies is 'Baby Baby', the narrator of *Rock N Roll Babes*. The trappings of adulthood are of little interest to Jaivin; she cultivates an adolescent image — swooning as she speaks of 'mosh pits', '*kyool* bands', and of the sexual appeal of 'slackers'. Similarly, she does not feel comfortable with the concept of committed relationships, shares a house with men who prop surfboards in otherwise empty bedrooms, and discusses 'wild' parties with the awe of a girl who was never asked to the prom. During one such event, she squeals, rose petals were being passed from tongue to tongue, the living room was so full of dancing bodies that all the furniture was pushed out into the corridor, and she was raised from hand to sweating hand above people's heads. One friend recalls wondering how Jaivin's then-purple beehive hairdo remained in place. Nix remembers feeling overwhelmed by the fact that men were openly undressing each other. The police were called; Jaivin awoke the next afternoon to find that raw eggs had been thrown by irate neighbours at her windows.

The flat itself is 'party city' — roomy, with a minimum of furniture and Indian throws over futons that double as beds for friends who 'crash'. The floor is littered with CDs. A Scrabble board is open on the wooden dining table; Jaivin and Nix play almost every day. In her bedroom are toy tigers, plastic dinosaurs, piles of glossy photographs, notes for her new novel, and nine bookshelves mostly crammed with Chinese texts and novels. Such urban bohemia is relished by her; it provides the backdrop not only to her romantic ideals, but to her novels, in which trains rumble past windows, lovers have a 'gamey' smell, drug-addled men are idealised as champions of anti-materialism, and depression masquerades as 'fun'.

'I find the slacker way really appealing,' she says with a shrug. 'I'm not attracted to ambition or pushiness or careerism in men or women. A lot of women find men in suits really attractive, whereas I look at a man in a suit and I don't see him. I do not see him as a man. It's bizarre. I don't go for that kind of —' and here her tone becomes uncharacteristically scathing — 'executive career *power* thing. It doesn't pull me. What pulls me is that very intelligent but kind of lazy I-don't-give-a-fuck-about-material-success-although-I-wouldn't-mind-if-I-had-enough-money-for-food-and-if-I-could-pay-my-rent attitude. There's something about that that *gets* me.'

Stylistically, *Rock N Roll Babes* reflects this love affair with apathy. The prose is deliberately and rhapsodically 'druggy'. An example? 'Acid. Speed. Booze. Speed. Dope. Speed. Hash. Speed. Ecstasy. Agony. Out there. In there. Here and there. Wheeeeee. Aliens. Wheeeeeeee.' Jaivin sees no harm in recreational drug use. 'I smoke dope from time to time if it's not mixed with tobacco,' she says simply. 'Tobacco sets my asthma off. I actually prefer to eat a hash cake or something. I don't take other drugs, but I have a lot of friends who *do* and I'm quite *fascinated* by hallucinogens. The kind of stories you hear from people who've taken LSD.' Her hands flare. 'I love it! I just *love* it! I *cannot* hear enough acid stories! I set that challenge for myself; I was trying to *imagine* myself into the drug state and I found that *enormously* fun.'

Given that her audience is primarily the youth market, it seems irresponsible of her not to consider the ramifications of effectively validating casual drug use, but Jaivin sees herself as light and optimistic, wild and free; any element of morality would, perhaps, be interpreted by her as authoritarianism. 'I've really only had pretty happy experiences!' she exclaims. 'I've never been *raped*, I've never been *abused* … I've been felt up by assholes or had them stick their tongues down my throat, but who *cares*? And because of that, I just can't write darkly. In effect, I don't have the emotional *depth* of somebody who's been through a hell of a lot of emotional shit. I have been very *lucky*. I haven't had, you know, really successful long-term relationships, but that fact does not make me unhappy.'

Her militant rejection of mainstream culture could be interpreted as a professional commitment in itself. 'I always feel like a *freak* in the quote/unquote straight world,' she says. 'The way I dress! If I walk into a party, I'll immediately become the object of *strange* attention to those sort of people. They can be very, very nice to me; but they totally *exhaust* me.' Her philosophy is best summarised by one of her fictional quotes: 'Live wild on the edge or die bored in the middle, that's what I say. The surf's never up in the great mainstream.' Such views seem simplistic for an academic of her obvious intelligence but like a child, Jaivin does not seem to understand delicate ambiguities. Beneath the chaos and the colour there is resentment in her with which she has not dealt, a raw determination to reject all that of which she was deprived.

It can be said that her attitude is a justification for the rage she still carries for the psychological scars inflicted on her by those of the 'straight' mindset.

Never a conventionally beautiful child or teenager, she was raised amongst the tightly-knit and very separate Jewish community in New London, Conneticut. Jaivin has always perceived 'the Jewish thing' as responsible for her feeling of alienation. Raised on tales of her Russian grandparents escaping pogroms, she was taught in Hebrew School by a man who not only terrified his prepubescent charges with films of the Holocaust and 'documentaries with skulls', but who, once a year, 'dragged out' his striped Auschwitz suit and discussed his persecution — an abusively macabre kind of show'n'tell. As a result, Jaivin quickly understood that she would never be assimilated into 'the great mainstream'. Not only were the parents of certain gentile friends disdainful towards her, but those of her faith were not permitted entry to select clubs. 'These things gave me a very strong awareness of myself as an

outsider,' she explains. 'The Holocaust certainly reinforced that
— you know, we were so *out* there that we got *killed* for it.'

The emphatic nature of American commercialism and its
attendant culture of perfection did not allow Jaivin to feel
accepted or acceptable and as a consequence, the only position
in which she feels comfortable is a marginal one. This is, as she
knows, reflected in her work. 'Why else would I write about
aliens?' she asks. Her dreams were of escape — 'very big visions
of travelling' — and fights against injustice. An ordinary girl
with an ordinary body, she was made to feel overweight, if not
ugly. 'Almost half my friends went and got *nose* jobs because the
Jewish nose does not conform to the WASP ideal,' she says with
the passion borne of justified anger. 'At that time it was very
hard to grow up looking like I do. If you didn't look like a
blonde, little WASP girl with, you know — the *tiniest* waist and
the little flippy nose, it was difficult. On the other hand, I must
have had some form of self esteem because I remember when
my parents asked me if I wanted a nose job, I said no.' She
plucks a black guitar pick from the rug and flicks it between
her fingers. 'The point is *I was offered a nose job*. That kind of
thing does not encourage a lot of self-confidence.'

Her self-perception changed when she moved to Taiwan. 'I
was suddenly seen as exotically *attractive!*' she cries. 'Chinese

men would say things like: "Oh, Chinese girls are too skinny! I *love* a fat ass!" And I suddenly thought: "Wow! It's good I've *got* one," you know?' Suddenly vulnerable, she pauses. 'When I left the States, I was running away from that whole Barbie Doll, *Seventeen* magazine way of growing up American. I remember I had this little bikini when I was thirteen and I'm sure I looked good in it, you know? But if you had one little *roll* of fat when you sat down — if your stomach folded, you were considered *fat.*'

She was made to experience profound feelings of guilt about her appetites. Food, for example. She cooks every day — for strangers, for lovers, for flatmates and friends. Helen Garner, who lives in the apartment upstairs, testifies to her neighbour's generosity. 'When you're sick,' she says, 'Linda is the kind of person who *always* brings you food.' Whilst writing, Jaivin's fantasies involve not erotic contortions, but the ingredients of the meal she plans to cook for supper. Nix again laughs wonderfully. 'Linda's relationship with food is *intense*,' he says. 'It is *committed*, an absolute *love* affair.' Jaivin believes that eating and lovemaking are 'the two top sensual activities'. Either can be functional or passionate; both can be done alone or shared. The forlorn intensity with which she discusses either activity suggests an emotional appetite which is impossible to satisfy. Owen Cook, Hum's twenty-two-year-old lead guitarist, chuckles. 'Linda is *ready*,' he says. 'She's out to get what she can from life.'

At the age of fourteen, the asthmatic Jaivin seriously dislocated her knee and was forced to rely on crutches and a brace to walk for some twelve months. Thus denied ordinary adolescent activities, she dedicated herself to a citizens' action group, had an epiphany in the parking lot of a synagogue about the way in which 'God was a kind of necessary construct', and from that moment on, regarded herself as an agnostic revolutionary. 'I think I was a rebel because my parents were very conservative politically.' She places the guitar pick on the coffee table beside her. 'Our opinions differed on the Vietnam War, Richard Nixon — all that stuff. *Big* political rebellion. I believed that I was going to dedicate my life to that sort of activism.'

In 1973 she enrolled at Brown University, where she studied political science and Asian history. She graduated four years later with the realisation that politics was not her destiny. 'To be quite honest,' she says, 'I just couldn't see things in black and white, the way you have to. Everything was just a bit too grey. And plus, I was getting completely intrigued by China. The complete *irrelevance* of it appealed to me.' On receiving her degree, she flew to Japan and then travelled to Taiwan, where she enrolled at the Normal University to study Mandarin. Once the year-long course was over and as a reaction against the fact that her beloved teacher resigned over a political issue, Jaivin began working for 'this completely lunatic little company' which published educational magazines in English and Chinese. She returned to the United States in 1979. 'I hadn't seen my parents for two years,' she says, 'and I thought, *what do I do now?* Going back to the States permanently didn't feel right, so I saved up money. A couple of months down the track I was in Hong Kong with no work visa, no contacts, nothing.'

A wealthy New Zealand couple employed her as a live-in maid. It is only when discussing these two months that Jaivin becomes so upset that she can barely articulate her thoughts. She pauses, stares blindly out of the window, seems to gag on her memories. 'When all that ended, it took me about *two years* before I would buy a pack of New Zealand *butter*,' she spits. Visibly traumatised, she again stops. Her jaw is set. And then: 'I thought they were *completely* horrible people. They thought it was very prestigious to have a *white*, university educated maid when everybody else's was Filipino. They were, like, business people, and I was *nothing* — it was just *awful*! Verbal abuse! They *bullied* me! I'm not an intellectual snob — I have friends from all levels of education — but they were not, let's say, extremely *literate* or intellectual people. They were shit-kicking *yobs*, as far as I was concerned — real, uncultured business people.'

With 'red and swollen eyes' after an altercation with her loathed employers, Jaivin 'snuck out' for a job interview with the head of the *very* civilised' Oxford University Press. She was immediately employed as an English textbook editor. It was during this time that she began freelancing for the Cathay Pacific in-flight magazine and *Asiaweek*. The literary criticism she wrote for the latter led to commissions for profiles which, in turn, led to her meeting Geremie Barmé, the Australian Sinologist who would later become her husband. 'We first met very briefly at the Peking Opera, but I don't think that he was the least bit interested in meeting some, you know, little western ... *idiot*,' she says. 'People like us all go through these stages — you don't even want to look at a white person. My relationships were with Chinese men. I preferred that they didn't speak English. That way it was more *interesting*.'

She would never have come to know Barmé had a mutual acquaintance not convinced a politically controversial actress to allow Jaivin to interview her. 'And so,' she giggles, 'this actress told Geremie to come and protect her from this big bad awful journalist. If I got scary, he was there to help her heavy me. And all he'd do was make these *little* side comments in the most *perfect* Mandarin I had ever heard come out of a foreigner's mouth, like — *stunning*! My Chinese was competent, but it was quite stilted and formal. So I'm there *panicking* and my Chinese is getting *worse* and *worse* and *worse* because Geremie just scared the *shit* out of me!' She shakes her head. 'He *totally* intimidated me!'

The two later 'hit it off' and remained friends until 1985, whereupon they became lovers and Jaivin was asked to be *Asiaweek*'s first bureau chief in Peking. 'I didn't realise that they really carefully *watch* a foreigner for the first three weeks, and that that determines their view of you,' she says, suddenly sitting up. 'So the first thing I did is have the … party … from … HELL! At that time, it was like a police state in China, and I invited *all* the dissidents — all the writers and artists and poets and underground this and underground that and there was *singing* and *dancing* —' as she speaks, she whirls her arms to illustrate — 'and *fucking* and *fighting* and *pissing* in the corners and *throwing* up — you know, it was THE WILD PARTY FROM HELL!' Her expression is insanely gleeful. 'It became a *legend*, and also resulted in my getting the ultimate, high-level twenty-four-hour surveillance, harassment of friends, recruitment of friends to spy on me — the full treatment. My big China dream: I get there; I move in; and within months, it is *so* hairy that I had a friend who was going to commit suicide because he did not want to inform on me and the police were heavying him so much.'

Jaivin resigned on principle. Not knowing where to go or what to do, she reluctantly agreed when Barmé suggested that they marry and return to Australia. The couple married in China in 1986 and moved to Canberra whilst Barmé completed his PhD. 'I would never have gotten married otherwise,' she tightly says. 'In my life. I never wanted to get married. I never wanted to have children and I never wanted to get married. I didn't like the fact that society approved of it.' *New Ghosts, Old Dreams: Chinese Rebel Voices*, the book Barme and Jaivin co-edited, was published by Times Books in New York in 1992, the year the couple separated. They divorced in 1994. 'It was hard to go through.' A slight tremor is audible as she speaks. 'It made me very sad and despite the fact that I'd never really believed in marriage as an institution, I had gone that far and I'd sort of come to believe that it was a permanent relationship. I was very depressed. I just realised that I couldn't have found a better Mister Right, you know what I mean?'

Since then, she has seized the day, lecturing on everything from Chinese censorship and the avant garde to homosexuality. She has subtitled Chinese films including *Farewell, My Concubine* and *Blue Kite*, contributed to radio programmes and newspapers, acted as a curator for the Museum of Contemporary Art and as a consultant for the Refugee Review Tribunal, and her collection of essays, *Confessions of an S&M Virgin*, is scheduled for publication in October. And then, of course, there is her well-documented penchant for 'much younger' men. Jaivin claims that this attraction is not an emotional safety measure from the traumata of her divorce, but based on emotional identification. 'I'm *really* upfront and *really* passionate and I'm *vulnerable* and very *real*,' she says, as if defending herself. 'Older men seem to be up to more tricks, whereas with younger men, I know *exactly* where they're coming from. So my emotional equals are younger.' McCarthy is reluctant to discuss her friend's personal life, but remarks: 'I know she likes being *teased* by men. She likes men with a sense of humour. She also likes them young and beautiful — that's her thing. She likes them because everything's new and exciting to them.'

Newly separated, Jaivin was led to believe that she had 'more of a chance of being hijacked than finding a partner', and it was only after a fling with a considerably younger man that she realised that she had been limiting her options. This experience led to the first story in which the four female characters of *Eat Me* appeared. 'There was a long period without sex after that,' she says. 'And at that time I went to a doctor who said: "I think you might be four months pregnant!" And I said: "Well then, you believe in the immaculate conception!" ' Her laughter feverishly builds. 'I had, like, a uterus full of fibroid tumours and what was happening as a result was like —' she loudly blows a giant raspberry — '*massive* bleeding. It was pretty disgusting and it ended up in a partial hysterectomy. I still have my ovaries, so I cycle and get PMT, but I don't have a uterus or menstruate. But that's what he had discovered — this huge uterus, *full!*' She gestures as if cupping an imaginary and hugely swollen belly. '*The size of a four-month-old foetus!*'

The lightness with which she discusses this is disconcerting. She expresses no grief and her smile is vacant. Nix pauses before commenting on this facet of Jaivin's character. 'I think Linda has a tendency not to want to burden others with her pain,' he murmurs. 'Like all of us, she uses the common devices of alcohol, loud music, and good food to avoid it. She suffers very privately. Unless I manage to ferret it out of her, she keeps it to herself. Locked up.'

The Australian, 1997

PARTNER OF MY DREAMS

LORD HAVE MERCY, but the one thing most opinionated types have yet to learn is that the most heinous crime any writer can commit is to be boring. Boringness is that which strips the soul of its decorations, it is that which rots the molars of the mind, it is a dripping tap in the bathroom of hope, a wart on the nose of true art, a married man with a shoe fetish in the singles' bar of the imagination, it is an erosion of life, a waste of the spirit, a blister on the big toe of eternity, and really not the thing a person wishes to be exposed to on any occasion. This is the platinum rule of prose, and one which Yvonne Roberts callously defies in her new book, *Mad About Women*.

Ms Roberts is the sort of right-on long-haired bespectacled English journalist who thanks her 'partner' at the beginning of the book for being man enough to 'live for three months knee-deep in feminist literature without losing his sense of humour'. We should all be so lucky to have such a partner and I, for one, am profoundly grateful to Ms Roberts for stoking my faith that such men exist. She dutifully apologises for the 'frighteningly short' period required for the book's gestation and delivery before subjecting us all to a few hundred pages of killingly dull rubbish touted as the response to the backlash against feminism. I fear that *Mad About Women* is more about Ms Roberts' bank balance than it is about the backlash against feminism, but will refrain from further cynical speculation. Maybe. Let it only be said that the enchanting author is featured on the back cover in her big earrings and beside the bold-type question that keeps us all fitfully tossing beneath our Beatrix Potter bunny rugs at night: CAN THERE EVER BE FAIR PLAY BETWEEN THE SEXES?

Well, theoretically speaking, there *could* be, but if there were, persons such as Roberts and her nemesis Lyndon would have to become neo-Nazi pornographers in order to satisfy their deep-seated psychological urges to place themselves on the outskirts of society. Roberts poses her question and then goes on to answer it no more cogently than my brother Alexander, who is fifteen years old and who describes women he finds attractive as 'megababes'. In her fingernail-chewing foreword, Roberts declares: 'Feminism can only ever act as a barb in society's bum.'

This is an interesting declaration for a number of reasons, the first being the assumption that society *has* a bum, in which case I would be fascinated to know if Roberts believes this bum to be covered by the trousers of decorum or whether this bum is exposed in the full glory of its essential bumness — a bum, say, *crying out* for a barb; a bum naked as the Good Lord intended bums to be, a bum firm with juice, packed with potential, a perfectly formed set of globes pushed together. Were this the case I would then put forth the argument that a bum is an innocent thing, a thing which sits in beauty like the night and is undeserving of barbs or smacks or ridicule. The second reason Roberts' declaration is so interesting is because it incorporates the assumption that feminism is a thing *separate* from society, as if society were, by definition, indifferent or alien or hostile to feminism. Both are assumptions that I, as a thunderingly ordinary member of the lumpenproletariat with my deep and abiding belief in bums and barbs and feminism and that men are genetically predisposed to buying diamonds, bestowing orchids upon their love objects, and uncomplainingly carrying their women up flights of stairs, find bewildering. I also find it bewildering that Roberts can make such a resoundingly stupid comment, that she can begin so badly and so tellingly on the wrong buttock, given that even if feminism *were* a barb and if society *had* a bum, it would be rather strange to say the least for feminism to *only ever* act as a barb for this bum of society's. Were this the case, feminism would become synonymous with anarchy, and then Ms Roberts would have to renounce not only the concept of acknowledgement, but her nice big earrings.

Neil Lyndon understandably has a problem with barbs such as Roberts', identifying as he does with society's bum. Lyndon, author of *No More Sex War — The Failures of Feminism*, is awesomely wise, a cogent thinker who appreciates two spoonfuls of grey with his cup of black and white, a man of many gifts, an intellectual who weights his arguments with substantial research and a subtlety I have to admit impressed me as wonderfully original. To quote: 'The cardinal tenets of feminism add up to a totem of bunkum' (page 6); 'The pseudo-Marxist tenets of modern feminism' (page 7); 'The more pustulent lines of piss in the crock of cant which is modern feminism' (page 48); 'An egg of scrambled Marxian dogma … fertilised by the darting pin-head of Freudian theory' (page 126); 'Pea-brained cant' (page 134); 'We have been chased up the totemic gum-tree … the whip has been cracked by those Marxian feminist criminologists' (page 156); 'The rape fantasies of the sisterhood' (page 156). And as if this lot were not adequate, Lyndon sweeps us off our feet with the philosophical mastery of page 23: 'He is the filthy sod in the thigh-high Doc

Martens, torn demins and AC/DC T-shirt who ... leers over the tits in the *Sun* while he is waiting to collect his packet of dole [with] his greasy fingers, sticking the remains up the cunts of whores.'

Susan Sontag, *move over*! After reading this book I sat back in my armchair at my local pea-brained feminist criminologists meeting, reluctantly pushed all rape fantasies out of my tiny mind, and tried to image Neil Lyndon beside me at the altar in his thigh-high Doc Martens, bulging cod-piece and AC/DC T-shirt, the cracking whip of his mind keeping me in place, the darting pin-head of his extensive vocabulary doing whatever it is that darting pin-heads do, his eyes burning with the light of genius, his cheeks illuminated by the light allowed by the stained glass windows, as outside, up totemic gum-trees and in Jungian saucepans, the Marxian koalas and poached eggs of modern thought both cling ... and in the distance, that single mournful poignant note as Roberts' barb pierces society's tender bum ...

When I set off to find the crock of cant at the end of the rainbow, there is only one partner I will want by my side ... Neil Lyndon, will you marry me?

The Sydney Morning Herald, 1993

FEAR OF DYING: ERICA JONG

UNSMILINGLY, THE WOMAN whom the novelist Paul Theroux referred to in print as 'a mammoth pudenda' opens the door of her Sydney Regent hotel suite, her breathing that of an overburdened mule, her left hand fluttering against her heaving breast, and begins braying for a doctor. Staring straight through me, she sternly addresses her publicist: 'Have you found a doctor yet? Because it's *really* critical.' To me, she suggests: 'Can you put that cigarette out? Normally I don't mind, but today is different. So can you put it out? *Now*?'

At the age of fifty-two, Erica Jong — the delicious, the predatory, the humorous — still exercises all the charm and ferocity of the truly celebrated. Her first and best-known novel, *Fear of Flying*, published when she was thirty, sold over ten million copies and was translated into twenty-two languages. Its ribald female voice incited both outrage and adoration and shot its author, then a romantic PhD student, into the firmament of public consciousness. Since then, she has written over a dozen novels and collections of poetry — some bestsellers, some remaindered, a few ridiculous, all of them Rabelaisian. She is in Sydney to promote her most recent effort, *Fear of Fifty*, a book she describes as her 'mid-life memoir'. As a memoir, mid-life or otherwise, it is selective in its candour and nothing like the brute unvarnished truth. This selectivity could be due to Jong's protectiveness towards her sixteen-year-old daughter Molly, whom she takes pains not to embarrass. Another explanation is Jong's unwillingness to perceive or to portray herself as anything but the most vulnerable of heroines.

She slams down onto one of the apricot-coloured sofas, surrounded by potted Alexander palms, the Opera House framed by the broad bow window behind her. Her voice is low and slow, New York patronising, intelligently deliberate. 'I mean,' she growls, fixing her publicist with a death-ray stare, 'it's *not* a joke. I was *gasping* for breath. I could not *breathe* on that staircase, all *right*? It's *really* critical. I was never so scared in my *life*.' The hapless publicist manages precisely two words before she loudly interrupts him. 'I couldn't get any *air* in my lungs, *okay*?' Her gnarled fat little hands angrily gesture. 'If it's like an asthmatic thing that just arrived out of *nowhere*, I just want to know what to *do*.' She sighs, exasperated. *'Okay?'* Her publicist bites his lip, nods, and leaves the room. Jong turns to me.

Her stare is bizarre — myopic and blue, huge and desperate, emphasised by close-set round blue-tinted spectacles that make her look like the demented scientist in early Looney Tunes shorts. She stares at me as she would at an indistinct but compelling point in the distance — an unidentifiable flying object, say, or a piece of lint on the Aubusson. She is a tiny woman, elegantly dressed in a loose black silk shift and opaque black stockings which flatter her cactus legs. She wears two watches, one of them with two faces, each face adjusted to a different time-zone. Garish rings are squeezed over most of her fingers — one a quail-egg opal ringed by diamonds, another a gold daisy with a diamond as its centrepiece, another a Haight-Ashbury assortment of semi-precious stones, all of them enormous. These fortune-telling-gypsy rings seem to be all that remain of her former Flowing Universal honeypot persona (the one who 'got laid', loved stoned orgasms in the hot tub, and had virile younger lovers pull her tampons out with their teeth). The new model Jong is a Power Broad: pearls, padded shoulders, arms folded, defined by a lot of black.

'I mean,' she insists with a lipsticked grimace, 'I've been *sick*! He [the publicist] doesn't *understand*. I mean, what do they *expect*? I mean, I've been *really* sick for about ten *days*! Last time this happened, I just lost my voice *totally*, but they just don't believe you! *He just didn't believe me!*' Her eyes are wild and she leans forward, as if reporting a crime to a police officer. 'I *told* him that my voice shorts out! I said: *you've gotta give me breathing space!* And they just *don't* — they just don't *believe* you!'

She rations me three words before interrupting. 'I mean, do you know that I haven't had lunch or *supper* today?' Her voice has risen to an indignant squeal. '*How* are you supposed to get up and get the energy for a speech when you're *sick*?' Another exasperated sigh. 'I mean, they're just *maaaad*! I've been on tour for four *months*! And you know who really killed me? You know who was the *worst*? My dear Italian publisher. Which is in *utter* chaos. I *arrived* in Milan,' she exhales, beside herself with the iniquity of it all, 'they gave me *no* schedule, so I never knew what to *wear*. It was freezing, I was dressed in woolly scarves, and they said: *Right! We're going to Rome!* We get on the plane. There's a strike at the airport. It was 100 degrees. I did a TV show. We went *back* to Milan. We waited at the airport for another three hours. I mean,' she says, gathering steam, 'it was just un-*fucking* believable! *Nobody* thought about telling me what to *wear*; *nobody* brought a sweater or cape; *nobody* had any interest. I mean, *that* was where I got *sick*.'

I manage two words before she cuts in again — enraged, despairing, dying, abandoned. 'When *Fear of Flying* was published, it was *possible* for a book to come out of nowhere and sell by word of mouth.' She stands to pluck a tangerine from the minaret of fruit on the table and then repositions herself as far from the tape recorder as possible. 'The reason for that was because publishers didn't pay for shelf-space. *Now* everything is presold. The bookstores are *paid* for the front-of-the-store display. So the whole system is now payola, like the record business, and the public doesn't *know* it.' Passionately ripping the skin from the fruit, she then stuffs a segment of the pulp into her mouth and chews it as she speaks. 'They pay off the stores [pronounced 'stawers'] for the *display* space. So *Fear of Flying* couldn't happen today, 'cause *Fear of Flying* was made by the audience.'

'You know,' she continues as she spits some seeds into her fleshy palm, 'I write only for me. I don't think about the audience. All my effort is concentrated on —' she looks up, distracted by the doorbell, and stands to answer it. A portly, terrified bellhop enters with her afternoon tea. '*Yeeeeeeeah*,' Jong approves. 'Would you like to put it here? The glass table, *here*?' Whilst indicating, she almost knocks her cup over and girlishly exclaims: '*Oooooops!*' And then, reflectively: '*Sandwiches.*' And to me: 'I ordered Lapsang Souchong because I *love* it. Would you like to have some sandwiches?' To the bellhop: 'Could we have, um, a coupla *clean* plates?' The bellhop shoots her a look, as if to say: *what, as opposed to the usual filthy ones?*, but Jong misses his expression and primly points, the privileged princess of a fairytale, to the corner. 'I think there're some plates over there. And *napkins*. Do you have some hot *water*? Great. Leave a plate *there*. Right. Thanks.'

A single word escapes my lips before she overrides me. 'Isn't this *great*?' she comments, offering me the plate of finger sandwiches. 'They actually do it very well here.' She waits for me, the nodding mute, to select some sandwiches, chooses three for herself, dramatically coughs without covering her mouth, and then pours herself some tea. Again, the dinky, '*Oooooooops!*' as she almost spills it, and then, with a *comme il faut* intonation, advises: 'Have a cucumber sandwich. They're *great*. You know,' she says, contently beginning to munch, oblivious to all but her pressing needs, 'you know, it was *terrible* — I just couldn't catch my *breath*, and that has never happened to me before. My *air* pipes were blocked! I was *soooooo* frightened! I just can't *tell* you how *scary* it was!'

Raised on Manhattan's Upper West Side, Jong is the second of three daughters to a painter mother and jazz-drummer-cum-*tchotchke*-salesman father. It was an unusual family — wealthy, Jewish and bohemian. Her mother, quoted as saying that, 'Erica always finds a reason to scream at me', and her father, who was less than faithful to his wife and more than convinced of his middle daughter's transcendent genius, provided an eccentric model of marriage. '*What* difficulty with my father?' Jong barks, sharply slamming the lid of the teapot at my timid suggestion. 'He absolutely doted and dotes on me. I was *fixated* on him; I was in *love* with him. I mean, I just had a very protracted Electra complex. He and my grandfather *absolutely adored* me and favoured me above my sisters, who hated me because they felt I was favoured. And my mother was *enraged* that her father nurtured me like a mommy, because he had abandoned her. So the love of these men came with a very high price tag.'

However expensive, their love also gave her the confidence to complete an MA at Columbia University at a time when few women did and to pursue, however nervously at first, a career in writing. As she leans over the biscuit plate her decolletage sags, exposing her loose brown cleavage and her lingerie. 'It just seems to me *stoopid* if you wanna accomplish something to let yourself be brought down by *fools*,' she says through a mouthful of biscuit. 'At bottom, my determination is sheer orneriness and cussedness. I mean, when you think of the pathetically small fraction of the population that even reads a bestseller, you really have to *despair*. We've misconstrued democracy to mean the *lowest*,' and here she nearly gurgles with contempt, '*gruntiest* person gets to determine what we should see, read or *hear*.'

Jong, who has penned lines such as the immortal, 'I could look up his nostrils and see eternity', considers herself to be a writer of literature, a poet, a feminist pioneer, a worthy intellectual. In *Fear of Fifty*, she posits: 'If you have a baby at home that you are nursing and you come into the boardroom wearing a filmy blouse and your breasts are leaking milk, who is going to tell you that you shouldn't be there? Not the men, who might be slightly turned on, but the *women*.'

Perhaps Jong would also advocate the cutting of deals by merchant bankers clad in filmy trousers stained with semen or Hilary Rodham Clinton debating health care issues whilst standing in a pool of her own menstrual blood. Never able to comprehend why she is not taken seriously as a thinker, Jong has always dismissed criticism as 'envy' or anti-feminism or as the spite of grunty little art haters. The great beauty of her work lies not in its intellectual weight, but in its wonderfully intense and comforting foolishness. If style, as Schopenhauer believed, is the physiognomy of the mind, then Jong's ganglia must look something like Mae West.

Her private life has been every bit, if not more, picaresque than her novels. At twenty-one, she married a brilliant fellow student who disintegrated into brilliant schizophrenia. The feisty Jong did her darnedest to make the marriage work but understood that it was over when her husband declared that he could walk on water. The marriage was annulled. At twenty-four, she married a Chinese-American psychiatrist, whose surname she still bears. Nine years later, they divorced. In 1977, she married the novelist Jonathan Fast, six years her junior. They produced the red-haired Molly Miranda, and then divorced in 1983. 'When my marriage to Jon broke up,' she soberly says, 'I remember driving dead drunk. I remember throwing myself in front of the wheels of his car to stop him from leaving. I think I went through a period when my marriage ended when I was in *despair* and I abused *everything*. I abused alcohol, I overworked, I abused my body — it was a grief reaction. I would say that my main addiction thought my life, though, has been workaholism. I can get into sex addiction, but at some point I'll say: *Okay! OUT! I have to write!*'

Jong's satirical documentation of this 'sex addiction' is that which made her famous. She has explicitly written about sexual combinations that would give the average person whiplash. 'I don't think I've ever been to an orgy,' she says, suddenly — and surprisingly — shy. And then, in the soft, disappointed tones of a woman who deplores her hostess' taste in china, she says: 'Jon and I went to Plato's Retreat [a defunct New York sex club], which was *so* awful. We said: *We've gotta do this! Are we cultural reporters or ain't we? Let's go!* So we went into the mat room, and there were all these sweaty, greasy people with *pimples* — it was totally anti-erotic, it was just a crock. Jon couldn't get it up, and I can't blame him. There was *scum* on the water in the *hot* tub!'

Her novels are also studded with robotic sapphic episodes. When asked for the most interesting feature of lesbian sex, Jong explodes in a sexual laugh, a laugh which transforms her, a laugh which renders her deliriously attractive, an attractiveness which evaporates with her reply. *'No COCK!'* she neighs, looking very pleased with herself.

It is precisely this kind of shallow and vulgar comment that has denied her the respectable reputation she sometimes seems to crave. *Fear of Fifty* is the first book in which she has depicted a lover (in this case, her most recent husband Ken Burrows) as something more than a set of genitals to be appraised and categorised. 'At a certain point,' she muses, sipping her tea, 'romantic satyr-type men began to seem so *repetitive* to me. There came a point where I couldn't even feel sexually attracted to them.' Suddenly engaged, she nods. 'There was always the *incipient* attraction, but I could see what was on the other side of it. I came to see that I was going to wind up — *yet again* — with someone who was,' and here she adopts a bored sing-song, '*wonderful* in bed, who was *lying* to the woman he lived with, and I was in some way *implicated* in the lying, and I'm not a liar, and I don't *enjoy* lying, and it just became *dreary*, because I had *changed*.'

She kicks off her black leather pumps and with a flourish of thighs, brings her feet up on the sofa. 'Maybe I was able to find a man like Ken because I was able to *believe* in him — to *believe* in his possible existence, whereas I wasn't before.' Burrows, a wealthy lawyer and amateur pilot, provides Jong with a support many say has steadied her. 'People ask me,' she says, widening her eyes, 'why I wrote about [his impotence] early in our relationship, but that was part of the *story*. Because men are vulnerable, too. Nobody is Superman or Superwoman. And I was *forever* running away from him and finding reasons to get on a plane. Um, so we were both running away from the relationship as much as we were running *towards* it.'

Her heroines have always been vulnerable artists who are deceived and hurt by ruthless and impressively-endowed brutes, and yet implicit in all her narratives is a clinical judgment which reduces her male characters to emotionally inert objects. 'I think I had a very deep *contempt* for men,' she admits for what perhaps is the first time, 'a deep *condescension*. You know, southern women are deeply sexist. They condescend to men by acting as though they're little boys. And I think I had it. I batted my eyelashes at men. I connected on one level, but on another level, I could never connect because I thought of them as *children*.' She removes the demented-scientist glasses to reveal extraordinarily arresting eyes. 'I thought — well, you need them in bed because they've got the *cock*, but they're not really human. I thought I could do everything — that I could have babies, I could write books, I could make money, I could take care of myself ... what did I need *them* for? I was really, *deeply*, a female chauvinist.'

The doorbell rings, and she leaps up to answer it. The publicist explains that the only time the doctor can see her is after 5.30 pm, and that she is due to speak at Sydney University at 6 pm. Jong questions him and bristles ('I don't *talk* for twenty-five minutes — I *perform*. You *have* to understand that I do what I *do*, right? If you want to sell any books — which is probably your *wish* here ...' et cetera). When she has finished, she returns to the sofa and, irritated, sips some more tea. 'Writers *are* hysterical,' she says, shrugging. 'I mean, you make yourself into a skinless membrane — which is an oxymoron — and then you go out into the world, and there's no protection between you and what you experience. So naturally, you experience everything very, very intensely.' She stops to cough. 'As a writer,' she concludes, 'the better you are at what you do, the more unfit you are for life.'

Elle, 1995

THE GETTING OF WISDOM:

MARK MATOUSEK

THERE IS A sweetness to the man. The response to *Sex, Death, Enlightenment*, the book which has established him as an archetype of the late twentieth century, has touched him; he joyously smiles — American teeth, eloquent leaf-coloured eyes — when discussing its impact around the world. A woman in Alaska, he says, wrote to thank him for writing the first account of a spiritual journey that did not make her physically sick. Those who have flocked to his readings are effusive in their praise of his self-deprecating honesty. The gay communities of the United States, Britain and America have embraced him. His publicist can't get enough of him. Even the expressionlessly courteous waiter in this, a private room (tapestried banquettes, discreet lighting) on the ground floor of Sydney's Sebel Townhouse, is charmed by his extravagant gestures and unforced compassion.

Now forty, Mark Matousek photographs like a Moroccan bruiser moonlighting as an existentialist, but in the flesh is handsome and his nimble movements impart the illusion of slightness. Dressed in cream and white that seems whiter against the butterscotch of his skin, he orders coffee and waves his hands as he exasperatedly recounts trying experiences with journalists. 'They ask me how I can believe that pain is a good thing!' he exclaims, rolling his eyes. 'I think that pain is a good insofar that it offers opportunities for change. If you *accept* it, pain is grace — a savage grace, but grace nonetheless.'

Matousek was diagnosed as HIV-positive in 1989. In his case, terminal illness was more than a metaphor; it allowed him to feel human for the first time in his life. A senior editor at Andy Warhol's *Interview*, he had transcended the relative poverty of a dysfunctional single-parent home in California for bacchanalian promiscuity, drug and alcohol abuse, seventy-hour working weeks, and daily interaction with the international leaders of every field — financial, social, artistic, athletic and intellectual. 'Bumping into Grace Jones coming out of the can,' he writes in the first chapter, 'did give me a feeling that I was becoming famous too.'

Glittering high-level nihilism was the religion of the eighties and Matousek was an avid acolyte. 'Warhol,' he remarks, glancing at the waiter as he places the silver tray on the table, 'is a perfect example of the way in which we have come to mock the sublime. I think Andy articulated and consolidated what was already there — he saw the lowest common denominator and cashed in on it. People want their moment in the sun, and Andy was a kind of revolving spotlight; if you stood close to him long enough, the spotlight would come to you.' His smile is almost apologetic. 'He was in the middle of that whole explosion of drugs and partying. Also, Andy was compulsively attracted to beautiful people, young people, rich people ... *lost* people ... and they became his groupies.'

Warhol embodied the spiritual vacuity of our civilisation to Matousek, who recalls the artist as emotionally frigid and exploitative, materialistic and pathologically detached. Their association began with a handshake ('[His hand was] strangely mushy — like boiled chicken'), and ignominiously ended when Warhol ordered an assistant to escort Matousek from the premises to ensure that he didn't 'steal' anything. 'Andy was the grand vizier of meaninglessness,' he explains, 'and the appeal of meaninglessness to lost people is only a sense of confirmation of what they have always suspected, which is this kind of nihilistic vision of the world — and not only does it confirm it, but it *celebrates* it.' Here he leans forward, his eyes torched. 'I mean, fame is the greatest illusion of all! It doesn't exist! A friend of mine says that fame is what other people *think* of your life.'

Matousek documents his paradigm shift with humorous severity: the celebrity which he had imagined to be his goal was, in fact, no more than the starting point of his quest for wisdom. Exposure to 'stars' such as Jean-Michel Basquiat ('At heart, just a street kid [who] was always around the office smoking pot'), Shirley Maclaine ('I wrote something she didn't like and she got on the phone and *screamed*'), Annie Lennox ('An *alien* creature'), and John Travolta ('A *wonderful* human being ... Richard Gere has a career because of the movies John turned down'), contributed to his understanding of the limitations of material success.

'I've seen people *ruin* themselves when they get too famous,' he says, raising his brows. 'Fame acts as a magnifying glass to human flaws. Insecure people get *pathologically* insecure. Mickey Rourke was a great example. I mean, my first lover picked Mickey up when he was a bouncer at a New York Club and saw his potential. Mickey has real talent as an actor but he has this very violent side, added to which were well-documented drug and drink problems. And as he became more famous, he started to take advantage of people and just got *crazier*.'

It was when he realised that American success had all the symptoms of a nervous breakdown that he began to take stock of his capacities, beliefs, and dreams. Matousek did not crave an escape from the twentieth century, but a redefinition of his place in it. The panic attacks and depression had been a feature of his life for too many years. 'People are *starving* for transcendence!' he cries as he thumps back into his chair. 'People are *starving* for a sense of unity! And if there's a pill you can pop, well — it's a lot easier than sitting around on a meditation cushion.'

His own experiences of excess brought him to the conclusion that neurotic behaviour was only a manifestation of spiritual deprivation. 'I mean,' he says, 'the number one drug here is ecstasy. Think about it. It's not *accidental* that they call MDMA — which is just a kind of amphetamine — ecstasy. And similarly, for people who have no spiritual inclinations, sex is the *door* — it is the *peak* experience, their one means of transcendence. The one thing we haven't been able to solve is that magical thing that happens between two bodies. *That* is the essence of the metaphysical. Sex is beyond rationality, which is why some people become addicted to it; it is the only place they can go where they are out of themselves, where they can experience that kind of true ecstasy.'

In this respect, Matousek was representative of his generation: sexual ecstasy was the only ecstasy he had ever known. His Jewish Bronx-raised mother, 'Ida the Tits', who welcomed the lung cancer which killed her in 1994, perceived herself in terms of sexual function and nothing more. This philosophy — transhistorically that of the sexually abused — was, in turn, passed on to her son. It is in writing of his later pilgrimage to India and of his mother that Matousek displays his prose skills at their finest: 'Six mornings a week, I opened my eyes half-expecting Ida to be dead. I'd wake up in hot, piss-soaked sheets and look over to her bed in the dark, where she lay smoking a cigarette. I'd fix my eyes on the ash, and when it changed colour as she inhaled, glowing orange to yellow-white, I knew that she was still breathing.'

Conceived in 'that hour of fabulous lust' when his compulsively promiscuous mother seduced the plumber who would later marry and then leave her, Matousek was raised in an atmosphere of despair, violence, rage, lasciviousness, and neglect. He never again heard from his father after he left. At the age of fifteen, his older sister, Joyce, was delivered of a baby who soon died. His eldest sister, Marcia, was committed to a mental hospital after an unsuccessful marriage and, after she had been released on their mother's insistence, committed suicide. For his part, the twelve-year-old Matousek was unwittingly introduced by Joyce to 'Harold', a notorious paedophile.

He pauses to deeply inhale. 'Harold had a ring of boy-prostitutes, and he used to film amateur video-porno stuff,' he eventually says. 'I never did anything on film and never actually hustled there, but I was a pretty boy and he wanted pretty boys around.' An absence of bitterness characterises his recollections. 'As far as I'm concerned, Harold should be in jail. I mean, I couldn't stand him *then* — but there were drugs, there were other little boys. I was looking for my peers. You have to understand, this was just *recreation* to me. I wasn't trying to get ahead in the world — it was, like: *what do I do this afternoon?* Part of my motivation was getting away from Ida. So anything that got me out of the house was, you know, *okay*.'

The dehumanisation, he reasoned, was 'better than nothing'. However obscene the attention, it was still a form of attention over which he exercised some measure of control. One of his most chilling memories is the evening he was picked up on the Santa Monica Boulevard by a crowd of 'tennis-playing rich kids' and driven to a party which featured — as its entertainment — a double-jointed cocaine-addicted septuagenarian. For the first time during the interview, he shifts awkwardly in his chair and the rhythm of his breathing changes. 'We were all doing liquid LSD,' he says, quickly sipping his coffee, 'and then Daisy appeared — naked, with her ankles around her neck, and with this guy holding her up. I mean, this guy —' he sharply laughs, shocked — 'this guy was walking around the *room* with her! Naked! Spread-*eagled*! I mean, she was an *old* lady! It was bizarre! Here were these well-to-do Palm Springs rich kids and this old, bony, naked woman with her vagina visible, and this guy would come and *stick* her vagina in everyone's face! It was just —' covering his eyes, he shudders — 'it was just like *Satyricon*. And she was *laughing*, stoned out of her mind. People are *twisted* — I mean, you gotta know this.'

He believes that as a culture, we have lost our sense of sacredness, and that the 'strong transcendent tradition of the founding fathers' has been dismissed in favour of what is speciously known as 'originality'. And so in 1986, when the English poet, Alexander Maxwell, asked him to accompany him on a trip to India, Matousek accepted. Essentially, he wanted to discover or recover his sense of wonder. 'People in the west are absolutely *terrified* of spirituality,' he says. 'We are taught that human intelligence is the be-all and end-all of experience and the suggestion that there may be something greater is terrifying. It makes us feel out of control. But you can only get so far with the intellectual faculty. To get beyond it, you have to stop thinking and start *feeling*.'

On their arrival in Paris, Maxwell informed him that they would be stopping in Germany en route to India to visit a woman he would not name. The woman was Mother Meera, the psychic spiritual leader to whom *Sex, Death, Enlightenment* is dedicated. At this point, Matousek was unaware of his HIV status; he knew only that his spirit needed healing, and Mother Meera was his first experience of human serenity. On the afternoon of his departure for India, Matousek lay his head on the pillow upon which Mother Meera rested her feet and implored the empty room: 'Please, if you have any power at all, help me change.'

India (which he lyrically describes as smelling of 'barbecued bones and flowers') permanently altered his perception. Matousek was never again able to return to his regime of self-destruction. In the book he documents his first disastrous attempt to engage in loveless sex following eight months of celibacy. After 'fervid squirming and apologies', he listened as the boy beside him said: 'You know, you're different ... you used to be hotter. But I like you more now.' Matousek likens the softening of his heart to a callus dissolving, and writes of the new experience of walking through the streets of New York City without 'wanting to fuck' the beautiful men and women who surrounded him. The predatory instinct which had enabled his survival was no longer necessary.

It was at this time that he felt able to deal with the results of the blood test he had been avoiding. 'The terror,' he writes, 'brought on by the knowledge of the virus circulating in my bloodstream, came in waves.' His attempts to 'purify his system' are faithfully reported. During Sunday meditation sessions at a Zen monastery, he sat 'miserably staring at a wall while a bald nun walked around whacking people on the shoulder blades'. He enrolled in a nine-day silent *vissipana*, about which he writes: 'Sitting perfectly still on a hard cushion in a cold room for fourteen hours a day might be the path to one's true nature … but after several days … I wasn't sure I wanted to find mine.' He attended the Radiant Light Ministry in San Francisco, ate cabbage soup under a photograph of a master yogi clutching his own intestines at a yoga retreat, paid to partake in a *kundalini* initiation, isolated himself for two summers in a cabin in the woods ('I would be forced to settle down and see in the Zen way … what I saw, in actuality, was that I was going berserk') and attended meetings of Love and Sex Addicts Anonymous. The only real answers he found were through volunteer work at a hospital, where he was confronted by the prosaic nature of death.

'When you really address how little time we have and how *precious* it is,' he tenderly says, '*everything* changes. Most people live with this illusion of immortality, which creates toughness instead of the vulnerability that comes of realising how fragile everything is. If I look at you as a dying person, I see you through very, very different eyes. Mortality can, I think, increase love and feeling for other people and for yourself.' Awareness of his own mortality forced Matousek to face a fear of truly feeling. 'There are very few times in your life when you're looking at the truth, *naked*. Death is one of those times. When you become aware that you are going to die, you are really saying — this is *me*; this is *me* dying. It shakes you up and also, in a strange way, brings you to life. There is something *exhilarating* about death. It forces you to rise.'

Finishing his cup of coffee, he looks up. 'I feel sorry for the boy I used to be,' he murmurs. 'Were he in front of me, I would tell him that it's going to change. I never thought it would, you see.' His pause is textured. 'Like all children, I was a magical kid. My mother always told me that I was a bastard like my father and as a consequence, I lost belief in myself as a loving person. I am a loving person. I was innocent and never knew it, because I always thought I was a freak.' His voice thickens. 'And,' he quietly continues through tears he wipes from his eyes with nervous hands, 'more importantly, I would tell that boy that it wasn't his *fault*.'

Whatever it takes to break a human heart and rouse the spirit is, Mark Matousek believes, real grace.

HQ, 1997

CAESAR'S PALACE:

COLLEEN MCCULLOUGH

WHEN COLLEEN MCCULLOUGH loves, it is with ferocity and tenacity and tenderness, a profoundly moving tenderness. The wounds she has inevitably suffered are concealed; she protects herself with stoicism. Nevertheless, her passion is evident in her will, in her devotion to her writing, her scholarship, her remarkable marriage. These appetites — sexual, emotional, intellectual — are prodigious; her opinions are informed with the same intensity. The garrulous persona behind which she hides allows her time to evaluate people and situations. Her cries of 'Awwwwwww — *shit!*' and Liberty-print sack-suits, her one-of-the-boys thigh-slapping and seismic laugh, her barroom humour and canine relentlessness defend a rare sensitivity and acuity of perception. Now fifty-eight, Colleen McCullough is and has always been a heroine in the great Romantic tradition, a heroine initially impeded by a carnivorous intellect and hard life, her public behaviour governed by a body her father told her was 'ugly' and destined her for work as 'a manual hand in a laundry'.

The 8000 square feet of whitewashed house she shares with her husband on Norfolk Island are as eclectic as their chatelaine. Within: Brobdingagian leopardskin-print armchairs, imitation Tiffany lamps, framed astrological charts, geological specimens, a Magritte, flying pig mobiles, a commercial cappuccino machine, scarlet heart-shaped soaps in a truly nightmarish black-and-gold bathroom, mirrored tiles, exquisite gilt-edged Hutschen Reuther tableware, 'probably' the largest privately-owned library on the Roman Republic in the world, marble floors and stained glass bow windows. She talks literature, medicine, history, politics, art, the occult, local gossip. She cooks, paints and designs. She and her husband, Ric Robinson, play one thousand games of Scrabble every year. Thirteen years her junior, he tells people that of his three children, she is the youngest. McCullough may be a rainbow unto herself, but she has suffered for her liberty.

'In all her life,' she wrote in *The Thorn Birds*, 'Justine seemed only to have loved Dane. No one else, even herself.' The character of Dane, McCullough admits, was based on her brother, Carl, who was discovered dead at the age of twenty-five after saving two women from drowning off the coast of Crete. Thirty years later, she still weeps at his mention. Seated amongst the feathery greenery and opaque glass windchimes of the 'patio'. — a room opened to the lush ocean-scented afternoon, she is immobile, her tears slowly dropping onto her crumpled hands. 'I don't think I have very many fears,' she says after a long pause. 'When my brother died, I realised that I'd gone through the worst thing that could ever have happened to me. I lost my *fear*. Of everything. I went through hell. There is *nothing* else in my life — and that even includes Ric — that could be worse; in its own way, it was the most amazing emancipation.'

Like a child, she wipes the tears from her cheeks with the backs of her hands. 'Carl was my anchor, you see,' she says. 'He was my *only* anchor. And so losing him was to be cast adrift. It was the kind of security I suppose I have with Ric, but it was *blood*. My immediate response was to put myself on Librium, which was a life *saver*.' As her father refused to pay the $8000 required to fly her brother's body home, it was, for eight years, lost. McCullough has never visited the gravesite. An obsessive writer since childhood, she was unable to 'write a word' for seven years. 'But it was *ten* years,' she explains as she lights one of the eighty or so low-tar cigarettes she smokes a day, 'before I looked at men again and even then, I wound up in two fruitless relationships. One was with a surgeon, the other with a chap who later suicided. I suffered *terribly*, and expressed it through writing.'

McCullough's prose is accessible, charged with feeling, and inspires in her fans a strange fanaticism. *The Thorn Birds* sold over eleven million copies and her novels — the newly released *Caesar's Women* brings the tally to nine — earn their stellar advances in pre-publication orders alone. *Business Review Weekly* estimates her earnings 'from the rights, screenplays and sales associated with fiction writing' to be between $20 and $35 million, although McCullough (derisively) cackles when quoted such figures. Money has never been her god. She refused $10 million to write *Son of Thorn Birds* because the themes no longer interested her. 'I need variety to stop myself getting into a rut,' she says, gesturing with her cigarette. 'If you start getting bored with what you're doing as a writer, you lose it. You lose the magic.'

The proud author of what sniffy critics have dismissed as 'low brow' fiction, she has never perceived herself as belonging to the international literary network. 'It seems to me,' and here she pauses to smile, 'that of all the other [successful novelists] who surrounded me at the time of *The Thorn Birds*, I was the only one to emerge unscathed. Fame makes people go batty.' She ripples with laughter as she recalls meeting Germaine Greer ('Germs') at the Frankfurt Book Fair: 'She had posters of her genitalia plastered up all over the place!' And the notoriously egocentric Erica Jong — 'a right bitch' — was equally memorable. 'She sent me a message that she wanted to see me,' McCullough says with a comic grimace. 'When I went, she cut me dead. I think she just wanted to cut me dead in a restaurant full of people. I was left standing there like an idiot. Ric was furious.'

She believes that detachment from the process of fame and dedication to her craft 'saved her bacon'. McCullough has never been given to star turns or networking. Glamour only makes her laugh. There are times she works three days at a stretch, only to then collapse for eighteen hours. She produces up to 20,000 words a day. The first two drafts of Caesar's Women (696 pages) were written in six weeks. Each of her novels is drafted five to ten times. Her limitations are, she feels, transcended through her work. 'I have never been somebody who shows pain readily, no!' The intensity of her statement almost surprises her, and she leans forward. 'Absolutely not! Books and writing have always been my escape and so I evince pain, if you like, simply in escape. I never feel consciously sad because I am busy, always. To this day, I remain too busy to think about myself, and that is my technique.'

One of her favourite sayings is that her 'idea of hell is forty seconds on a lounge by the pool with a daiquiri'. 'The mind,' she says as she stubs her cigarette out into an ashtray, 'has to be occupied, all the time. Otherwise, I guess I'd go *crazy*.'

She was conferred with a Degree of Doctor of Letters (Honoris Causa) at Macquarie University, where she is a board member of the Foundation of the Study of Ancient Cultures. She is a Consultant Emeritus in clinical neurophysiology at Sydney's Royal North Shore Hospital, an honorary founding governor at the Prince of Wales Medical Research Institute, a patron of the Geronotology Foundation of Australia, the Monash Medical Centre Literary Program, and the Continence Foundation of Australia. Of the latter, she evenly says: 'What people don't understand is that the two worst side effects of menopause are that you cease to sleep and that you have bladder urgency. I believe in getting up on television and saying — *yeah, I gotta wear a pad 'cause I dribble!*' The pragmatism with which she approaches her 'physical disabilities' — hypothyroidism, glaucoma, osteoporosis and diabetes — evolved in her peripatetic childhood.

Before her mother settled in Sydney when McCullough was twelve, the family 'moved about from one rural district to another ... the wheat ... and sheep country of New South Wales, the sugar country of far north Queensland'. An unusually gifted child, McCullough was given the opportunity to excel at Sydney's Holy Cross College but never praised. 'I always just wanted to be famous,' she comments, sinking her chin into her hands. 'I wanted some *acknowledge*ment. *Abs*olutely. I never had it, on any level. Even when I excelled academically, there was no appreciation. No. Funny, that. Very odd.' She inclines her head. 'I was born into a family of jockstraps, you see. They adulated sports and seemed to forget that the country is in *despe*rate need of intellectuals.' Suddenly sitting up, she enthuses: 'I've always *liked* the world of academics! Hey — they can talk Schopenhauer! They can talk *obscure* medieval philosophers! They've been there, done that, read everything … their minds are just *open* and *groping* for everything and I *love* that!'

Her interests and abilities were not shared by her early peers. 'I was never very popular at school,' she says. 'I always equated popularity with *dimples*. I always thought that they would be the most *wonder*ful things to have — dimples and black patent-leather shoes. With bows on them.' McCullough remembers herself as a leader, deliberate in her thinking, a loner. 'I suppose,' she says as she lights another cigarette, 'that having produced a girl as a first child, my mother wanted a cute gorgeous little thing that would be feminine and da-de-da, and I *wasn't*. I was *not* a happy child, mostly because life seemed to be an endless procession to doctors to see if they could do something with my weight.'

There was a marked withholding of love in the family, a withholding McCullough learned to accept. 'I didn't feel *loved* by my mother,' she says as she exhales smoke, her elbows firmly on the tabletop. 'I knew she loved me on a primitive plane — that tigress kind of thing — but there was no real under*standing*.' With humorous sarcasm, she says: 'I don't *like* her. She never *let* me like her. A friend of mine said that she feels intensely sorry for children who are smarter than their parents. That was the story of my childhood, you might say. There was nobody except my brother who was proud of me.'

McCullough's father, a 'terribly attractive' Irishman who took work where he could find it, tormented his two children with his indifference. It was only after his death that McCullough discovered he had various other wives around the country. 'My father was a peripheral figure,' she explains as she smokes. 'He wasn't *there* and when he was there, it was just *rows* … not with Carl and me, he never noticed *us* — but with Mother. They were,' she wryly continues, 'determined to *kill* each other. There was no physical violence, just verbal. Very *fierce* verbal. *Always*. Carl and I just used to cling together and hide. It was miserable. Just misery.' A cup of coffee is brought in by her assistant and she cradles it as she speaks. 'I thought of marriage as something *abominable*. Artificial. Unnatural.' She finishes her cigarette, sips her coffee, smiles.

Consistent early disparagement about her appearance had liberated her from 'traditional female fantasies', but it was not until she enrolled at Sydney University that she realised she was attractive to men. 'Discovering this pulled me out of that frame of self-hate that a lot of fat women have for themselves,' she says. 'Nevertheless, I proceeded to do to men what men traditionally do to women: I used them and threw them aside. Before Ric, writing simply engaged my *affections* a great deal more. It gave me a *return*; I never really got returns out of men. Mostly because I wouldn't let them, you see. I just couldn't be bothered with them. If they had existed on a more personal plane in my life, I would then have had to deviate from my chosen course and I wasn't about to do that.'

Although she was studying to be 'a great doctor and medical scientist', her 'chosen course' was her writing. Deeply amused, she sets her coffee cup on the table. 'A friend told me that she had never seen anyone so cold-bloodedly lose their virginity,' she says. 'I just decided that it was going to happen because if I wanted to write novels, I would have to understand that aspect of life. I could no longer remain a virgin. I was twenty-one. There was a chap who had been putting the hard word on me for ages and I just said: *okay*.' Her smile cracks into laughter.

'My heart was not engaged at all, not at all. There was a myth that it only hurts once. That *certainly* was not true for me. Because of my glandular problems, I didn't produce lubricating juices.'

Financial difficulties made it impossible for McCullough to continue at Sydney, and she completed her BSc at the University of New South Wales at night whilst working days in the field of neurophysiology. She then left for London, where she worked at the Great Ormond Street Hospital for Sick Children, finished an MSc at the Institute of Child Health at London University, and was asked to join the Department of Neurology at the Yale School of Internal Medicine. Both *Tim* (the first novel she wrote after her brother's death) and *The Thorn Birds* were written at Yale. Whilst her colleagues slept, McCullough was up chain-smoking and invoking the heat and dust of rural Australia, oblivious to the past and future and intrigued only by her present. Years later and to escape her renown, she moved to Norfolk with the same desire for silence, exile, cunning. The last thing she expected to find was love.

Her new suitors courted her with bananas and parcels of fish. McCullough chuckles so violently that she half-chokes on her coffee. 'Fish is very *precious* here, you see,' she says, patting her lips with a napkin. 'Most of it is immediately sold to restaurants. So I'd come home and find parcels of fish in the front seat of my car or wretchedly enormous bunches of bananas by my door. There is,' she drily adds, 'a limit to the bananas one can eat.' When Ric Robinson, a planter who was odd-jobbing as he waited for his Kentia Palm crop to mature, arrived to paint her house, McCullough told a friend that she had met 'the only attractive man on the island'. 'It wasn't love at first sight,' she says, 'but I *felt* something.' Robinson was then still married to his first wife (by whom he has a son and daughter), and it was not until she left him that his relationship with McCullough developed. 'He began to drink,' she says with compassion, 'and we got to know each other. From that moment on, it just *went*.'

The response of the media to their 1984 marriage was coruscating. Time and again, McCullough was asked why she thought Robinson had married her, whether she questioned his motives, whether she wondered of his fidelity. Such questions would never have been asked of a slim and stupid woman and at one point, McCullough poignantly asked a journalist: 'Don't I have more to offer than *money*?' 'Everybody,' she sighs, 'says that Ric married me for my money and that I married him for his dick. It's so trite. Some thought I should have married Lord Muck of Dunghill Hall or some sort of ersatz Keating. I should not have married this wonderful, ordinary, *terrific* bloke that I saw the potential in and nobody else had, *ever*.'

Robinson — a tall, broad-shouldered, intelligent and powerfully emotional man — is protective of his wife and their privacy, and has always refused to be interviewed. McCullough still finds it difficult to control her excitement when she speaks of him. Almost bounding in her chair, she begins to gesture, her black eyes lit. 'Ric is the only man I've ever met who is completely secure in his masculinity,' she breathlessly says, 'and I'm still hopelessly in love with him. I saw in him the most wonderful security and sense of completion. I think real love is very much a thing of tremendous friendship and the fact that you've found the person with whom you can stand back-to-back and fight off the whole world — what the Ancient Greeks called a "shield companion".'

On a stand a few feet behind her is the reproduction of the Vatican bust of Julius Caesar she ordered from an advertisement in *Architectural Digest*. The extreme resemblance between the bust and her husband is energetically denied by McCullough. 'Not at all!' she cries. 'And I try very carefully not to borrow events from our marriage for my fiction. I *really* make an effort, because it would *insult* him.' Whilst she may not directly mine her marriage for her fiction, there are still echoes. *Caesar's Women* has as its axis the compulsive sexual relationship between Julius Caesar and Brutus' mother, Servilia, who tells him: 'Before you, all other men were *insulsus* [tasteless]. And after you, all other men are *insulsus*.'

Which is — as are a number of statements in the book — what McCullough has always said of her husband.

Depicting passion has never been difficult. The critics have been the problem. One wrote: 'Although she is setting out her monumental vision of Ancient Rome, McCullough's language tends to undermine the *dignitas* of fortune's favourites ... we therefore have Caesar slopping around in backless clogs saying "Hello, dad!". Pompey the Great saying "Bye-bye!" and "Last one in's a rotten egg!" and ... Queen Oradaltis is made to say ... "Diddums!" ' McCullough pauses to sip her coffee. 'I try to avoid anachronisms,' she explains. 'I excuse myself "electrifying" because the ancient Greeks knew that if you rubbed amber with fur you would create electricity. Their language, as it existed, was very explicit and crisp. So all I've done is couch their conversation in modern language. I can't *stand* these novels where I *thinkest this* and I *thinkest that* ... awwwwwwww, *shit!*' Her laughter rings throughout the room. 'And the Romans were not mealy-mouthed at *all!* I've never forgotten the time that I first found that wonderful witticism of Cicero's about Cato.' She gently gestures to illustrate her words. 'They're in the Senate and Cicero whispers to his neighbour: *Oh, Cato! You'd think he lived in Plato's republic rather than Romulus' sink!* And the alarm bells started to ring. So I looked at the Latin text. And that was *not* what he said. What he said was Romulus' *shit*-heap.'

The tortuous, legalistic, litigious, quarrelsome and destructive nature of Ancient Rome fascinates McCullough, who never loses an opportunity to dream. 'I think the *visual* — movies, videos — gives people a world they cannot interpret for themselves,' she states, 'and that's why I have the thought of the book dying. I speak of the inner eye, of the imagination. People should be encouraged to *read*. I think the emphasis upon the visual is part of the depersonalising of the individual, which is the great crime of egalitarianism.' She believes that the purpose of egalitarianism is 'to level everybody down to the *same* exact common denominator: homogenisation'. 'It's *awful!*' she insists. 'And you see it so much! These days people all want to be the *same*. To me the great beauty — and I gave an address at Macquarie University on this — is *dif*ference.'

Colleen McCullough has never known what it is not to be true to herself. Understanding this and over the opaque music of glass windchimes, she laughs. She lights another cigarette, sits back in her leopardskin chair, and laughs.

Elle, 1996

THE KITCHENS
OF MADISON COUNTY

THERE WALK AMONGST us the deluded few who, after
ingesting the serotonin re-uptake inhibitors that dull awareness of
their excised minds, keen and pine for a novel to rival the ball-
breaking banality of *The Bridges of Madison County*. Said
individuals will exult as they welcome *Necessary Madness*, the
wee and 'brilliantly perceptive' tale of Gloria, a thirty-year-old
American who loses her English husband, Bill, to leukaemia after
a 'scant eight years of marriage' and is left alone to raise their son,
Curran. The rest of us will have to settle for responding with
intestinal cramps followed by discreet regurgitation.

The fact that this novel is set in England, a country our
seventeen-year-old author, Jenn Crowell, had never visited, is,

we are told, 'astonishing' as she captures London 'perfectly'. Given that her descriptions of the city amount to a few vague adjectives applied to its climate, this 'perfection' appears to be what is known as 'hyperbole'. Crowell is also howlingly ignorant of the colloquialisms appropriate to the socio-economic status of her characters. Englishness, to her, entails prefacing every statement with 'love', the description of unusual behaviour as 'barmy', and the consumption of curry whenever one is not drinking 'ale' in a pub. Witness sensitive artist-martyr Bill's mating-call to the dislocated Gloria: 'Come over for dinner. It's a grotty madhouse, but one of my mates makes a dead good boil-in-the-bag curry.'

Now: the sort of Englishman who uses the expression 'dead good' would rather hammer hat-pins through his eyeballs than invite a woman 'over for dinner'; 'dead good' Englishmen ask their birds 'round for tea'. Equally, an Englishman would never preface 'madhouse' with 'grotty', for that would be, as every Englishman knows, over-egging the custard. And then there is the 'boil-in-the-bag curry' conundrum to consider. Those of a British persuasion who consume 'boil-in-the-bag curry' do not have 'mates'; 'mates' are that which sweating Australian thugs furiously fondle on mud-rich rugby pitches. 'Boil-in-the-bag curry' Englishmen are 'lads' and 'lads' are not Islington-dwelling artistes who bestow titles such as *Necessary Madness* upon their works. 'Lads' sneer at art, shag slappers, watch the football, indulge in bevvies down the pub and never, but *never*, open conversations with the word 'say' (as our Bill does on page 81).

Such churlish pedantry aside, one must consider Crowell's handling of Big Chief Universal Themes. It can be said that when a thirty-year-old woman, Pennsylvanian or otherwise, loses the man she deliriously loves, her thoughts are not — as they are for most of this novel — with her parents. To the bereaved, the world serves only as a reminder of their loss, whereas to Gloria, her loss serves only as a reminder of the world. Crowell is too immature to understand such differentiation. Poor old boil-in-the-bag-Bill is no more than a wooden prop dragged out to steady Gloria's feverish reminiscences about her adolescence and those nutty, nutty folks back home.

The one truly astonishing aspect of this book is not the author's age and nor is it the many, many thousands for which the rights were sold. None but a careful reading will betray the bizarre truth: Crowell's stomach is the narrator. The desire that straddles her Ethiopian narrative is not for Bill to burst forth like Lazarus, for a better publicity campaign, or for innocence restored — Crowell's yearning is for *food*. Peanut butter and jelly sandwiches, say. An obscene hot dog. Pecan Pie. Brownies fragrant from the oven. Baked Alaska. Venison fresh from them there woods.

Consider, then, the damning evidence.

The book opens. Curran (Currant?) discerns 'the hunger' in his mother at his father's funeral. Gloria is then beseeched to 'come up to lunch'. Guts gurgling, she recalls that her parents would 'stare at their plates, scrape the last bites of food into their mouths, [and] gulp water'. On page 15, she smacks her chops as she imagines 'the hungry hour of my conception'. Her mother's stomach is understood by her as an 'empty bowl', her father's heart as a 'pomegranate cave'. 'A clinging hunger' drives her on page 45; she then admits that 'grief is essentially hunger'. Her father, ostensibly a fellow weight-watcher, gazes at her with 'sad, pitiable hunger'. She tells of having felt like the sum of her 'stark hunger', of being 'bones when the universe demanded flesh'. Page 93 has her confessing that she hadn't realised 'how hungry' she had been. Curran-the-Currant then nervously warns her: 'You're getting dead skinny, Mum. You should eat more.'

When she travels to Angel on the tube, the Northern Line graffiti reminds Gloria 'of … my kitchen'. (Another error. Anyone living in Islington's Theberton Street would catch the Victoria Line to Highbury and Islington station, not the Northern Line to Angel.) Having never read *Fat Is A Feminist Issue*, she decides on page 100 that being 'complicated meant … full of bad hunger'. The transference is completed by her assumption that she can *feel* another's 'hunger'. By page 161, her grip on reality slipping, she is 'driven by desperate hunger'. She wanders the streets, a woman crazed: 'As I passed … kitchen-gadget stores … I thought, oh, God.' Her new suitor is then informed by her that she 'married the last man who was in the kitchen with me'. He is perturbed, but not enough. 'I imagine a million couples,' she continues, 'eating tandoori … and I seethe.' Appropriately enough, she is then encouraged to 'forget the bleeding kitchen'. But does she listen? Does she hell. 'Winter is coming,' her stomach insists, 'and we will have to gorge ourselves now before the famine.'

So much for mourning. A mere four months into the 'madness' of her heartfelt grief (read: diet), she not only gets it on with her husband's persistent and equally-bereaved colleague but neatly patches the troubled relationship with her shrewish mother, whom she is moved to thank: 'For vegetable soup. For trying.' (Crowell's characters would forgive Hitler for a plate of well-poached eggs.) 'We ate in silence,' she concludes with a full mouth, 'crossing a border together into a room where the end was only the beginning.'

The bucket, please.

The Australian, 1997

TIGER, TIGER BURNING BRIGHT: TRENT NATHAN

AT THE AGE of fifty-four, Trent Nathan is still commandingly beautiful. His hands are weathered and his figure has lost the elasticity of youth, but his face is a source of energy in itself — powerfully shaped by broad cheekbones, a Persian mouth, and great green orbs which invariably dictate the tone of his conversations. These eyes of his range in expression from an almost predatory alertness to real tenderness. They are sleepy in reflection, but when the topic of his fashion empire arises, they flash dangerously, immediately dominate. His beauty is, above all, that of strength, and it has been both a blessing and the greatest alienating factor of his life.

'Has my beauty given me all this?' he asks wonderingly, gesturing as he walks through his immaculate Sydney warehouse. 'Has it given me all *this*? What has it done for me? It has opened every *door*! Whatever country I'm in, whatever shop I've walked into, whichever restaurant, whatever plane, wherever I go …' Reaching his small, stark, whitewashed office, he pauses to close the door behind himself. 'In my youth,' he says, 'my physical beauty made me feel alone. I have a photograph of myself in Cubs — the rest of them are on one side of the picture, and there I was: *by myself*. I would be *distant*.' He gracefully sits down in one of his two director's chairs, his back to the clouded afternoon. 'But do I really *attract* anybody? My telephone has nevah rung hot with invitations. *Nev-ah!* Mr Popular? No no no no *no*! My youngest nephew tells me that I *frighten* people. He tells me that they're *petrified* of me. I look at pictures of myself when I was young and think: *God, I was a good-looking young man!*' He pauses, arches one dramatically sculpted brow. 'I knew I was different, but I never *felt* beautiful. I've been in solitude since I was nineteen years of age, which is when my business first hit jackpot.'

With the exception of two early liquidations, Nathan's business has been hitting 'jackpot' for thirty-five years. His label has become synonymous with understated elegance, his private life with outrage. 'The drugs were interfering with his life,' comments his friend and mentor Robert Chu, a practitioner of Chinese soft tissue massage and Chi manipulation. 'He was a very social person — he drank a lot and took a lot of drugs, like many people under stress. His life was not what he wanted it to be. He has changed remarkably. He is now a very content soul.'

Nathan's excesses were legendary within the industry. For twenty years, he never once appeared on a television programme without having anaesthetised himself with marijuana; when he did not collect an award at fashion ceremonies, he would vomit with frustration; he worked eighteen-hour days, was ruthless with his verbal abuse, openly contemptuous of his peers, and partied *hard*. 'Trent was the wildest,' an associate recalls, 'but he has always had guts. He has an incredible talent. You don't get to where he is by chance. He is an absolute survivor — in a commercial sense, in a personal sense. He is an *amazing* man.'

His determination has paid impressive dividends. Beginning with women's clothes, he has expanded into lingerie, men's business shirts, ties, scarves, hosiery, costume jewellery, sunglasses, and now luggage. The figures reflect his phenomenal progress: retail sales now exceed $35 million per annum. Nathan takes great delight in his company's growth, but also retains an unusual humility. He acknowledges the creative, financial, and philosophical impact of others on his work; he no longer takes all the credit. 'I don't have to make out that I know everything any more,' he says with a pliant smile. 'I'm happy to be stupid. I'm dumb. *Open*. Uncluttered. That inner emptiness has brought me peace.'

In his denim jeans and shirt, Gucci loafers, and wearing a gold signet ring, he is the picture of languid European chic. Nathan's sinuous voice is camp, but covers a potential roar. He can stretch any word to a hiss of significance, and emphasises every point with his fluidly expressive hands. 'My parents,' he says with an arch look, 'had *great* sex. MODEL MARRIES WHARFIE! My father was a hunk. A *hunk*!' He throws his hands up, rolls his eyes. 'He had a tattoo of a koala on his inside elbow. He was physically strong, but an insecure man. He had a great passion for my mother. He was a little jealous of the love and affection she gave me. I had,' he continues with the satisfaction of the cat who got the cream, *'one hundred per cent* of her attention! So I grew up with two people who had a wonderful sexual relationship, but also with confusion. A woman who was so ambitious, and a man who was left out.'

Nathan's mother died last year; his father, 'twenty or so years ago'. He speaks of his parents with an oddly compassionate detachment, although it is obvious that in a certain sense, their deaths released him. 'When my mother died,' he admits, 'the cord was actually cut. The cord was *cut*.'

Raised in Homebush (a blue-collar suburb of Sydney), Nathan was the second of two children. However nurturing, his mother's love also seemed to entail tremendous emotional pressure. 'She made sure that I identified with her,' he says, shaking his head. 'My father wanted to call me *Wesley*, but she chose my name. The identification between the two of us was *radical.*' Again, he throws his hands up and whistles. '*Radical.* I worked with her *every day* for thirty years. She called me *every morning* of her life, but only ever to talk business. Not: *Wow! Isn't that beautiful!*, but to give *advice.*'

These days he prefers to focus on the positive aspects of his upbringing; in the past, Nathan was clear about how his parents would 'rubbish' his dreams and how he had to struggle against their parochialism — in particular, that of his remote father. 'I didn't come into contact with men much, as I had fifteen or sixteen girl cousins,' he says. 'It was all *girls*. It was all *clothing*. Christmas time was the only contact I had with men. I remember wearing *stretch lycra Italian swimsuits*. And there would be my uncles — *bush horsemen!* — staring at me in confusion. They just didn't *get* it.'

'It' was essentially Nathan's contempt for sexual stereotypes, although he never acknowledged it as such. 'Corduroy pants and desert boots?' he yelps. '*No!* Mum would make me these wonderful yuppie clothes, and you can imagine the response of the private school girls: *whoooooooooooah*! They adored me. *Adored* me.'

The adolescent Nathan had discovered the two forms of creative expression which elicited approval from those he respected — clothing and sport. In effect, his success at both was his interpretation of teenage rebellion. For seven years he held the Australian Junior Swimming Championship (over 100 yards). He was also a member of the Junior Davis Cup tennis squad. 'Whatever I attempted in sport,' he shrugs, 'I *won*.'

What he never won was an open expression of love from his father. He was instead sexually molested by father-figures. 'My first sexual experience — if you could call it that — was the minister trying to touch my dick under the church. I was thirteen.' Nathan's gaze steadies, and his sarcasm is chilling. '*Come into the church, Trent* ... this "straight" minister ... I ran away; I laughed; didn't affect me at all. And then on the Manly ferry, another man tried to touch my dick. I was a good-looking, lovely young boy, you know? No big deal. That didn't freak me. I wasn't raped.'

His verbal indifference reflects the questionable response of his mother to his molestation. 'I'd go home and tell mum and she'd say: *oh, well — are you right?* And I'd say: *yeah, it was nothing*. No big deal. *Laughed*. Because,' he says, his tone suddenly sharpening, 'they were usually *sick*-looking things, you know? You could punch them and run. They were *weak*. I've never had trouble with perverts, never! *PISS OFF!*' he shouts in recollection. 'And they'd run. Because I was *loud*.'

As an adult, his reaction to unwanted attention remains the same. 'As a twenty-six year old, I went to cocktail parties — posh, posh Melbourne,' he explains, calmly folding his hands in his lap. 'On one occasion, a "straight" man tried to feel my dick and I shouted: *PISS OFF! Haaaaazel — he just tried to feel my DICK!*' The offender was so humiliated that he left. Nathan's oldest nephew and MD, Shane Barr, smiles a dry smile when asked about his uncle's volatile temperament. 'He's very generous and supportive and nurturing to *some*, and rude and callous and hard to those who underestimate him.'

The love Nathan had received from the women around him gave him the strength to assert himself, and the strength of this self-assertion also betrays the strength of encountered opposition. 'I always *knew* I would do well,' he insists. 'I never even *thought* of failure. There was no question. Didn't even *register*. Don't know the *feeling*.' Then ashamed of being a 'Westie', he longed to be part of the upper class milieu — 'the regatta people, the polo crowd' — people he perceived as being successful. 'I became part of that set,' he says. 'Did I enjoy it? No. But I thought that was what you had to do to make it. I was always *frightfully* ambitious. Amazing! I thought success was *money*. I didn't know about freedom in those days.'

The perfect conduit for his mother's drive, he left school at sixteen to become a trainee buyer at a department store, where he was taught to 'answer telephones and work cash registers'. His co-workers nicknamed him 'The Perpetual Moaner'. The mundanity of the work infuriated him. He resigned after four years, the 'last straw' being a request that he help demonstrate a sick bed by lying on it and being wheeled around the floor. 'Such a *humiliating* experience!' he recalls with distaste. 'Those bad experiences taught me so much.'

His mother refused his plea to work with her in manufacturing the White Collar Girl range and told him to 'go out and learn the trade'. Nathan spent the following year learning to be a cutter, and then set up his own label in an inner-city factory. The experience instilled in him an aversion to the actual *making* of clothes; he just wanted to design and supervise. 'That's been my whole journey,' he says, closing his eyes, *'frustration*. Frustration after frustration after frustration. Some people always have the same frustration, whereas I conquer one only to have another one come up. I was *always* frustrated.'

The company operated as a partnership for twenty-three years until Nathan bought out his partners in 1984.

Throughout those years, he worked himself to the point of exhaustion, fuelled by the terror of failure. His life was fraught with anxiety. 'If I was at an awards-giving ceremony where I didn't win, I would panic,' he says. 'That ambition to be the best! I'd *drink*. I would be *loud*. I would become so frustrated I'd *vomit*. And seeing what I had done was not good enough and no one had to tell me that it wasn't good enough because I *knew* it wasn't good enough. I *still* feel that I'm not good enough. You have no idea what I *used* to be like.'

There were few occasions on which he didn't win an award; despite his extravagantly emotional personality, Nathan had secured the respect of both the industry and the market. He attributes his understanding of women's fashion needs to his lack of sexual desire for them. 'Sexual desire *absolutely* gets in the way of empathy!' he says, madly waving his hands. 'Of *course* it does! Male or female, all you can think is: *they turn me on … they turn me on … THEY TURN ME ON*. You can't even get into a conversation! I know *women*. Look how close I get to women because they don't feel *threatened*! I'm their best friend. They love me.' He pauses, smoothes his jeans with a tidy little gesture and then looks up, all eyes. 'That's when I'm not being *rude* to them. I'm only rude to them when they behave like smartarses. I don't like it,' he says, 'when they play little *hunting* games with me, looking at my lips and not into my eyes.

Literally looking at my mouth as they tried to do lines for me. When they'd try to be sexy with me, I'd be *ruthless*.'

The easiest way for Nathan to disguise his fear of vulnerability was to indulge in kaleidoscopic temper tantrums and drug abuse. His other nephew and sales executive, Chris Barr, screams with delight. 'When Trent wanted to have a go at somebody, he'd stand a foot away and *just let them have it*. He swore. He was *terrifying*. They would quiver, go red, begin to cry, and then have a complete breakdown. Deadset true,' he laughs.

'I thought marijuana made me more creative,' Nathan says. 'I thought it made me more vivacious. I wanted to have the gift of the gab. I liked being that alone in my head. I felt I wasn't vivacious enough.' Chris Barr remembers that when his uncle bought a house in Palm Beach, he decided that the white walls were 'dull' and painted 'murals of palm trees and nude men — he was right into painting nude men on the walls when he was stoned.' Barr pauses, and with great affection, says: 'The walls, need I add, have since been repainted white although one of the men he painted keeps seeping through, no matter how many coats of white are put over him.'

A friend recalls Nathan's televised interview with the phlegmatic Clive Robertson. 'Trent was *out* of it, just *rambling*. Clive was staring at him as if he'd just landed from another planet.' Nathan's humour is evident as he agrees. 'Oh, *yes*. I always used to have joints before I went on television. Dope makes you *talk*. It was a matter of being stoned and having a rave. I probably didn't go to an awards ceremony without smoking dope. I used to sit and roll *all the time*, starting at 7.30 am. I used to smoke all day, every day.' When asked a serious question during a television interview, Nathan had a policy of replying: *Think Green*. 'He did talk a lot of hogwash when stoned,' Chris Barr comments, 'but I was never worried because I knew that with a snap of his fingers, he could conquer any habit.'

Nathan never stopped working, even when he was high. 'When I look back now,' he says, 'I see I wasn't as centred or focused, I was kidding myself. I was numbing myself. I was numbing that *anxiety*. I was numbing the feeling that *there had to be something else in life*.' He used to 'smoke joints like cigarettes', having up to five in two hours. 'I had people come around,' he exclaims as he leans forward in his chair, 'and after a smoke, they'd try to walk out of the room, fall flat on their faces, and I'd still be going. My tolerance was unbelievable. People would spin out and I'd *still* be talking.'

Another long-term addiction had been his workaholism, which was often manic. 'I *definitely* worked as hard as I did to cover emotion,' he says, his features working. 'What was I covering? My homosexuality. There was absolutely nothing else in my life to cover.' From 1940 to 1960, Nathan wasn't even aware that there was a term for his sexual preference. He tried kissing girls, only to discover that it didn't do *'anything'* for him. Very gently, he says: 'I always knew. From *dot*. I'm not talking about drag queens or gays. I'm a *man*, absolutely. But "gay"? Who cares about sexual playacting? It was *extremely* difficult — *extremely*. Some commit suicide because they never let it out. Look at the alcoholics on the streets — the men who piss themselves, you know, who mess around with one another — most of them are gay. They live with this *trauma* ...' The expression in his feral eyes softens, and he shakes his head. 'Poor things. Poor *things*.'

His one emotional stab at heterosexuality was in 1971, when he announced his engagement to Jane Blundell, a socialite shoe designer. The engagement lasted a week. 'I pretended until I was thirty-one,' he says. 'The *repression*! It was terrible. You had to cover it up. Homosexual? *Hideous* connotations. The worst element was my own head trip. You know how some men go like this —' his shoulders suddenly square, he puffs his chest out, and his voice drops to a baritone — 'and then as soon as they're with The Boys, they become *big queens*! I've *nev*-ah done that! I've never played two roles.'

'I used to deny myself externally, but inside ... *whooooooah*!' His eyes flare as he bounces back into his seat. 'A *tiger*! An absolute *tiger*! I've always said that I could relate to Jeffrey Dahmer, the guy who cut penises off and kept them in the top drawer. I told my friends: *I can relate to that!* Meaning, how if I weren't strong and focused and mentally stable, how that *rejection* could ...' He trails off, and after a charged pause, continues. 'I can understand that. If I were a psychiatrist, I would be able to listen to him, you know?'

Peter Chadwick, the MD of Chadwick's Modelling Agency, remembers Nathan as being 'wild, a heap of fun, and *totally* unpredictable'. Despite this wildness, Nathan has never been promiscuous and did not practise penetration. This restraint may have saved his life. 'I didn't have sex,' he says, almost affronted. 'I just used to ejaculate. Insertion? *Insertion?* Eughhhhhh! And thank *God!* *Thank God!* Because it was all the good-looking ones that got it, you know?' He is unable to bring himself to mention AIDS, having lost too many associates to the disease. 'But *sex?*' he suddenly cries, adding with a flourish: 'Oh, ejaculate! Oh, don't we feel close now that we've all ejaculated, oooooooooh!' In full flight, and completely deadpan, he continues, hands everywhere. '*I love you forever!* Don't I feel better now that I've *ejaculated! Now* I can talk to you!' Again, he shakes his head. '*Radical* concept. My God, what an awful way to feel — that to get close to someone, you have to *do* that. *Love* is a better word for me, not sex. For God's sake! Sex! *Eugh!*'

The sexual and financial decadence of the eighties was disturbing to Nathan, and he retreated to his sparsely furnished Palm Beach home, where he meditated, practised yoga, and adhered to a strict diet. 'The eighties were *amazing!*' he exclaims. 'I look back and think: *riiiiiiiiiight* — *billionaires! trillionaires!* And then all of a sudden, most of them are in jail. You must never let material wealth overtake your life; it is the biggest downfall of the human race. I visited the Marcos home in the sixties. It was *awful!* That level of greed would make me *shudder!* To hear them say: *yes*, darling! *Trent*, darling — you *creative* designer!' He lifts his shoulders in a theatrical shiver. 'Women carrying lizard bags with *the heads still attached*! That's why I dropped out, I couldn't stand it.'

Artifice no longer holds any lure for him, and this change is reflected in his classic designs. 'I saw a woman with a fake Cartier on the other day and thought: why *bother*? Go out and buy a *Swatch!*' He inclines his big head, and purrs: 'I know these women — how they learn to talk private school ... very subtle; very subtle and discreet. How they learn to talk as if they know all about money *to the man*. They know,' he says, illustrating each statement with its corresponding gesture, 'how to tie that Hermes; they know their Gucci; they know how to casually put their jeans on to go to the polo. But the real McCoy will always give it a twist. The *real* McCoy is not one who relies on hubby to pay for everything. There is a *fine* line between real style and the bourgeois.'

He has no desire to float his company internationally as it would be 'too demanding' an enterprise, and prays that the empire will not go the way of the Gucci family, who are 'all at war'. He wants to continue making all his business decisions on instinct — 'decisions worth *millions* of dollars' — and may or may not open a Trent Nathan flagship boutique which handles all his products. Now that money is no longer an issue, Nathan regards his work as an expression of his creativity rather than as an exercise in ambition.

'The work is my truth,' he says. '*Always* the truth. Some people used to keep away from me because I was so honest. If a guy was suppressing his gayness, he'd keep *right* away from me, oh yes! Because otherwise, I'd try to bring it out, to help it *emerge*, absolutely! People lie to themselves because they are afraid. Because they don't love themselves. That's a hard one, to learn to love and be true to yourself, hard. Oy oy oy oy *oy*! And it is the most important lesson: to love is to forgive. We must learn to *forgive*. It's as simple as that.'

Mode, 1994

LEER OF THE WHITE WORM:

GENE SIMMONS

LOVINGLY RETAINED IN the bowels of all newspaper libraries and, I imagine, in thousands of crammed scrapbooks throughout the world, is a certain photograph of a certain man in the prime of his very special life — a man who has become a hero to the uncertain and the simplistic, to the doubting and the desperate, to the young and the restless. Originally known as Chaim Witz, then as Chaim Klein, then as Gene Klein, this man is now revered as Gene Simmons.

In the photograph and against a backdrop over which the word KISS is spelt out by versicoloured light bulbs, Gene is hunched. He is plucking a bass guitar shaped like a medieval axe; his jaw juts out, canines exposed; his face is painted white, his lips are black, and black demon wings flare over his menacing eyes. Perhaps to disguise what appears to be a receding hairline, an inverted black triangle is painted on his forehead, and his steel-wool hair is pulled back into a Shinto top-knot. He is wearing the kind of glittering rocket-shouldered jacket Joan Collins made famous, a jewelled and bulging cod-piece, black stretch-fit pants, and a gargantuan pair of foil-wrapped platform boots in the shape of dinosaur paws. Understandably, he does not look agile. The effect is odd. He looks possessed. In short, he looks completely mad.

This is the man for whom so many have haunted the lobby of the Melbourne Hilton for so long. It can be said that many KISS fans look like nothing so much as water-tower snipers or Internet perverts. Bug-eyed, they pollute the grand lobby with their frayed black metal-head *couture*. They worship Gene because he is the man they would all be if they only had the courage to confront the world in foil-wrapped boots in the shape of dinosaur paws. They see him as a man who could stick chips in his nostrils and never get busted; a man who is rewarded with approval for boasting of 'fucking [his] brains out' with 'over' 3000 women; a man who can, with a flick of his tongue, tie knots in lengths of industrial tubing. They see him as the man who needs no dad. He is, in fact, the dad of their dreams — a wild man, nothing like their real dads who browbeat them and forced them to eat broccoli. Gene doesn't care if they eat broccoli; he wants them to eat *pussy*.

The subsequent KISS ALIVE WORLDWIDE tour is, the press release will tell you, a '100 per cent sellout'. Whether this 'sellout' is ideological or financial is not specified. That which is specified follows: KISS hysteria is sweeping the globe! Over ten million people have bought tickets! Four Madison Square Gardens shows sold out in less than an hour! Tickets in Chicago sold out in *six minutes*! KISS will use over forty-four pounds of theatrical makeup on the tour! The stage production will require over 1.8 million volts of electricity! 228, 334 feet of cable will be needed! More than 15,100 guitar picks will be used! Over 41,500 guitar strings will be played! In the interests of showmanship, musical excellence, and Ibanez shares, frontman Paul Stanley will smash 350 guitars into pieces! And Gene, well — Gene will breathe fire and regurgitate 158 pounds of 'blood' in twenty-six countries.

I ride the elevator to the eighteenth floor, where I will be interviewing this man, a man who named his first band Wicked Lester. I sit in an empty lounge, light a cigarette, and wait. And wait. He is an hour late. Punctuality cannot be expected of Gene, a man who has so much sexual energy to expel. Well into my third glass of water, I hear a noise and look up. It is Gene. He has a face like a bag full of chopped liver. He is very tall and broad. His dyed black hair looks like the aftermath of a bushfire. It is two o'clock in the afternoon and the man is delirious, he is exhausted. 'I'm sorry I'm late,' he says, 'but I was up all night fucking.'

His voice is very deep and he speaks very slowly. He is accompanied by his macro-goon, a walking planet in high-tops. Staring at me, Gene becomes intense. Intensity is to Gene as the ukulele was to Tiny Tim. He makes a long, low, rumbling sound and suddenly grabs a fistful of my hair. '*Mmmmmnnnnn* ...' he murmurs as he evaluates its texture, 'long *hair*.' The macro-goon, who has undoubtedly heard this spiel before, mindlessly gazes out of the window at the empty Melbourne Cricket Ground. 'Nothin' goin' on in this place,' he sadly says. Gene's stare becomes liquid. '*Goooooooood*,' he decides. 'You have thick lips.' I am uncharacteristically unresponsive. I am scared that if I respond, he may attempt to mount me. He leans down to slowly — *very* slowly — run his hand up the shin of my boot. '*Mmmmmnnnnn* ...' he again murmurs, holding my attention with what I imagine he thinks is a seductive expression, 'I *like* boots.'

I am extremely fortunate in that Gene appears to approve of both my features and my apparel. The only aspect of me that he finds distressing is my lack of bulk. He pinches my arm through the jacket and frowns. 'Too *thin*,' is his verdict. Later, when I ask him why he has jumped from his chair to peer down my shirt, he will reply: 'I want to see your tits.' These have his approval, but the rest — well, the rest needs work. I am too scrawny. Gene likes his women to look like WOMEN. Gene likes nothing better than to grab great handfuls of thigh, of breast, of buttock. Gene's fantasy must be to suffocate under the blonde tonnage of Anna Nicole Smith. His partner of a decade, a former Playmate Of The Year and soft-porn queen, is built like one of the better suspension bridges. Gene wants his women to explode from their fish-net body-stockings, he wants them to burst out of their boots, he wants them to quiver beneath him like swimming pools filled with *blancmange*. No starving waifs for Gene. He ain't no faggot.

We walk into an executive boardroom and sit down. There are vases of delicate lilies, mirrors, tastefully framed prints. Gene almost looks uncomfortable, but this discomfort is immediately mastered. He is wearing a light and shiny black Nike wind-jacket, a jacket unzipped to reveal the rolling hills and forested dales of his forty-five-year-old chest. His skin-tight pants are unpalatably worn at the crotch. 'They stretch both ways,' he explains, suddenly boyish, as he offers me a feel of the versatile fabric. 'Very thin, very comfortable. I can just pop them into the washing machine.' His big and pointy cowboy boots are black and made from python skin. His many rings (embossed with spiders, snakes, et cetera) are all presents from devotees. Around his neck and hanging from a thick silver chain, a lock with the skull and crossbones in bas-relief. A silver hoop punctures each earlobe, and crusty remnants of the previous night's eyeliner sugar his eyelashes. The way in which Gene presents himself is not only a statement, but a very astute marketing ploy. It must be said that Gene The Demon King has never been a dum-dum.

'The things,' he says as he pours water from a jug into a glass packed with ice-cubes, 'women are fascinated by are beautiful yet *trivial*. The whole world of it — fashion, make-up, all of it. A rock band should make sure that its male following pays complete disregard to the female point of view. If the core of your audience is female, the clock [of your popularity] is ticking and it's over before it's begun, because for them it's *fashion*. There's no loyalty. There is no loyalty.' He takes a careful sip of his water and eases back into his leather chair.

I light a cigarette and point out that fashion and make-up are pretty much the bases of his success. After all, where would Chaim Witz be today without the greasepaint, demon wings and dinosaur paw boots? Hasn't KISS always been a case of clever marketing? Pausing, he places his glass on the table and smiles with his eyes. 'In which case,' he says, 'it's a very good story. In which case, you have something to write about. In which case, if it weren't so, you wouldn't be here talking to me. *Elle* is all about fluff, anyway. Faggots who design clothes, the eternal search for beauty. You don't even pronounce the last letter of its name, so what the fuck is that?' He kicks his pointy boots up onto the chair opposite him. 'It's a complete waste of time. That French stuff! Smoking cigarettes backwards and wearing little berets … you're fucked. Eating frogs' legs … as soon as you get into that French world, oh boy!'

He is not pleased. The concept of marketing is one Gene would prefer not to publicly explore. KISS have, after all, sold seventy-five million albums (albums with names such as *Love Gun*, *Lick It Up* and *Kiss My Ass*). Gold, platinum, multi-platinum — KISS have done them all. Were it to be made obvious to KISS fans that their vaudevillian idols were primarily in it for the money, Gene could find that KISS comic books, KISS transistor radios, KISS back-to-school books, KISS jeans, KISS garbage pails, KISS dolls, KISS Bally pinball machines, KISS bubblegum cards, KISS jackets, KISS albums, and the 4.5 kg book KISSTORY would not shift as many 'units' as he would wish. Given this, it seems interesting that he doesn't even feign enthrallment with his music.

His old pal, Paul Stanley, recently said: 'We must have hit upon something sonically, because every time [our new] songs come on, my balls jiggle.' Gene's balls, it seems, jiggle to a different drum. 'I get satisfaction from music,' he shrugs, 'but music is not the be-all and end-all for me. I'm no Mozart or Beethoven. I don't have that kind of passion. I don't live, breathe, and dream music *at all*. If it wasn't music, I'd do something else. Other [musicians] lie because they have to toe the line. A lot of people say things they think others wanna hear.' He fixes me with the *danse macabre* of his eyes. 'It's like seducing a woman — tell her what's inside of you, and even if it's disagreeable, she will respond to it more.'

Adroitly, he has steered the conversation back to his favourite topic. Gene can talk about women for hours. Sexual modesty is not a blot on his escutcheon. He describes his 'appetite' for women as if they were thickshakes or cheeseburgers. He expounds on his admiration of their 'intelligence', and yet is essentially indifferent to what they say. 'The word "no",' he says, slowly arching his left eyebrow, 'means *nothing* to me. It is just another step towards "yes", and "yes" means everything and "no" means nothing. To this day, I get rejected — *all the time* — but it means nothing. All it means is that they just don't see my greatness.'

When I suggest that if 'no' means nothing the question was irrelevant, he eyes me like a thousand-year-old lizard. 'It's just a lack on their part of not recognising what's good about me. Some guys feel that there's something wrong with them when a girl rejects them. The woman should have *nothing* to do with it. *Nothing.*' His expression changes as he watches me light another cigarette. 'To me,' he says with some consternation, 'smoking is what truck drivers do. I've never understood the fascination women have with it. It's some kind of *penis* fixation. I keep telling them that they don't need to smoke — they can have my dick any time they want.'

While I am wondering how kindly the American Truck Drivers' Association would take to his suggestion that many of them have penis fixations, he continues. 'When the band first went on tour,' he says, 'I was *astonished* and amazed that there was an endless supply of women — *endless!*' There is an approximation of surprise in his voice. 'Like somehow the tap went all the way to heaven and God was up there saying: *It's all yours — have as much as you want!* I felt … *blessed.*'

Gene may not always feel blessed, but he certainly feels whomever is within his reach. 'I want to press your lip to see if it's as soft as it looks,' he says. My blood turns to ice as his index finger caresses my mouth. I am as still as Sam Neill was when the T-Rex pressed its snout against the windscreen of his car. 'Oh, I could fuck that *all* night …' he purrs, digging his heels into the chair. And then, with a billowing sigh: 'I'm romantic. To me, women are *amazing* life forms … *complete* contradictions. They cry when they're happy, they say "no" when they mean "yes" … they always smell good, always.' He shakes his head. 'Even when they *sweat*, it's like the way a baby sweats; it's not like men … *stink*.' He pauses to deliver unto me a meaningful look. 'With me, it's not so much sex — there's always a lot of kissing and holding and stuff. I *look* and am amazed by how *different* you are. I'm just like a little kid.'

With an Oedipal Complex the size of the Greater London Area.

At this point his publicist bursts in, her eyes moist. She breathlessly recounts the tale of the young cancer victim who had lost the will to live until Gene rang him and 'returned' it. 'His mother didn't have the words to thank him!' she says, all choked up. 'She was crying! The whole family were absolutely beside themselves with emotion! It was like a *miracle*!'

Saint Gene of the Bass Guitar has forgotten her before she has even left the room. 'You know,' he casually says, 'I could put a blush on your face like —' and here he jazzily clicks his fingers — '*that*. I could fuck you on the spot. I could do you — especially with those —' here he indicates my breasts — 'like *that*.' I nervously light another cigarette. '*Mmmmmmmnnnnn …*' he growls, 'you *need* a man.' I am beginning to agree. A *police*man.

A catwalk model present at a party thrown by a woman for KISS in 1980 remembers Gene well. 'The woman holding the party,' she chuckles, 'was rumoured to run a high-class call-girl ring. Gene was with Diana Ross at the time. He came after me in a big way. I'll never forget his words: *We'd have beautiful babies together*.' Gene has never pretended to be monogamous. He refuses to marry the mother of his two children, Shannon Tweed, because he feels that it would be a 'lie' (in June, 1995, this 'lie' became truth, and the couple now live 'quietly' in Beverly Hills). When I ask him why he is so promiscuous when he has a former Playmate Of The Year at home, he shrugs. 'Why are all men?' he asks in reply. I then ask him whether, in this age of AIDS, Shannon minds his forays into free love. 'I think that all women mind,' he indifferently says. And then: 'Shannon is beautiful. She is *strong*. She is *super*woman.'

He has been publicly linked with many superwomen. Cher, Diana Ross, and Liza Minelli have all dissolved before Gene's lizard-stare. The fact that they enjoyed relationships with Gene is more a reflection of them than it is of him. 'Diana,' he says, 'is beautiful. She is *strong*. Cher is beautiful. And *strong*. Liza is *strong*. And beautiful. I'm attracted to strong, strong women. I don't appreciate unintelligent women. I love women who don't define themselves by,' and his lip voluptuously curls, 'men.'

I stub the evidence of my penis fixation out in the ashtray. Gene watches me. 'Fucking Miss Nude Australia last night — whatever her name is — was *delicious*,' he drawls. 'It was beautiful. *Romantic.*' Later in the day I call the Queensland-based Miss Melinda Lee, otherwise known as Miss Nude Australia. There is an awful silence as she listens to Gene's allegations. And then, in a hurt and cynical voice, she says: 'Guys are always saying that. Sex with Gene Simmons? *In his dreams.* I've never met the guy in my *life.*' Bewildered, I then ring Gene's publicist. 'It, uh, may have been the runner-up or something,' she anxiously says. '*Gene* wouldn't know. How did you get hold of Miss Nude Australia anyway?'

Aside from his tongue and foil-wrapped dinosaur paw boots, Gene is most famous for the boast that he has 'done' over 3000 women. This is a big call, even for the most obsessive-compulsive old satyromaniac. Given the number of women he's 'done', I ask, hasn't he ever caught a venereal disease or ten? For the first time during the interview, Gene stiffens. 'No,' he replies very calmly as he pulls his nose. I question the veracity of his answer. '*No*,' he repeats, 'never. No crabs or venereal disease of … *any* kind. And I, uh, wear a *rain*coat.' I silently consider the kind of woman who would gravitate towards Gene — the many metal groupies, the strippers, the raree-show divas. Not one of them gave him a venereal disease! The statisticians would have a field day. For some reason, Gene is becoming mildly discomfited. 'You know,' he says, somewhat nonsensically, 'I like my women to *bathe.*'

Surprisingly, Gene wants to change the subject. Pubic lice, it seems, are not terribly cool. He begins to discuss his legendary Polaroid collection, the one he keeps in 'portfolios protected from oxygen'. 'I wanted to take photos of [all my conquests],' he says with emphasis, 'because I got the sense that it may not last forever. Every once in a while I take them out and look at them and it's *beautiful*. I don't think I'm weird. The only difference between me and the rest of the male population is that I don't go to newsstands and buy pornography. To me, pornography is just a pale second to having a real, hot woman in front of you.'

I wonder out loud at the effect of all this bragging and posturing on his six-year-old son and later, on his two-year-old daughter. Gene dismisses this as ludicrous. 'I mean,' he exclaims, 'for God's *sake*! Their mom was a foldout — a whatdoyoucallit — Playmate Of The Year, whatever year it was! She makes tons of — I don't know, something like thirty — movies, and some of them are *very* steamy. And even though we don't sit there and, you know, *watch* them, I'm very open and so is she about human sexuality.' His face grows stern. 'It's very healthy and *should* be that way,' he says in an admonishing tone. 'When Nicholas was two or three, he said: *Mommy, I have a penis and you have a vagina!* It was very clear.'

A lubricious prodigy, he admits his sexual awareness was premature. 'I *always* wanted to fuck everything that moved,' he says. At the age of twelve, Gene was studying to be a rabbi at a theological seminary. He and his divorced Hungarian mother were living in a New York ghetto. 'I remember looking out the window one day,' he says, 'and there was this Spanish girl with long, black, THICK hair all the way down to her butt.' The young rabbi-in-training watched as this girl jumped rope, his eyes hanging out of his head. 'Whenever she jumped,' he says with wanton relish, 'it looked like her hair was slapping her butt, and it was the most remarkably erotic thing I've *ever* seen.'

He kicks his boots off the chair and neatly crosses his long leathery legs. 'It was at that point,' he says, 'that I thought: *This is better than God!* This thing *moves*, it's in front of me, it may as well be saying: *This can be yours, Gene!*' Unaware that his terminology ('this thing', 'it') is that of a serial rapist, he continues his rhapsody. 'And I remember that in sixth grade all the girls would come up to me and say: *Do that strange thing!* So I'd stick my tongue out and wiggle it, and they'd all start giggling.'

Curious to see this fabled tongue of his, I ask him to display it. Gene complies. A glistening purple thing the length of a baby's forearm rolls out of his mouth. It looks like a jellied eel or something that lives on the floor of the ocean. He rolls it back in. 'I never knew what made them giggle,' he wonderingly says. 'I thought: *Gee, is it so strange?* And I'd look in the mirror and start wiggling and think: *What's the big deal? It's just my tongue!* I figured it must just be funny. What I *didn't* know,' and here his eyes flatten to slits, 'is that they were pressing their *knees* together for the rest of the day.'

It then seems logical, I say, to assume that he began KISS as a showcase for his tongue. 'No,' he replies, perfectly sombre, 'I was *so* in love with the Beatles. My mother thought they were silly-looking, and I figured that the more my mother hated something, the more I liked it.' Gene's mother, a Holocaust survivor, left her husband in Israel when her only child was six and moved with him to America. Her neglect of her son was an economic necessity, and could explain both his determined self-reliance and near-psychotic self-belief. 'She worked from 7 am to 7 pm, six days a week, picking lint from jackets in a factory. She was paid fifteen dollars a week. We lived in a ghetto. But I always had jam and bread and butter, and with a glass of milk, I thought I was in heaven. And then,' he says with more excitement than I have seen him muster for music, metal molls, or his many millions, 'I discovered *peanut* butter and I just fell in *love*! Every day — morning, noon, and night — I had peanut butter and jelly sandwiches!'

I try to picture Chaim Witz, a boy who spoke no English, a boy with no relatives, a boy with no father, a boy whose mother must have been socially ostracised for her divorce, a boy with no one to guide him, a boy whose self-belief was all that he had. However morally reprehensible Gene Simmons may be, however vulgar and bizarre, he is a man of great resilience. 'There is,' he says, 'a song I wrote called "I".' He clears his throat and then begins to sing in a thin and tuneless voice:

> *I believe in me;*
> *I believe in something more than you can understand.*
> *I don't need to get wasted;*
> *It only holds me down.*
> *'Cause I got a will o' my own*
> *And the guts to stand alone —*
> *Yes, I believe in me.*

When he has finished singing, he coughs ferociously. The macro-goon waddles in. I shake Gene's hand and thank him for his time. Once outside, I ask the Hilton's lounge manager for her opinion of the man. Is it possible that his behaviour is simply an elaborate and lucrative joke? Her eyes widen and she laughingly shudders. 'Oh, no,' she says, 'he's like that all day long. Trust me, it's for real. Hard to believe, isn't it?'

Elle, 1995

SURVIVOR OF SURVIVORS:
AUSTEN TAYSHUS

HE CUTS AN incongruous figure amongst the dainty lunching ladies in the Lobby Lounge of Sydney's chandelier-rich Ritz-Carlton. Tall and imposingly shouldered, he is dressed in a long black coat, worn blue jeans, a crumpled shirt, and sharp black riding boots. His large, smooth hands are those of a reader, and unusually formed: the tips of his long fingers curl backwards, creating the effect of pale Persian slippers. He looks down at his hands, demonstrates their span by spreading them, and shrugs. 'They're big,' he agrees, 'but my penis is bigger.'

Sandy Gutman removes his wraparound shades, the trademark of his alter-ego, Austen Tayshus, and glances around the room. His closely-set dark eyes are the one tentative feature in an otherwise craggy and dominating face and he acknowledges that yes, these soft eyes of his are 'the mirrors' of his soul which is why he must disguise them when he is on stage. The character that made Gutman a household name is anything but tentative, anything but soft. Austen Tayshus is ruthlessly fast and funny, sometimes crass, often vicious, always reckless, and famed for opening shows with the line: 'Settle down, motherfuckers!' A national hero, he was the character who delivered 'Australiana' (the best-selling Australian single of all time), and the creation of a man widely acknowledged as both a comic genius and a nightmare.

The prospect of a heavy lunch makes Gutman feel queasy. He has just had an 'enormous' breakfast over which he signed the contract for his latest album, *Alive and Schticking*, to be released by Laughing Stock Records. After so many years of personal, professional, and financial humiliation, Gutman's star is again on the ascendant. The many problems that dogged him in the late eighties have made him cautious — not only with others, but with himself. 'His biggest problem,' comments an associate, 'was his attitude. He burnt every single bridge. He was so self-destructive. Sandy had this *need* to stick it to everyone.' And then there was his drug problem, the obscenity charges, ugly public wrangles with everyone from Peter Garrett to P&O (who hired him as the *Fairstar*'s resident entertainer only to dump him in Suva after five days), his insensitive 'comic' assaults on the Third World, Catholicism, and the working classes, and, finally, his inevitable bankruptcy.

The sound and fury had to be silenced in order for Sandy Gutman to rediscover what it was that made him happy. Years of suppressed rage and the stresses of performing over 2500 shows had extracted their price. 'The real turning-point in Sandy's life,' explains a friend, 'was his marriage to Emma-Jane [Cromb], his polar opposite. She has given him stability. He has become a different man — calmer, far more reflective.' Sixteen years his junior, the twenty-four-year-old Emma-Jane is a tall and doe-like strawberry blonde. With a lovely laugh, she says: 'Our two years of marriage have been *mutually* beneficial. Sandy has opened my mind. He is passionate and sensitive, and an absolute gentleman at heart. He *can* get out of control, but only in public. In private, he is always considerate.' The brash image Gutman has presented to the world has, in many respects, been the wall behind which he has hidden.

With his hands folded in his lap he talks of his late father, in whose shadow he has always lived. 'As a child I was too *respectful* towards my father to … *really let him have it*.' Uncharacteristically awkward, he begins to breathe rapidly, uncomfortably. 'My father *did* cut me down, probably. My ideas had no free rein in our house. I could never compete with him.'

His voice suddenly drops to a thundering Polish-accented baritone: *'Hooooow can you imagine what the Holocaust was like? Hoooooow can I tell you? In Bergen-Belsen I was lying on the floor of the hut and I heard the Russians eating each other alive — the SCREAMS! I will always have it with me!'* His fingers knot, he looks up, and his voice is now his own. 'There was nothing to *compare* with such suffering. I ended up competing with the Holocaust for his attention. There was no contest. The Holocaust won, hands down.'

Born into an Orthodox Jewish family, Alexander Jacob Gutman was the eldest of two sons to Polish refugees Margaret and Isaac Gutman, a journalist and watch wholesaler respectively. The family lived in the wealthy Eastern suburbs of Sydney, where Gutman attended the Jewish Moriah College and then Vaucluse Boys' High. From the age of six, he had listened to the traumatic stories of his father, who had the need to share his horrific experiences with his young son. The premature awareness of such barbarity was to scar the boy and create a permanent sense of the world being polarised — a case of 'us' against 'them'. In all startled and wounded innocence, Gutman still points an accusing finger at all non-Jews. 'You *hate us*,' he says with conviction, 'and *we* don't hate you.' It was precisely this kind of indoctrination which led to Gutman's psychological 'split', to his need to protect himself against 'them' by creating a disguise.

'When I was very young, it seemed as if the sun was shining and didn't stop,' he says. 'There was a feeling of being *alive* and continuously happy. And then around 1970, my father *lost* it.' A light stammer becomes apparent as he continues. 'He went into some — some sort of p-p-p-psychological *slump* ... a very dark period, he started with the Valium ... the prescription drug cocktails. I remember seeing him coming down the stairs while he was on Mandrax, *slurring* words. I had never seen my father out of control, and it was *devastating*.'

He recalls eavesdropping at his father's bedroom door as the doctor explained the severity of his problem. 'The world,' he says, 'fell apart for me that moment.' Forced by his father's mental decline into an unwanted adulthood, the previously quiet and devout boy panicked and attempted to restore his father's authority in the only way he knew how: by shocking him into some show of responsibility. 'I felt a bit ... abandoned,' he murmurs, 'I just felt a bit ... *lost*, you know? There was nobody to turn to. I was really singled out by him, because my brother was so diplomatic. And when my father got angry with me, it was like pitting three against one, you know? He was big — six foot three, broad. He'd get so *angry* with me.' The Polish baritone returns: '*But SANDY! What do you WANT?*' He powerfully slaps his thigh to emphasise his words, '*BUT WHAT DO YOU WANT?*'

Although Isaac Gutman's tortured subconscious overwhelmed the family, the deep love he had for his eldest son gave the boy the strength to rebel. Sandy Gutman grew his hair, began to smoke marijuana, 'hung out with the guys', and was nearly expelled — anything to distract him from the grief and guilt of his home life. 'My father would always *stress* how careful we had to be in terms of the hatred others felt for us. And I listened to him. He was never that interested in listening to me.'

His father's violent mood swings imprinted an association between anger and instruction in Gutman's mind, an association he was later to practise on stage. Despite his problems with school authorities, he was awarded a Commonwealth Scholarship and enrolled at Sydney University to study dentistry, a profession his father regarded as 'safe'. He repeated his first year of dentistry because of his poor marks, 'switched over' to fine arts, political science and philosophy for a year, and then left to study at the Film & Television School, where he completed the three-year fulltime programme and graduated as a director. His new ambition was to be a lighting cameraman, but as he was 'useless with all the clapper-loading and putting the film in', he soon found himself unemployed.

'At uni,' he says, 'we smoked a lot of hashish, marijuana, we dropped acid, did mushrooms ... I smoked marijuana *constantly* for years.' Drugged and broke, Gutman was desperate for a new direction, and on the advice of a friend, began to perform comedy. 'It was only when I started doing comedy in 1981 that I got into cocaine. I did all my television appearances *heavily* coked. *Very* heavily coked. I had a fear of doing comedy. I had a great fear of letting myself down. I was worried about the quality of my work.'

His wife attests that he is *still* worried about the quality of his work. 'Sometimes,' she says, 'I wake up in the small hours and hear him pacing the floor. If he performs badly, he becomes *furious* with himself.' The high expectations Gutman had absorbed from his father nearly destroyed him. Profoundly ashamed at his lack of commercial success, he was on the dole and living in a seedy inner-city boarding house with his then-girlfriend. 'I was in the shower when she ran in to tell me that "Australiana" had gone to number one on the charts,' he explains. 'I just started to cry.' Once the initial shock had abated, Gutman let loose. 'I had such a fear of failure, such a fear of performing,' he says, 'so I took cocaine, because I thought it would alleviate my suffering. The problem built and built and built. There were nights I sat around with all of INXS … everybody doing it. I was doing two, three grams a day … a lot.' He pauses to clear his throat. 'I mean, the need to entertain is in itself a means of avoiding intimacy, of *course* it is.'

There were weeks when he earned over $25,000. He employed road managers, stayed in the best hotels, was relentlessly generous to all those around him. 'The whole thing, everything five-star,' he says softly. 'The turning point was an accident my girlfriend and I had. We hit this tractor on a sunny road on our way to a gig. The whole roof of the Jaguar was taken off and her face was completely carved up.' As he speaks, his eyes are heavy with regret. 'I was in the passenger seat and she was driving. One minute I was sitting there, and the next she was *covered* in blood. She hit the tractor as it was turning right. She hadn't seen it because the day was too bright; we weren't used to brightness. It was *devastating*. I knew I had to finish with drugs, with cigarettes, with alcohol. We had just been building towards some kind of climactic cathartic thing, and the accident was just the manifestation of all that *shit*.'

Gutman's emphasis on his own celebrity was, in essence, only an expression of his need to be important to his father — to *impress* him, to impact upon him. 'My career was absolutely a disappointment to him,' he says. 'He strongly wanted me to be a doctor or a dentist. During the Holocaust, professionals were singled out and survived because they could *do* things. He always believed that a professional would never have finan—' he chokes on the word, visibly pained.

At the height of his financial troubles, he again disguised his agony with humour. He immediately began touring — beginning with the *Bankruptcy Tour* and continuing with *The Good, The Bad and The Broke*. The work was useful to him as a means to provide income (however curtailed by his infamy), as a form of expression, and, primarily, as a distraction from his grief. His adored father had died of heart complications in 1990. 'I still miss him,' he says, 'I *still* miss him.'

The effect his father's death had on him was profound and may have, on a certain level, released him to become a man. Gutman returned to the traditional Judaism of his youth and took the previously unthinkable 'plunge' into marriage, an institution he had previously described as 'mundane' and 'for the birds'. The new couple travelled to Los Angeles, where Gutman experimented with stand-up work and performed a cameo in *Sliver*. 'In LA, I found most artists in my field to be contrived,' he says with a shrug. 'It was a supermarket — toothpaste comedy; ten minutes and you develop the attitude you have for your entire career. When they've completely sucked the tube, they throw you away. But working on *Sliver* was a fantastic experience. Sharon Stone and I became friends. She'd knock on the trailer door sometimes and say: *can I bludge a cigarette?* or, *can I sit on your face?* That sort of stuff.'

Gutman's chuckle is remarkably boyish, almost subdued, and it sweetens his face. No longer the freakishly angry youth, he has grown wiser. 'My wife is my soulmate,' he says by way of explanation. 'She is capable of taming the wild beast in me, and I have the ability to bring out the wild beast in her.' Again, the gentle chuckle and a private glitter in his eyes. 'Emma-Jane is a tactician, a diplomat, my opposite. She gets on with everybody, whereas I'm limited to about two people on the planet. She's one of them. You're the other.'

He slowly looks around the room — at the gilt, at the crystal, at the flowers, through the windows at the blue afternoon. 'I love to make her laugh,' he says. 'You know, I was never the funny one at home. It was my brother who could make my father laugh and laugh and laugh. It's a wonderful sound, isn't it?' His expression is tender and distant. 'The sound of laughter fills me with *warmth*.'

Mode, 1995

PINK TRIANGLE

AND CIRCULAR ARGUMENT

UNITED STATES: ESSAYS 1952 — 1992 competes with the Old Testament for shelf-space, its size a reflection of its author's self-importance. On the front, a reproduction of Jasper John's American flag; on the back, a portrait of the beautiful Gore, his aristocratic hands propping his formerly chiselled chin. Vanity, thy name is Vidal. After reading this work, one is left with the impression that the juxtaposition of the world's most recognisable flag and *il Signore* Vidal is an inadequate *homage* to his relentless cleverness; in a fairer world, his profile would feature on the national currency.

Vidal, an American expatriate now based in Rome, is a great wit, a bad novelist, ferociously learned, a failed politician, and a crackling (if not first-rate) essayist. Reading his prose is like listening to a benevolent despot orating to a minion who is feeding him peeled grapes. At his best, he is rapaciously funny ('You can spend your seed in a woman's bank and, if the moon is right, nine months later you will get an eight-pound dividend'); at his worst, he is neurotically hostile and his arguments are bruised. Vidal jeers to great effect but frequently jeers himself into a corner, rejecting, as he does, most everything that cannot be empirically proven. He ridicules the groundless assertions of others only to bombard the reader with his own. 'Most men,' he drawls, 'homo or hetero — given the opportunity to have sex with 500 different people would do so, gladly.' *Prove.* Or: 'Women today are more candid about their preference for other women.' Compared to women of what other period? The time of the Twelve Caesars? The Golden Age of Greece? The Renaissance? The Middle Ages? Last week? *Prove.*

'This simplistic view of history is a popular one, particularly among those who do not read history,' he snickers. Sadly enough, he goes on to base his arguments on the most stunningly simplistic of views. Take his stance on wedlock: 'Without children, there will be no reason for men and women to enter into lifetime contracts with each other and marriage … will come to an end.' *Prove.* And his stance on psychiatry: 'To one who locates psychiatry somewhere between astrology and phrenology on the scale of human gullibility, the cold-blooded desire to make money by giving one's fellows ... obvious advice and ... notions even sillier than the ones that made them suffers smacks of *Schadenfreude*.' Value judgment upon value judgment! *Prove*! He is at his most frightening on the topic of prostitution ('an arrangement necessary to the wellbeing of many millions'): 'As for the prostitutes themselves, they practise an art as legitimate as any other, somewhere between that of a masseur and a psychiatrist. The best are natural healers and, contrary to tribal superstition, they often enjoy their work.' Let me get this right — one minute he tells us that psychiatry is no more than so much snake oil; the next he refers to it as a 'legitimate' art; the next he appoints himself as the spokesperson for the Parlour Industries Association. Define 'art', Gore! Define 'healing'! *Prove* that prostitutes enjoy their work. *Explain* in what ways their services are 'necessary' to the 'wellbeing of many millions'. *Substantiate your arguments*. (And as for 'legitimacy', I'd wager that Vidal has never attended a White House dinner with a 42nd Street hooker in tow.)

Entertaining, yes; enlightening, sometimes. And as for categoric sexuality — the real rock to which our ruthless warrior is lashed — Vidal's declarations border on the absurd. 'Nevertheless, despite contexts, we are [all] bisexual.' *Prove*.

And, more grandly: 'Society wants [men] safely married so that they will be docile workers and loyal consumers,' in which case I would be fascinated to know how 'society' (the concept of which Vidal treats as reverently as his despised Christian fundamentalists treat their 'Skygod') exists *outside* men. Who constitutes 'society', Gore? Women? Children? 'Fag-baiters'? Norman *Mailer*?

Vidal demonstrates more 'cold-blooded desire' in these essays than any psychiatrist of my acquaintance, and his insistence on the myth of complete intellectual, sexual, and emotional 'freedom' (from what?) betrays the holocaust effect of his logic on his heart. Our warrior is so preoccupied with the arch retort and the wonder of his secular coolness that he fails to distinguish the subtler notes of the human psyche. In the end, it is only his floral and elegant prose that saves him from the ignominy of dismissal as just another knee-jerk inverse censor.

The Sydney Morning Herald, 1994

IN REMEMBERING FIRE

ON THE TWENTY-eighth of August this year, the man I was once to marry and with whom I still shared a profound bond — a highly successful, highly intelligent, shrewd, ambitious and handsome man — overdosed on cocaine and was discovered dead in the bed we used to share. A 'high-end' prostitute was said to have been with him. He was thirty-eight years old. He is now a lapful of ashes. Despite the fact that over two times the fatal dose of cocaine was found in his system, his family remains convinced that he could not have taken his own life. 'The guy had the world by the tail,' his brother told the *Daily Mail*, 'he was so happy.' My heart was silenced by the way in which the English newspapers, globally renowned for the fine standard of their journalism, avoided confronting the truth of the life that led to such a sordid death. The *Times* reported that he had 'died suddenly in his sleep'. The *Daily Telegraph* decided that he 'died of sudden heart failure'. The coroner ruled it 'death by misadventure'. Half-truths and euphemisms. What remained unacknowledged was that the First World Dream was not, is not, and will never be enough.

This was a man who had assiduously followed the dictates of his civilisation, dictates which he had been assured would fulfil him, dictates which he believed would bring him that sense of satisfaction he so desperately sought. Death by misadventure. What could have been wrong? After all, the guy had the world by the tail — first-class travel and first-class hotels, money, glamour, women, social standing, power, talent, respect. *He was so happy.* He was so happy that he was seven stone overweight, a chain-smoker and an alcoholic. He was so happy that he chose to pay for sexual intercourse with a stranger. He was so happy that, like all happy people, he scored some cocaine and killed himself. Suicide was something of which he often spoke. When we were together, he used to sob in my arms with all force, all heart-energy. When I left him, he would sob on the telephone to me from London. I left him not because I did not love him, but because he was overwhelmed by pain and like all creatures in pain, clawed those who came too close to him. He was always surrounded by people and I have never known a lonelier man. Whilst patient with the traumata and depressions of those around him, he was incapable of confiding in his friends; he did not understand the world beyond 'I'. His griefs were hidden and because of this, his isolation was complete. In this respect, he was a textualist, the *GQ* man — seemingly confident, always ready to party. His life was the fire which eventually consumed him.

On hearing of his death, I was not only distraught, but angry — I was angry that those around him had not had the courage to seriously challenge his self-destructiveness; I was angry that he had not questioned that which he had been taught; I was angry that he had been encouraged to pursue a way of life which could ultimately only compound his depression; I was angry that I lived in a world in which the abuse of alcohol or narcotic drugs is, by many, considered to be 'creative' or 'interesting' or 'fun'. I remember one male 'friend' of his telling him that by attempting to stop him drinking, I was 'emasculating' him. This 'friend' always encouraged him to join him in taking drugs, in drinking to the point of incoherence. After his death, I rang his friend up and asked him: 'Is he enough of a man for you now?' But what angered me most of all was his dishonesty — he was dishonest with others in pretending that all was well with his life, and more grievously, he was dishonest with himself by denying his deep griefs, the hope that would have naturally evolved had he acknowledged them, and his capacity for a true love. When I told a girlfriend of his death, she replied that it was the third of which she had heard that week. The deceased in question were all male (those most vulnerable to the dictates of material success), all under the age of forty, all objects of envy and admiration — clever, wealthy, alpha males. One overdosed on cocaine, the other on heroin, the third was found with his wrists, ankles and abdomen slashed in his *Vogue Living* home. No man survives the death of hope.

We are all taught to look outside ourselves for validation and identity. We are all taught to exteriorise. Our quests are no longer spiritual, they are exclusively material and their only reward can be that of the mythological King Ixion, who was bound to an eternally revolving wheel in Hades. What we are not taught is that without hope and the love which fuels it, our ambitions are no more than distractions from the sense of alienation and despair that we all feel in the absence of hope and love.

Time magazine reported that suicide is the second most common cause of death among young adults in North America and that fifteen per cent of Americans have a clinical anxiety disorder. Rates of depression have been doubling in certain industrial countries every decade. The latest edition of the *Australian and New Zealand Journal of Psychiatry* published unhappy findings: sixty-two per cent of university students contemplate suicide. In this respect, Australians are ahead of their American cousins — suicide has overtaken car accidents as the most common cause of young deaths. Instead of encouraging widespread examination of our ways of being, instead of encouraging people to ask themselves which needs of theirs are not being met, these facts seem to excite only scientists, who trip over themselves in their efforts to save the world by isolating the genes which 'cause' depression, anxiety, schizophrenia, obsessive-compulsive behaviour, post-partum depression, alcoholism and drug abuse. We are bombarded by specious new 'discoveries' — the gambling gene, the dial-a-pizza gene, the shopping gene, the bad hair day gene, the illegal parking gene, the chocolate-binge gene. Last week, the University of Maryland held a conference to discuss the ethical implications of research seeking a genetic foundation of violence and other criminal behaviour. Long live Nazi eugenics! And how fantastically convenient for us to think destructive behaviour is *meaningless* — that is to say, not codified discontent but merely genetic freakishness. Isn't it reassuring to know that one day we will be able to be wheeled into theatre to have all those unpleasant little idiosyncracies surgically removed or altered? Up until that time, we will have to settle for medicating ourselves with alcohol, prescription drugs and illegal narcotics.

What amazes me is that so few people actually examine the messages communicated by anti-social behaviour. Instead of embracing the knowledge it offers, we shy away from it, as if from a vampire. The eleventh-century physician Avicenna was presented with a seriously downcast young man, and so took the man's pulse and asked him questions. When a nearby city was mentioned, the man's pulse became rapid. In pursuing his questioning, Avicenna noticed that the man's pulse became quickened when a certain street name was mentioned. A list of people who lived in the street was obtained. The young man's pulse did the salsa at the mention of a certain girl's name. The girl was called. The young man's despondency magically vanished. Love was recognised as a cure in the eleventh century. These days, the lovelorn youth would have been prescribed Prozac.

Teaching respect for achievement is not wrong, but teaching respect for achievement at the expense of emotional development is disastrous. Feelings are considered to be a secondary issue in our empirical society as they cannot be measured or weighed, but what is ignored is that the results of emotional repression are horribly tangible. Our spiritual pollution is reflected in our environmental pollution, in random acts of violence, in the high rates of brutal child abuse. Turning for comfort to the music and literature of our times, we are only dehumanised — confronted by contempt for thought, for art, for craftsmanship: deconstructionist theory, dissonance, the limping prose of Generation X, grunge — catabolism as the ideal. This nihilism is borne of unheard grief and its resultant apathy, and it is that which our generation is taught to regard as the apex of creativity, as enlightenment, as entertainment. We are no longer familiar with real esctasy; to understand it, we swallow its namesake tablet.

In the past, art was thought to be synonymous with truth or beauty and was created to inspire, awe, educate and to bestow hope; nowadays, art is the refuse bin of talents *manqué*.

Kurt Cobain, the musical hero of Generation X and a chronic depressive who ended his life with a gun, made himself impressive to the world by refusing to hope. His awful widow, Courtney Love, has taken it upon herself to promote auditory, visual and behavioural ugliness. Michael Stipe, of the popular band REM, justifies what some would refer to as psychopathological sexual behaviour by encouraging others to 'experiment' as he has with what Love calls his 'pansexuality'. The beermat novels of Generation X are remarkable only as testimonies to their authors' talentlessness and sharp absence of intellect. Nihilists insist on action being stripped of meaning, for meaning is an affront to those in denial. We live in a society in which the average person watches twenty-eight — and I repeat, ladies and gentlemen, twenty-eight — hours of television every week, so such nihilism is to be expected. In coming to the end of the millennium, have we also come to the end of ourselves? Have we exhausted our capacity to hope?

Integral to the practise of Sufism is *Sama*, the Enraptured Dance. To the music of a flute, the Sufis spin in intense spiritual concentration, with one hand outstretched to the heavens to receive blessings and the other turned to the earth to transmit them. The meaning of this dance is beautiful: man is presented as the intermediary between the known and the unknown, between heaven and earth, of one and in the other. A sense of purpose is bestowed by that very definition — it is the dancer's power to receive and then to give, and also his pleasure to be the beneficiary of others' blessings. There is a rapture experienced in belonging and it is a rapture that we all seek. What could be more lyrical and more logical? And yet our world is one in which we are conditioned to hoard blessings — he who hoards the most blessings wins, and charity has become no more than a tax deduction.

The journalist Robert Wright postulated that 'natural selection has imbued our minds with an infrastructure for friendship ... affection, gratitude, and trust ... the machinery for "reciprocal altruism" '. Wright's use of the term 'machinery' is not inappropriate. Ours is the first generation to model itself on machines. Our worth, we are made to understand, is no more than our performance. Few of us question; questioning is seen to be as quaint a practice as saying grace before supper. Machines do not question. Few of us act for constructive change; acting for constructive change is understood to be *passé*. Machines do not act for constructive change. Few of us freely dream; dreaming is perceived to be the province of Coleridge and the dusty Decadents. Machines do not dream. Few of us hope; hope belongs to the ignorant, the naive, the primitive, the religious, the very young. Machines do not hope. Few of us acknowledge that such widespread destructiveness exists because as a civilisation, we are unhappy. This remains unacknowledged because such an explanation is simple and we no longer trust simplicity. Machines are valuable only for their complexity.

Our short and bow-legged ancestors battled acute poverty, rudimentary sanitation, disease, bad diets, natural disasters, unjust warfare. Many of their children died at birth, and the rest of them could expect the lifespan of a modern housecat. Our physical existence has improved immeasurably, but we ruin our lives by not trusting our hearts. Despair is our pestilence.

Until we learn to respect our deep, sweet, simple human needs, we are destined only to further erode our ability to enjoy our lives. Our history is filled with as much love, hope, courage, and kindness as it is with stupidity and cowardice. Until we recall those moral and ethical frameworks from the foreconscious, we can only feel impeded by our experience of the world. The 'I' whose grievances we ignore and whom we thus enrage must metamorphose into 'we' to be calmed and nurtured. The rapture of belonging is the right of every being. Jalal al-Din Rumi, the Sufi mystic, put it more elegantly than I ever could: 'One went to the door of the Beloved and knocked. A voice asked, "Who is there?" He answered, "It is I." The voice said, "There is no room for Me and Thee." The door was shut. After a year of solitude and deprivation he returned and knocked. A voice from within asked, "Who is there?" The man said, "It is Thee." '

The door was opened.

Speech for the 1995 Sydney University Union Annual Dinner